Make That Grade Marketing

Fourth Edition

Margaret Linehan and Thérèse Cadogan

 GILL EDUCATION

Gill Education
Hume Avenue, Park West
Dublin 12
www.gilleducation.ie

Gill Education is an imprint of M.H. Gill & Co.

978 07171 4982 7

Print origination in Ireland by Carole Lynch
Printed in Ireland by SPRINT-print Ltd.

*The paper used in this book is made from the wood pulp of
managed forests. For every tree felled, at least one tree
is planted, thereby renewing natural resources.*

CONTENTS

DIAGRAMS

TABLES

1
INTRODUCTION TO MARKETING

Chapter objectives

After reading this chapter you should be able to:
- Define marketing.
- Trace the historical development of marketing.
- Identify the elements of the marketing mix.
- Understand the marketing environment.
- Understand relationship marketing.

1.1 *Marketing defined*

This chapter begins with an examination of what is meant by the term 'marketing'. Kotler and Armstrong (2008) define **marketing** as 'a social and managerial process by which individuals and groups obtain what they need and want through creating and exchanging products and value with others'.

The definition of marketing given by the British Chartered Institute of Marketing is: 'Marketing is the management process responsible for identifying, anticipating and satisfying customers' requirements profitably.'

The American Marketing Association's definition of marketing (AMA, 1985) is: 'Marketing is the process of planning and executing the conception, pricing, promotion and distribution of ideas, goods and services to create exchange and satisfy individual and organisational objectives.'

These definitions show that:
- Marketing is a management process.
- Marketing is an activity geared towards giving customers what they want.
- Marketing identifies and anticipates customers' requirements.
- Marketing fulfils customers' requirements efficiently and profitably.
- Marketing facilitates exchange relationships.

Marketing occurs when people decide to satisfy needs and wants through exchange. *Human* **needs** are a state of felt deprivation, for example basic physical needs for food, clothing, warmth and safety. *Human* **wants** are shaped by culture and individual personality. Wants are described as objects that will satisfy needs: for example, a hungry person in the United States might want a hamburger, chips and cola. People have almost unlimited wants, but limited resources; when wants are supported by buying power, they become **demands.**

Exchange is the core concept of marketing. *Exchange* is the act of obtaining a desired object from someone by offering something in return. For an exchange to take place, certain conditions must exist. For example, (*a*) two or more individuals, groups or companies must participate, (*b*) each party must possess something of value that the other party desires, (*c*) each party must be willing to give up its 'something of value' to receive the 'something of value' held by the other party and (*d*) each party must be able to communicate and deliver.

The concept of exchange leads to the concept of *market.* A market is the set of actual and potential buyers of a product or service. These buyers share a particular need or want that can be satisfied through exchange. The size of a market therefore depends on the number of people who show the need, have resources to engage in exchange and are willing to offer resources in exchange for what they want.

1.2 *The historical development of marketing*

The idea of marketing is a fairly recent one but has been preceded by others, which are contrasted in Table 1.1. The basic idea of marketing as an exchange process has its roots in ancient history, when people began to produce crops or surplus goods, then bartered them for other things they wanted. During the late nineteenth and early twentieth centuries, goods were sufficiently scarce and competition sufficiently underdeveloped for producers not to really need marketing; they could sell whatever they produced. This became known as the *production era*, in which a production orientation was adopted.

The production era

The focus on production that began in the United States after the Civil War in 1865 and continued into the 1920s was fuelled by milestones such as Henry Ford's adoption of the assembly line and the more efficient work principles advanced by Frederick W. Taylor's scientific management movement. These two innovations made business managers aware that mass production resulted in steeply declining unit costs of production. In turn, the declining unit costs of production made profit possibilities look very achievable.

During this era it was thought that people would buy anything, provided it was cheap enough. The prevailing attitude among manufacturers was that getting production right was all that mattered. This was a period of mass production. For example, Henry Ford's objective was to perfect the production of the Ford Model T so that its costs could be reduced and more people could afford it. His marketing policy was: 'The customer can have any colour car he wants as long as it is black.' The production concept assumes that consumers are mostly interested in product availability at low prices; its marketing objectives are cheap, efficient production and intensive distribution. This is used when consumers are more interested in obtaining the product than they are in specific features and will buy what is available rather than wait for what they really want. Today companies use this concept in developing countries or in other situations in which the main objective is to expand the market. The rationale for mass production, however, seemed sound at the time of the production era. It was perceived that reduced production costs could lead to reduced selling prices and thus appeal to the largest segment of customers. Unfortunately, turbulent economic conditions associated with the late 1920s through the 1940s caused many companies to fail despite adopting this production-oriented philosophy of doing business. As a result, companies looked for other ways to improve the exchange process.

With increasing affluence, people are not prepared to accept standardised products, and as markets become more segmented, manufacturers realise that there are many benefits to be gained from providing specialised products.

The sales era

In the period from the mid-1920s to the early 1950s, manufacturers believed that customers needed to be persuaded to buy more of a firm's products. Companies found that they could no longer sell all the products they produced, even though prices were lowered through mass production. Firms now had to quickly sell their excess production in order to convert products into cash. This era was characterised by aggressive sales techniques, which created profit through quick turnover of high volume. The *sales era* was concerned with the needs of the seller, not with the needs of the buyer. During this period, personal selling and advertising were regarded as the most important promotional activities.

This approach does not consider customer satisfaction. When consumers are induced to buy products they do not want or need, they will not buy them again. They are also likely to communicate any dissatisfaction with the product through negative word of mouth that serves to dissuade potential consumers from making similar purchases. Today the selling concept is typically utilised by marketers of unsought goods (such as life insurance), by political parties 'selling' their candidates to uninterested voters and by companies that have excess inventory.

In the current competitive environment, most markets are buyer markets and sellers have to work hard for customers. People are inundated with graphic commercials, print advertisements, direct mail, telemarketing and sales calls. As a result, the public often identifies marketing with hard selling and advertising. Selling, however, is not the most important part of healthy marketing. Selling is only one part, although an essential part, of the marketing mix. As management and marketing scholar Peter Drucker states, 'There will always, one can assume, be a need for some selling. But the aim of marketing is to make selling superfluous. The aim of marketing is to know and understand the customer so well that the product or service fits him and sells itself. Ideally, marketing should result in a customer who is ready to buy. All that should be needed then is to make the product or service available.'

The marketing era

It was not really until the 1960s–70s that marketing generally moved from emphasising aggressive selling. Whereas the selling concept focuses on the needs of the *sellers* and on existing products, the marketing concept focuses on the needs of the *buyer*. The selling concept focuses on profits through sales volume; the marketing concept focuses on profits through customer satisfaction. In the 1980s companies began to move from the policy of selling what they could make towards finding out what the customer wants and then making it. Businesspeople began to recognise that customers are intelligent enough to know what they need, can recognise value for money and will not buy from a firm if they do not get value for money. Achieving organisational goals depends on determining the needs and wants of target markets and delivering the desired satisfactions more effectively and efficiently than competitors do. This is the basis of the **marketing concept**. Customers, therefore, took their place at the centre of a company's activities. In practice the marketing concept means finding out what a particular group of customers' needs and wants are, finding out what price they would be willing to pay and fitting the company's activities to meeting those needs and wants at the right price. The motivation is to find wants and fill them, rather than to create products and sell them.

If all of the organisation's functions are focused on customer needs, the marketing concept implies that profits can be achieved by satisfying those needs. The satisfaction of customer needs can be accomplished through product changes, pricing adjustments, increased customer service and distribution changes.

Understanding the nature of customers and their needs and wants, however, is only the first step. A company needs to act on that information in order to develop and implement marketing activities that actually deliver something of value to the customer. The means by which such ideas are turned into reality is the **marketing mix** (see section 1.3).

Concept	Focus	Means	Ends
Production	Mass production	Low-priced products	Profits from sales of standardised products
Sales	Existing products	Selling and promoting	Profits from sales volume
Marketing	Customer needs	Integrated marketing	Profits through satisfied customers
Social	Society's long-term well-being	'Green' marketing	Profits through providing for society's welfare

Table 1.1: *The production, sales, marketing and social concepts contrasted*

The social marketing concept

Social marketing developed as a discipline in the 1970s when promoters realised that the same marketing principles that were being used to sell products to consumers could be used to sell or promote ideas, attitudes and behaviours. Social marketing seeks to influence social behaviours in order to benefit the general society. This technique is used extensively in health programmes and for such diverse topics as reducing drug abuse or heart disease and in promoting organ donation – often where the social marketing 'product' is not a physical offering.

The **social marketing concept** holds that a company should determine the needs, wants and demands of its customers. It should then deliver the desired satisfaction more effectively and efficiently than competitors, in a way that maintains or improves the customer's and society's well-being. The social marketing concept calls on marketers to balance three considerations in setting their marketing policies: (*1*) company profits, (*2*) customers' wants and (*3*) society's interests. This concept need not conflict with the immediate needs of the company's customers. For example, the Body Shop operates a highly successful customer-oriented business while still promising and delivering low environmental impact. The company uses only vegetable-based materials for its products and it is also against animal testing. It supports community trade, promotes self-esteem, defends human rights and promotes overall protection of the planet.

Thus, a restructured definition of the marketing concept calls on marketers to *fulfil the needs of the target audience in ways that improve society as a whole, while fulfilling the objectives of the organisation.* According to the social marketing concept, fast-food restaurants should develop foods that contain less fat and starch and more nutrients, and marketers should not advertise alcoholic beverages or cigarettes to young people or use young models or professional athletes in liquor or tobacco advertisements because celebrities often serve as role models for the young.

The societal marketing concept

Societal marketing appeared during the 1970s in an attempt to provide marketing concepts that were more in tune with social needs and to establish more ethical practices. As more emphasis was placed on social responsibility, more companies moved toward business practices that supported these values. The unethical business practices of many companies became public knowledge, often leading to activities improving the company image and increased social responsibility – resulting in societal marketing.

While some businesses view corporate social responsibility as an image enhancement tool with no tangible benefits, many organisations are increasingly concerned about managing social issues to benefit stakeholder interests. In an increasingly competitive and changing marketplace, corporate social responsibility can become a competitive advantage.

One of the major goals of societal marketing is to improve brand image in the eyes of the consumer. For companies, this is referred to as corporate societal marketing. This type of marketing has several goals, including building the image of the brand, developing more community awareness of the brand, ensuring a sense of credibility in the brand, eliciting consumer feelings toward the brand and ultimately securing a customer–brand connection. When companies adopt societal marketing, they are choosing to maintain socially responsible practices that benefit consumers and the larger community. Companies using this type of marketing are concerned not only with immediate customer satisfaction, but also with the long-term impact on the customer and society. Many examples of societal marketing can now be seen with increased environmental awareness and the marketing of 'green' products.

Relationship marketing

Relationship marketing is defined as 'the development and maintenance of successful relational exchanges through interactive ongoing, two-way connections among customers, organisations, suppliers, and other parties for mutual benefit' (Harrell, 2002). Traditional marketing techniques are usually concerned with attracting new customers and preventing existing ones from being lured away by competition. It focuses on a business's ability to make a series of single sales to a group of potential customers. The more recent theoretical concept of relationship marketing focuses on building high levels of customer commitment by offering exceptional service levels over a long timescale and generating customers' loyalty by treating them as individuals rather than small elements of large markets.

The rationale for building relationships with customers is based on the long-term financial benefits that can accrue. It is based on two economic facts: (*1*) it is more expensive to obtain a new customer than to retain an existing customer and (*2*) the longer the period of the relationship, the more profitable the relationship becomes.

Many companies have established relationship marketing programmes (sometimes called *loyalty programmes)* to encourage usage loyalty and a commitment to their company's products and services. Relationship marketing programmes have been used in a wide variety of product and service categories. Many companies call their relationship programmes a club. Airlines and major hotel chains in particular use relationship marketing techniques by awarding points to frequent customers that can be used to obtain additional goods or services from the company. Relationship marketing is helped by ***database marketing***, which involves tracking consumers' buying habits very closely and crafting products and messages tailored precisely to people's wants and needs based on this information.

With the growth of the Internet and mobile platforms, relationship marketing has continued to evolve as technology opens more collaborative and social communication channels. Relationship marketing has also migrated back into direct mail, allowing marketers to take advantage of the technological capabilities of digital printing to produce unique or personalised pieces of communication for each recipient. Marketers can personalise documents with any information contained in their databases, including images, names, addresses, demographics, purchase history and many other variables. The result is a printed piece of communication that ideally reflects the individual needs and preferences of each recipient, increasing the relevance of the communication and increasing the response rate. Relationship marketing also includes social media and application development.

Exchange marketing	Relationship marketing
Importance of single sale	Importance of customer retention
Importance of product features	Importance of customer benefits
Short timescale	Longer timescale
Less emphasis on service	Higher customer service
Quality is concern of production	Quality is concern of all
Competitive commitment	High customer commitment
Persuasive communication	Regular customer communication

Table 1.2: *Differences between traditional and relationship marketing*

Social media marketing

Social media marketing is a recent addition to the communications plans of organisations. Social media uses web-based technologies to turn communication into interactive dialogues. The growth of social media has impacted on the way in which organisations communicate with their customers. With the emergence of Web 2.0, the Internet provides a set of tools that allow people to build social and business connections and to share information.

Social media are primarily Internet-based tools for sharing and discussing information among people. Social media marketing programmes usually centre on efforts to create content that attracts attention and encourages readers to share that content with their social networks. A corporate message spreads quickly from user to user and is a powerful source of marketing because it is coming from a trusted individual, as opposed to the brand or organisation itself being the source. Social media is a relatively inexpensive platform for organisations to implement marketing campaigns and to receive direct feedback from customers and from targeted markets. Some of the most popular of these platforms include Facebook, YouTube, LinkedIn, Twitter and MySpace.

In conclusion, marketers strive to initiate exchanges and build relationships; therefore, marketing can be viewed as an activity involved in *getting* and *keeping* customers. It is the marketer's job to use the resources of the entire organisation to create, interpret, and maintain the relationship between the company and the customer.

1.3 *The traditional marketing mix ('four Ps')*

The *marketing mix* concept is derived from the 1950s US corporate marketing world. The marketing mix is the combination of four major tools of marketing, known as the 'four Ps': *product*, *price*, *place* and *promotion* (see Fig. 1.1 and Table 1.3). The four Ps represent a framework that can be used in developing strategies for marketing managers.

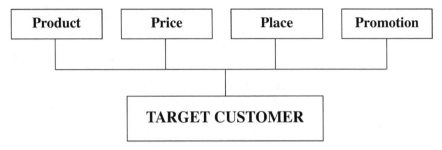

Fig. 1.1: *The elements of the marketing mix*

Faced with a wide choice of product features, prices, distribution methods and promotional messages, the marketing manager must select and combine ingredients to create a marketing mix that will achieve corporate objectives.

Product

A *product* is anything that can be offered to a market for attention, acquisition, use or consumption and that might satisfy a want or need. It need not be a physical thing but in marketing terms is viewed as a good, a service or an idea. A *good* is a physical entity that can be touched, for example a car, a camera or a bar of chocolate. A *service* is an activity or benefit that can be offered for sale, for example a haircut, a concert or a bus journey. An *idea* is a concept or a policy, for example the importance of parents reading to their children; other marketers of ideas include political parties, churches and schools.

The product the customer receives in the exchange process is the result of a number of product strategy decisions. Product strategies must take into consideration the other three elements of the marketing mix. (See Chapter 7 for further detail on products.)

Price

The amount of money given in exchange for something is its *price*, that is, what is exchanged for the product. To a buyer, price is the value placed on what is exchanged.

Marketers must determine the best price for their products. To do so they must ascertain a product's value, or what it is worth to customers in monetary terms. Once the value of a product is established, the marketer knows what price to charge. Because customers' evaluation of a product's worth changes over time, prices are also subject to change. Price may be described in different ways for different exchanges. For example, insurance companies charge a *premium*, a solicitor charges a *fee*, a taxi driver charges a *fare* and a *toll* may be charged for the use of motorways. Although price may be expressed in a variety of ways, it is important to remember that the purpose of this concept is to quantify and express the value of the items in a market exchange in a way the consumer can understand. (See Chapter 8 for further detail on prices.)

Place (distribution)

Determining how goods reach the customer, how quickly and in what condition involves *place*, or distribution strategy. To satisfy customers, products must be available at the right time and at a convenient place. The marketer has to decide on the structure of *channels of distribution*, from mail-order companies that deal directly with the final customer to long and complex chains that involve goods passing between several intermediaries (wholesalers, retailers and dealers) before they reach the consumer. A marketing manager may also become involved in establishing and maintaining stock control procedures and developing and managing transport and storage systems. (See Chapter 9 for further detail on place.)

Promotion (marketing communication)

Promotion is the means by which marketers communicate with both existing and potential customers. The promotional mix is the direct way in which a company attempts to communicate with various target audiences. A company's promotional mix consists of five main elements: sales promotion, direct marketing, advertising, personal selling and public relations. Promotion can be aimed at increasing public awareness of a company and of new or existing products. (See Chapter 10 for further detail on promotion.)

Product	Price	Place	Promotion
Functionality	List price	Locations	Advertising
Appearance	Discounts	Logistics	Personal selling
Quality	Financing	Market coverage	Public relations
Brand	Leasing options	Distribution	Media
Warranty	Seasonal pricing	channels	Budget
Service/support	Wholesale pricing	Warehousing	Sales force
Safety	Suggested retail	Transportation	Promotional
	price	Inventory	strategy
		management	

Table 1.3: *Summary of marketing mix decisions*

The extended marketing mix for services ('seven Ps')

The *extended marketing mix* for services is: product, price, place and promotion, plus an additional three variables or 'Ps', namely: people, physical evidence and process.

People

The majority of services depend on direct, personal interaction between customers and the company's employees. For example, in a bank, one customer is being served at the desk, other customers are being served at the same time or else are waiting in a queue and employees are providing the service (service providers). These interactions with other people in a service situation may influence a customer's perceptions and expectations of service quality. Service companies such as retailers should, therefore, concentrate on providing a good level of customer service by recruiting the right staff, investing in staff training and delegating some level of authority to the front-line staff.

Physical evidence

The design of an appropriate physical environment is essential for the delivery of a service so as to compensate for its intangible nature. Physical evidence includes uniforms, reception areas, appearance of buildings, signage, forms, furniture, equipment, brochures, lighting, landscaping, printed materials and any other visible cues. These provide tangible evidence of an organisation's service style and quality. For example, uniforms are a way of reassuring the customer of the roles and skills of the service providers.

Process

This refers to a particular method of operations or series of actions, usually involving steps that need to occur in a defined sequence. Poorly designed processes will result in customer dissatisfaction because of slow and ineffective service delivery. Services, therefore, need to be easily accessible and conveniently presented. Clear and easy procedures can help to make the service more efficient.

1.4 *The marketing environment*

The *marketing environment* consists of forces that directly or indirectly influence a company's ability to develop and maintain successful transactions with target customers. The marketing environment consists of a *macro-environment* and a *micro-environment*. The macro-environment consists of the larger social forces that affect all micro-environments and are generally outside the control of the company. The micro-environment consists of the forces close to the company that affect its ability to serve its customers. Table 1.4 illustrates the marketing environment.

Macro-environment	Micro-environment
• Sociocultural	• Company
• Technological	• Suppliers
• Economic	• Customers
• Political and legal	• Marketing intermediaries
• Natural	• Competitors
	• Publics

Table 1.4: *The marketing environment*

The company's macro-environment

Sociocultural environment

The *sociocultural environment* can be further divided into (*a*) demographics, (*b*) culture, (*c*) attitudes and (*d*) current issues. **Demography** is the study of human population according to size, density, location, age, gender, nationality and occupation. **Cultural forces** affect society's basic values, perceptions, preferences and behaviour. The sociocultural environment also looks at the way in which consumers' attitudes and opinions are formed and how they evolve. **Current issues** include a large increase in the number of foreign nationals living in Ireland, which has seen the introduction of a variety of speciality products and shops to cater for these needs, for example Polish food and drink. The sociocultural environment is of particular concern to marketers, as it has a direct effect on their understanding of customers and what their needs and wants are.

Technological environment

The **technological environment** consists of forces that create new technologies and so create new product and market opportunities. Computer technology has had a profound effect on marketing activities. For example, it helps to make warehouse management more efficient and therefore less expensive. Computer technology has aided product design, quality control, the production of advertising and other promotional material and the management and analysis of customer information.

Technology has also brought a new way of communication and new advertising tools, for example mobile phones, podcasts and virtual online worlds. Marketers can use these tools to connect with selected customers with carefully targeted messages. Customers can learn about design through e-commerce and can order and pay for products and services without leaving their homes. Then, through express delivery, they can receive their purchase within 24 hours.

Economic environment

The **economic environment** influences the decisions and activities of marketers and customers. When an economic outlook remains prosperous, customers are generally willing to buy. Marketers take advantage of this forecast and often expand their markets to take advantage of the increased buying power. On the other hand, if there is a period of recession, during which unemployment rises, customers' ability and willingness to buy many kinds of products decline.

The European Union is now the largest economy in the world and is the world's largest exporter and the second largest importer. Achieving greater economic integration among member states is a goal of the European Union. The single market has implications for marketers and consumers. Efficient firms can benefit from increased competitiveness, lower costs, profitability and the ability to compete globally.

Political and legal environment

The **political and legal environment** consists of forces controlled by laws enforced by governments and local authorities. The political and legal environment is influenced by sociocultural factors, pressure groups, the media and public opinion. Marketers need to know about the main laws protecting competition, customers and society. International marketers should also be aware of regional, national and local regulations that affect their international marketing activities.

Legislation affecting businesses around the world has increased steadily over the years. The European Commission has been active in establishing a new framework of laws covering competitive behaviour, fair trade practices, environmental protection, product standards, product liability and commercial transactions for nations of the European Union. The EU Directive on Privacy and Electronic Communications, for example, aims to crack down on e-mail spam by giving government agencies the power to prosecute firms that send unsolicited e-mails.

Natural environment

The ***natural environment*** involves natural resources that are needed as inputs by marketers or are affected by marketing activities. Ecological and geographical factors have come to the forefront of marketing strategies over the past 10 years. The increasing scarcity of raw materials, the problem of disposing of waste materials and the difficulty in finding appropriate sites for industrial complexes (particularly those with a significant environmental impact) are all factors that are seriously affecting the marketer.

All kinds of external effects of production and consumption have gradually become visible in the environment. River and sea water have become unsuitable for swimming, forests suffer from acid rain and beaches are polluted with oil. On the positive side, a number of companies participate in the application of environmental innovations to production processes. Examples of environment-friendly behaviour include buying free-range eggs, phosphate-free detergents and lead-free and water-based paints.

The natural environment work of An Taisce focuses on the conservation of Ireland's rich natural and built heritage. Aspects of Ireland's natural heritage include clean air and water; ecological communities (ecosystems), e.g. woods and wetlands; lakes and rivers; the variability among all types of living organisms (biodiversity); green spaces shared by people and wildlife; and Ireland's coastline.

The company's micro-environment

The company

In making marketing plans, marketers take other departments of ***the company*** into consideration, including the top management, finance, research and development, purchasing and manufacturing. All these interconnected groups form part of the micro-environment. Under the marketing concept, all these departments must 'think customer' and they should work together to provide superior customer value and satisfaction.

Suppliers

Suppliers are firms and individuals that provide the resources needed by the company and its competitors to produce goods and services. The marketer must monitor the availability of supplies, the price of their supply costs and their terms for supplying resources. Losing an important supplier can mean that production flow is interrupted or that a lower-quality or more expensive substitute has to be made.

Companies must decide on issues such as who should supply them with products or services, on the responsibility they take for these suppliers and on the terms and conditions they adopt. Some firms take quite an aggressive attitude towards their suppliers by trying to push down purchase prices and to delay payments. Others view the relationship more as a partnership in which they work together with suppliers, even helping each other so that both supplier and receiver can benefit.

Customers

Customers are vital for the success of a company. Marketers need to be able to find customers, to establish what they want and then communicate their messages to them. Marketers aim to deliver the right product at the right time at the right price and in the right place and to follow up to ensure that customers are satisfied.

Managers must monitor customer needs and try to anticipate how these will develop so that they can meet these requirements effectively, now and in the future. To better understand their customers, firms are increasingly trying to gather information on customers through mechanisms such as loyalty cards. By gathering data on shopping patterns and matching these to data on individual shoppers, firms can build up detailed pictures of buyers and then offer them more appropriate deals.

Marketing intermediaries

Marketing intermediaries are firms that help a company to promote, sell and distribute its goods. They include **retailers**, **physical distribution firms** and **market research firms**. Physical distribution firms – for example, warehouse and transport firms – enable companies to stock and move goods from their point of origin to their destination. The marketer must decide on the best way to store and deliver goods, considering such factors as cost, delivery, speed and safety. (See Chapter 9 for further detail on distribution.)

Competitors

Customers will make comparisons between different products and will listen to messages from **competitors**. The marketing manager has to both monitor what competitors are doing now and try to anticipate what they will do in the future in order to position their own products strongly against competitors' products in the minds of customers. (See Chapter 4 for further details.)

Public

Finally, some of a company's public form part of the micro-environment. A **public** is any group, including employees, that has actual or potential impact or interest in a company. A range of publics can include **financial publics**, for example banks, insurance companies and shareholders. **Local publics** consist mainly of a company's neighbours. Local people and organisations may put pressure on the company to take local action, for example to clean up pollution or to sponsor local charities. **Media publics** include newspapers, magazines and radio and television stations that carry news, features and opinion.

Important terms and concepts

Case study: Live, breathe and wear passion: Diesel

Diesel is a global clothing and lifestyle brand. With a history stretching back over 30 years, the company now employs some 2,200 people globally with a turnover of €1.3 billion in 2009 and its products are available in more than 5,000 outlets in subsidiaries across Europe, Asia and the Americas. The story begins with a young Renzo Rosso, who was passionate about his clothes but disappointed in the options available to him in his hometown of Molvena in Italy. Acting on impulse, he decided to use his passion to make the clothes he wanted to wear. Renzo was drawn to the rebellious fabric of the 1960s and to rock 'n' roll denim. It inspired him to create jeans that would allow him and others to express themselves in ways other clothing simply could not.

Proving popular, Renzo made more and more of his handcrafted creations, selling them around Italy from the back of his little van. Renzo is today the proud owner and CEO of Diesel, which suggests that his impulse and passion have paid off.

Product

The reason Diesel has grown is because it knows it is about a lot more than just selling attractive jeans. Diesel is marketed as a lifestyle so that you might like to buy those products if that lifestyle appeals to you. Renzo describes this approach as turning away from traditional marketing 'violence' towards the customer, which virtually forced them to buy rather than involving them in the lifestyle. The Diesel brand promises to entertain and to introduce customers to new, experimental experiences. Its product line expanded beyond premium jeans to include fragrances, sunglasses and even bike helmets. These products complement, convey and support the promises of passion and experience made by the Diesel brand. The marketing team at Diesel is passionate about their creations, helping them to be even more creative. As employees deliberately absorb the Diesel brand into their own lifestyles, their design and marketing creativity is more organic, spontaneous and relevant.

Price

The price of a product is so much more than a number on a tag. The price of a product is the most direct and immediate tool a business can use to convey the quality of its product at the point of sale. If done right, price reinforces the rest of the marketing process, drawing in target customers by conveying the appropriate quality.

Diesel uses a model based on premium pricing. Through the vision and passion of Renzo Rosso, the company has created a whole new approach to engaging with its customers. The price of Diesel's products needs to reflect the substance and value of that experience. A strategy such as penetration pricing used by businesses making high-volume but relatively low-margin products would be inappropriate for Diesel, as it would undermine its association with quality and thus devalue the brand and the experience.

People do not pay a premium price for Diesel jeans just because they are of premium quality; that is taken for granted. People pay a premium price because the jeans and the brand fit in with and even encourage a premium and dynamic lifestyle built 'for successful living', as Diesel phrases it.

Place

A way of describing 'place' in the marketing mix is the distribution channel. The way a business chooses to offer its products to customers has a huge impact on its success. Only around 300 of the 5,000 global outlets selling Diesel products are owned and managed by the company itself. The majority of the outlets are large department stores offering many other brands or boutiques with a specific style of their own. Marketers need to examine how they can successfully maintain the quality of a product and successfully communicate when dealing with so many different partners and distribution channels.

Diesel addresses this challenge through endeavouring to maintain a strong culture. Every employee is able to communicate the brand appropriately in their given role within the company. Therefore, the managers of Diesel-branded outlets know that their function is to act as a flagship. Employees in each of the stores all know the campaigns intimately and are very aware of the image they should put across to customers entering their stores. Retail partners, such as department stores, are a crucial link in the chain. Diesel works closely with partners to ensure they express the same level of passion when offering their products. This is done through customised and individual campaigns. These provide visitors with a unique experience which again encourages them to get involved with the Diesel lifestyle as opposed to forcing products on them.

This approach to distribution can be seen as a mix of exclusive and selective distribution over intensive distribution. Exclusive distribution involves limiting distribution to single outlets, such as Diesel flagship stores. Selective distribution involves using a small number of retail outlets and partners to maintain a high level of presentation and communication to the customer. This approach contrasts with intensive distribution, which is commonly used to distribute low-price or impulse-purchased goods, such as sweets or chocolate.

Promotion

Promotion and marketing at Diesel are quite different from the approach in many mainstream companies. At Diesel it is about engaging with the customer as opposed to selling at them: creating an enjoyable two-way dialogue as opposed to a shallow one-way effort. All elements of Diesel's promotion aim to engage the customer with the lifestyle. If customers like the lifestyle, they are more prone to like the products.

For example, the Diesel team saw music as an inseparable part of that lifestyle and realised that exploring new music and new artists was all part of trying something different and of experimenting with the unusual. Diesel:U:Music is now a global music support collaborative, giving unsigned bands a place where they can be heard and an opportunity to have their talent recognised. It's not about selling, it's about giving people something they will enjoy and interact with.

An online radio station is now connected to Diesel:U:Music. This is another example where Diesel has created something unconventional that promotes conceptions. The radio station takes a rather unusual approach of not having a traditional play list, but rather gives the choice to the resident DJ. This freedom is reflected in the unusual mix of music played on the station.

In promotion and marketing, above-the-line and below-the-line marketing are methods of reaching consumers. Above-the-line marketing is aimed at a mass audience through media such as television or radio. Below-the-line marketing takes a more individual, targeted approach using incentives to purchase via various promotions. In this case, passion again acts to blur the boundaries between the two approaches. If Diesel had to define this approach in terms of theory, they would call it 'through-the-line', i.e. a blend of the two. The passion and energy embodied by the Diesel lifestyle are communicated through a mix of above-the-line and below-the-line approaches. The balance and composition of that mix is what the Diesel team hands over to their passion and feel for the company and brand.

To understand the full marketing experience of Diesel, it is necessary to look at the emotional elements of business that are less often discussed. Diesel declares that it has built its existence around that touchy-feely passion, with every one of its 2,200 employees living the Diesel brand.

Diesel grew into a global household name for premium clothing after one man wanted to do something unusual. He stubbornly stuck to his belief in doing the unusual, creating a global company whose products are now enjoyed by millions. More importantly, this has created a lifestyle – a whole new approach to the way we see a brand. Diesel is an experience that interacts with and entertains customers with a far deeper relationship than what they get from most other brands.

Being driven by passion and the desire to do something special are combined here. Understanding theory, like the marketing mix in a company like Diesel, can be difficult if we expect the elements of price, place, product and promotion to be distinct from each other. It becomes easier if we look beyond the formal theory and realise that all of these elements are inseparably bound together by the passion of people like Renzo Rosso who have dedicated their lives to treating their work as an artistic expression of their feelings.

Source: Adapted from www.thetimes100.co.uk/case-study--live-breathe-and-wear-passion--159-414-1.php [accessed 19 March 2011].

Case study: The marketing mix in the food industry: McCain

McCain Foods was founded in 1957 in Canada by the McCain brothers. McCain Foods is now the largest chip producer in the world with a market share of almost 33 per cent and more than 20,000 employees working in 57 locations worldwide. Since 1968, McCain Great Britain has been operating from its base in North Yorkshire. McCain prides itself on the quality and convenience of its product range, and for over three decades has been making healthier versions of favourite staple foods.

The McCain brothers had a simple philosophy: 'good ethics is good business'. This lies behind the McCain 'It's All Good' brand message, as it is not just the food that is good. The philosophy also refers to the way McCain works with its suppliers and the way it builds relationships with customers. McCain believes it is important to take care of the environment, the community and its people. The company works with around 300 farmers in Britain, chosen for the quality of their potato crop. McCain factories are also located in key potato-growing areas, helping to reduce food miles.

Product

McCain Foods is one of the world's leading manufacturers of frozen potato products. While McCain is perhaps best known for producing oven chips, its product lines are much wider. In Britain, McCain products include other potato products such as wedges, home roasts, sweet potato and microwave pizza. In other countries, McCain includes frozen vegetables, ready meals and desserts. Some products, such as their oven chips, immediately captured the public imagination and continue to sell well without needing to be changed. Other products change through time or are adapted to create new variations, for example curly fries or thin and crispy fries. Changes in the range are driven by a number of different factors. Microwaveable snacks, for example, take account of changing lifestyles, where people are looking for food that does not take long to prepare. McCain has also been responsive to market needs for healthier options.

Price

A business must consider four elements when pricing its products.

1. **Business objectives:** A business may set its pricing to achieve a number of objectives, including:
   - Maximising profits.
   - Achieving a target return on investment.
   - Achieving a target sales figure.
   - Achieving a target market share.
   - Matching the competition.
2. **Costs:** In order to make a profit, a business must make sure that its products are priced above their cost. The total cost of a product includes overheads, such as research and development, and investment in equipment, people and technology as well as direct costs, such as raw materials, ingredients, wages and salaries.
3. **Competitors:** If there is no competition, a business can set whatever price it chooses. On the other hand, if there is perfect competition, then the business must accept the market price for its products. In most cases the reality is somewhere in between.
4. **Customers:** The business needs to consider what customer expectations will be. In some cases, customers may be prepared to pay more for a product that is unique or produced in an ethical and sustainable manner. This would place it as a premium brand above its competitors.

McCain uses a range of pricing strategies associated with adding value for money. 'Extra-fill' packs, for example, can give the customer up to 30 per cent extra free. This rewards regular buyers of a particular product. McCain may also offer its products at a special promotional price using price-marked packs to encourage people to try the product.

Place

Place describes the channels McCain uses to position its products in the marketplace. As a business-to-business (B2B) organisation, McCain does not sell directly to consumers. Instead, it places its products with wholesalers and retailers, such as major supermarket chains. McCain may then be able to influence how its products reach the consumer at the point of sale. For example, it may secure key positions for its products in stores. By paying for end-of-shelf positions for its products, customers are more likely to see and buy them.

McCain does not use its own vehicles to distribute products to its customers. Instead, delivery transportation is outsourced to other organisations. Products are delivered directly to central depots belonging to retailers for onward distribution to individual stores. Alternatively, products may go to wholesalers, who sell them on to other businesses such as restaurants. McCain takes the need for sustainability and for reducing its impact on the environment into consideration for transporting products. This typically includes using:

- Local farm product where possible to reduce food miles.
- Double-decker trucks, saving in the region of 2,000 lorry journeys a year.
- Lorries with built-in solar panels, helping to provide additional power for internal lifting mechanisms.

Promotion

The 'It's All Good' ethos of McCain Foods supports its ethical stance on promotion. McCain makes a commitment not to advertise to children under 12 years old. It also ensures that the retail labelling on its products carries clear information on levels of fat, saturated fat, salt and sugar to help shoppers choose healthier options.

Above-the-line promotion is paid for and includes traditional advertising routes such as television, radio and the press. These are good for carrying marketing messages to a large audience. It is less easy, however, to measure the impact of these channels, for example if a TV advertisement has increased sales. Special displays or positioning in stores or advertising on supermarket trolleys are also examples of above-the-line promotional activity of McCain Foods.

McCain also uses below-the-line promotion, which can take many forms and is usually controlled by the particular business outlet. Typical examples include events or direct mail. McCain uses a combination of below-the-line activities, including:

- Door-to-door leaflet drops or books of vouchers which give customers discounts over a period of time. These help to attract consumers and to establish brand loyalty so that the consumer buys the product again.
- E-mail newsletter for consumers. This creates a relationship with consumers, which is unusual for a B2B organisation. It not only allows McCain to communicate directly with and to listen to consumers, it also enables the business to collect information, e.g. about their lifestyles and product choices. This information is used for feedback, research and promotions.

Finally, 'It's All Good' is a message that is embedded in all aspects of the McCain marketing mix. Not only are the products designed to look and taste good, they are produced from good-quality crops in a way that addresses people's concerns about issues such as health and knowing the origin of their food. This helps McCain to be a trusted brand.

Source: Adapted from www.thetimes100.co.uk/case-study—the marketing-mix-in-the-food-industry—101-401-1.php [accessed 19 March 2011].

Questions for review

1. What essential concepts should a definition of marketing include?
2. Explain what is meant by the description of marketing as an 'exchange process'.
3. Trace the historical development of the marketing concept.
4. Briefly explain what the 'four Ps' of the marketing mix refer to.
5. List the main elements in a company's macro-environment that can influence how the company operates.
6. What are the main elements in a company's micro-environment that can influence how the company operates?
7. 'Marketing is a process that provides needed direction for production and helps make sure that the right products are produced and find their way to consumers.' Discuss whether or not this is a good description of marketing.
8. Compare and contrast the sales concept and the marketing concept.
9. What does the term 'extended marketing mix for services' refer to?

2
CONSUMER AND ORGANISATIONAL BUYING BEHAVIOUR

Chapter objectives

After reading this chapter you should be able to:
- Define consumer buying behaviour.
- Recognise the stages of the consumer buying decision process.
- Understand how decision-making processes differ between consumer and organisational buying situations.
- Understand the influences that affect consumers' buying behaviour.
- Explain impulse purchases.

2.1 *Consumer buying behaviour defined*

While it is relatively simple for a company to work out who is buying what, from where and when or how much they buy, the reasons *why* people buy are usually far less clear. It is not always obvious why people respond in the ways they do to the products that are available to them or how they make the choices they are confronted with. By studying buyer behaviour, marketers aim to find out how people make their buying decisions and identify the factors that influence those decisions.

Consumer buying behaviour is defined as the study of the buying units and the exchange processes involved in acquiring, consuming and disposing of goods, services, experiences and ideas (Mowen, 1995). Within this simple definition a number of important concepts are introduced, such as the word 'exchange'. A consumer is at one end of an *exchange process* in which resources are transferred between two parties. Notice that the term '*buying units*' is used rather than 'consumers'; this is because purchases can be made by either individuals or groups.

Exchange is the core concept of consumer behaviour. Several conditions must be satisfied for an exchange to take place. There must be at least two parties and each must have something of value to the other. Each party must also want to deal with the other party and each must be free to accept or reject the other's offer. Finally, each party must be able to communicate and deliver. These conditions simply make exchange possible. A successful exchange depends on the parties coming to an agreement.

The definition of consumer behaviour also reveals that the exchange process involves a series of steps, beginning with acquiring the product (the *acquisition phase*), moving to consumption and ending with disposing of the product or service. When investigating the acquisition phase, researchers analyse the factors that influence the product and service choices of consumers. During the *consumption phase* the researcher analyses how a consumer uses a product or service and the experiences the consumer obtains from such use. The investigation of the consumption process is particularly important for service industries, for example restaurants, amusement parks, and concerts, where the consumption experience is the reason for the purchase. The *disposition phase* refers to what consumers do with a product once they have completed their use of it. In addition, it includes the level of satisfaction or dissatisfaction that consumers experience after the purchase of a good or service.

Consumer behaviour, therefore, focuses on how individuals make decisions to spend their available resources (time, money, effort) on consumption-related items. That includes what they buy, why they buy it, when they buy it, where they buy it, how often they buy it, how often they use it, how they evaluate it after the purchase and the impact of such evaluations on future purchases, and how they dispose of it.

The term *buying behaviour* describes two different kinds of buyers: the personal buyer and the organisational buyer. The *personal buyer* buys goods and services for his or her own use, for the use of the household or as a gift. In each of these contexts, the products are bought for final use by individuals, who are referred to as *end users*. The second category of buyer is the *organisational buyer*, which includes profit and not-for-profit businesses, government agencies (local and national) and institutions (e.g. hospitals, prisons and schools), all of which must buy products, equipment and services in order to run their organisations.

2.2 *The consumer decision-making process*

The *consumer decision-making process* can be divided into the following stages: problem recognition, information search, evaluation of alternatives, purchase decision and post-purchase behaviour, as shown in Fig. 2.1.

Stage 1: Problem recognition

The buying process starts with the buyer recognising a problem or a need. The buyer realises that there is a difference between his or her ***actual state*** and some ***desired state***. Being hungry, for example, leads to a drive to find food. Other purchases may be triggered by a problem: for example, if part of a car is faulty, the driver soon becomes aware of the nature of the problem and the kind of purchase that will provide a solution to the problem. If the need is sufficiently strong, it may motivate the person to enter the second stage of the consumer decision-making process: the search for information. The search for information can be either extensive or limited, depending on the involvement level of the consumer (high or low involvement).

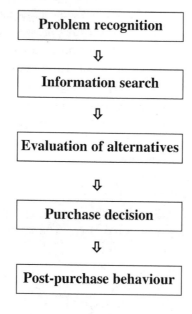

Fig. 2.1: *Stages of the consumer decision-making process*

Stage 2: Information search

The questions to be answered at this stage can include enquiries regarding what kind of purchase will solve the problem, where and how it can be obtained, what information is needed to arrive at a decision and where that information is available. The consumer can obtain information from several sources, including:

- *Personal sources* – family, friends, neighbours, acquaintances.
- *Commercial sources* – salespeople, advertising, dealers, packaging.
- *Public sources* – mass media, consumer-rating companies, the Internet.
- *Experiential sources* – handling, examining, using the product.

Information search can generally be divided into two forms: *internal search* and *external search*. Internal search involves consumers remembering previous experiences and thinking about what they have heard about the product category. The internal search is sufficient, for example, for a consumer who needs to buy biscuits. The consumer will easily remember what his or her favourite brand tastes like and will also remember where it is on the supermarket shelf. Buying a car, on the other hand, involves external search, which includes shopping around, reading manufacturers' advertisements and test-driving the car. The purpose of this exercise is to reduce risk. Buying the wrong brand of biscuits involves very little risk, since the financial commitment is low, but buying the wrong car could prove to be an expensive mistake. The Internet has had a great impact on pre-purchase search. Rather than visiting a shop to find out about a product, manufacturers' websites can provide consumers with much of the information they need about the products and services they are considering.

Stage 3: Evaluation of alternatives

This is the stage of the buying decision process at which the consumer uses information to evaluate alternative brands in a *consideration set*, which is the group of products that would most closely meet their needs. Having learned about several competing brands, the consumer will evaluate the alternatives according to the information collected or remembered. Certain basic concepts help to explain consumer evaluation processes: for example, a consumer will typically have a clear idea of the acceptable price range for the product. The consumer is trying to satisfy some need and is looking for certain *benefits* that can be acquired by buying a product or service. Each consumer sees a product as a bundle of *product attributes*, with varying capacities for delivering these benefits and satisfying the need. For mobile phones, product attributes might include keypad, camera, memory card, Bluetooth, interface, MP3 player, USB and price. Consumers will differ on the priority of the attributes that they consider relevant and will pay most attention to those attributes connected with satisfying their needs.

When a company knows that consumers will be evaluating alternatives, it sometimes advertises in a way that recommends criteria that consumers should use in assessing product or service options. When consumers compare or evaluate different brands or models of a product, they choose the product that feels, looks or performs best for them. Research shows that when consumers discuss such 'right products', there is little or no mention of price or brand names. The product often reflects personality characteristics or even childhood experiences.

Stage 4: Purchase decision

This is the fourth stage of the buying decision process, in which the consumer actually buys the product. The consumer will find the required brand, choose a retailer he or she has most faith in and also select an appropriate payment method. Purchase intention is also influenced by **unexpected situational factors**. These include in-store promotions (for example eye-catching posters for other brands) and unexpected information.

Consumers make three types of purchase: **trial purchases**, **repeat purchases** and **long-term commitment purchases**. When a consumer purchases a product for the first time and buys a smaller quantity than usual, this purchase would be considered a trial. A trial, therefore, is the exploratory phase of purchase behaviour in which consumers attempt to evaluate a product through direct use. Consumers can also be encouraged to try a new product through such promotional tactics as free samples, coupons or sale prices.

When a new brand in an established product category, for example crisps or chocolate, is found by trial to be better than other brands, consumers are likely to repeat the purchase. Unlike a trial, in which the consumer uses the product on a small scale and without any commitment, a repeat purchase usually signifies that the product meets with the consumer's approval and that he or she is willing to use it again and in larger quantities. This signifies a commitment to the product and is closely related to the concept of **brand loyalty**, which most organisations try to encourage because it contributes to greater stability in the marketplace.

A consumer's decision to change, postpone or avoid a purchase decision is influenced by **perceived risk**. Many purchases involve some risk-taking. The amount of perceived risk varies with the amount of money at stake, the amount of purchase uncertainty and the amount of consumer self-confidence. A consumer can take certain actions to reduce risk, such as avoiding purchase decisions, gathering more information or looking for national brand names and products with guarantees.

Stage 5: Post-purchase behaviour

Post-purchase behaviour is the final stage in the consumer decision-making process. After buying the product, the consumer will be satisfied or dissatisfied. Post-purchase behaviour usually involves a comparison between what the consumer was expecting to receive and what was actually received. If the product falls short of expectations, the evaluation leads to *post-purchase dissonance* or *post-purchase conflict*. Whether a consumer is satisfied or dissatisfied with a purchase is determined by the relationship between the expectations and the product's perceived performance. Consumers base their expectations on messages they receive from sellers, friends and other information sources. If the product meets expectations, the consumer is satisfied. If the product exceeds expectations, the consumer is very happy. The most effective way of reducing post-purchase dissonance is to provide a product that meets the consumer's expectations. A failure to solve problems raised by post-purchase dissonance will ultimately lead to irreparable damage to a company's reputation.

The degree of post-purchase analysis that consumers undertake depends on the importance of the product decision and the experience acquired in using the product. When the product lives up to expectations, consumers will probably buy it again. The consumer's post-purchase evaluation acts as experience and serves to influence future related decisions. When the product's performance is disappointing or does not meet expectations, however, consumers will search for a more suitable option.

The consumer decision-making process, as described above, can involve all or some of the five stages of purchasing. In more routine purchases, however, consumers skip or reverse some stages.

2.3 Types of consumer involvement in different buying situations

The level of a consumer's *involvement* is influenced by the perceived personal importance and interest in a buying decision. Personal importance increases as the perceived risk of purchasing increases. *Low involvement* occurs in the purchase of a low-risk, routine purchase, for example toothpaste or milk. In contrast, *high involvement* occurs where an item is expensive, can have serious social consequences or could reflect on one's social image. When a consumer's involvement level increases, they begin to process information about the product in more depth. This means that they are more likely to think about a purchase decision under such circumstances. As the product or service under consideration becomes more expensive, socially visible and risky to purchase, a consumer's involvement in the purchase is likely to increase. The involvement concept is important for marketers in order to understand consumer behaviour. The level of involvement influences the amount of information processing and attitude formation and change before a consumer buys a product. Fig. 2.2 illustrates the decision-making process for high-involvement and low-involvement products.

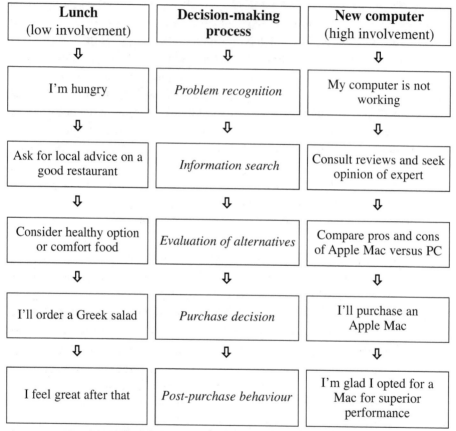

Fig. 2.2: *The decision-making process for lunch (low involvement) versus a new computer (high involvement)*

Impulse purchases

An *impulse purchase* has been defined as a 'buying action undertaken without a problem having been previously recognised or a buying intention formed prior to entering the store' (Langer and Imba, 1980). Impulse purchases, therefore, are made with no planning. An impulse purchase may be described as a choice made on the spur of the moment based upon the development of a strong positive feeling regarding an object. The visual stimulus of seeing a product available on a shelf is what prompts a person to buy. The motivation is sudden and instant, and consequently such purchases can lead to feelings of guilt. Emotions and feelings play a decisive role in purchasing, triggered by seeing the product or upon exposure to a well-crafted promotional message. Marketers and retailers tend to exploit impulses for instant gratification.

Various studies have found that as many as 39 per cent of department store purchases and 67 per cent of grocery store purchases may be unplanned (Mowen, 1995). After the purchase has been made, consumers may realise that they have little need for the product and may regret the failure to evaluate more carefully (though this may not deter them from making a similar purchase in the future). The powerful urge to buy seems to override conscious rationality. Marketers have long recognised the potential for impulse purchase of non-essential items such as confectionery and magazines at supermarket check-outs. Faced with a short wait in a queue, shoppers are ideally placed to pick up the visual stimuli from such items, which are unlikely to have been on their shopping lists and would otherwise have been passed by in the aisles.

Addictive consumption

Consumer addiction is a physiological and/or psychological dependency on products or services. While most people equate addiction with drugs, virtually any product or service can be seen as relieving some problem or satisfying some need to the point where reliance on it becomes extreme. Indeed, some psychologists are even raising concerns about Internet addiction, where people (particularly college students) become obsessed with online chat rooms to the point that their 'virtual' lives take priority over their real ones.

Compulsive consumption

For some consumers, the expression 'born to shop' is taken quite literally. These consumers shop because they are compelled to do so, rather than because shopping is a pleasurable or functional task. *Compulsive consumption* refers to repetitive shopping, often excessive, as an antidote to tension, anxiety, depression, or boredom. 'Shopaholics' turn to shopping much the same way as addicted people turn to drugs or alcohol. While shopping, compulsive shoppers may report feeling intensely excited, happy and powerful. These emotions are frequently followed by distress or guilt. Compulsive shoppers may return purchases or hide them in wardrobes or attics, never to be used.

Compulsive consumption is different from impulse buying. The impulse to buy a specific item is temporary and it centres on a specific product at a particular moment. In contrast, compulsive buying is an enduring behaviour that centres on the process of buying, not on the purchases themselves.

2.4 *Influences on the buying decision*

The main influences on the buying decision are:
- Personal factors.
- Psychological factors.
- Social factors.

The **personal factors** that influence buying decisions include individual characteristics such as age, gender, nationality, occupation, income and life style. People change the choice of goods and services they buy over their lifetime. For instance, their taste in clothes, music and leisure activities are age related. Many needs are age dependent, for example baby food. **Life style** covers not only demographic characteristics but also attitudes to life, beliefs and aspirations, hobbies, sports interests and opinions. A person's occupation and economic situation will also affect product choice: for example, a managing director will buy expensive clothes for work, whereas a factory worker will buy utility clothing and utility shoes.

Psychological factors that influence buying decisions include perception, attitude, learning, motivation and personality. **Perception** is the process by which people analyse, select, organise and interpret information in order to make sense of it. No two people will interpret the same information in the same way, whether it is a product's package or its taste or smell. Perception is of interest to marketers because of the influence it can have on consumers' decision-making generally and on the way it can affect the understanding of marketing communication. Consumers are very selective regarding their environmental perceptions. A person may look at some things, ignore others and turn away from other things. Because the brain's capacity to process information is limited, consumers are very selective about what they pay attention to. **Perceptual selectivity** means that people attend to only a small portion of things to which they are exposed. They pick and choose among items so as to avoid being overwhelmed by advertising clutter.

This over-abundance of advertising illustrates two important aspects of perceptual selectivity as they relate to consumer behaviour: exposure and attention. **Exposure** is the degree to which people notice a stimulus. A **stimulus** is anything that has an input to any of the senses: examples include products, packets, brand names and advertisements. *Selective exposure* occurs when consumers actively seek out messages that they find pleasant while they actively avoid painful or threatening messages. The smoker therefore avoids articles that point out the link between cigarette smoking and cancer. Consumers also selectively expose themselves to advertisements that reassure them of the wisdom of their purchasing decisions.

Attention is the degree to which consumers concentrate on stimuli that meet their needs or interests. This can register minimal awareness of stimuli that are irrelevant to their needs. Consumers are therefore likely to notice advertisements for products that would satisfy their needs and for stores in which they shop and to disregard advertisements in which they have no interest. A vivid packet, for example, is one way of actively gaining attention.

Attitude is a person's favourable or unfavourable feelings and tendencies towards a product or service. Attitudes are learned, which means that attitudes relevant to purchasing behaviour are formed as a result of direct experience with the product, information acquired from others or promotions. Another characteristic of attitudes is that they are relatively consistent, as they tend to endure over time, but they are often difficult to change. Consumers' attitudes to products can be complex. They can develop attitudes to any kind of product or service, or indeed to any aspect of the marketing mix, and these attitudes will affect behaviour. Changing consumers' attitudes is an important strategy consideration for marketers who are not market leaders.

Social factors also influence consumers' behaviour, for example *peer groups*, *family* and *status*. Peer groups will exert a particular type of behaviour and put pressure on the person to conform. Research has shown, for example, that smokers begin to smoke as a result of pressure from their friends when they are young teenagers. The desire to be a fully accepted member of the group is far stronger than any health warnings. Peer pressure contributes to buying for materialistic or social reasons, for example keeping up with social pressure or not to seem to be the odd one out.

Family members can also have a strong influence on buyers' behaviour. Different family members frequently take over the role of buyer for specific product categories: for example, older children may decide on food, choosing environmentally responsible alternatives. Another reason for the family's importance is its role as a *socialisation agent*. Socialisation may be defined as *the process by which people acquire knowledge and skills that enable them to participate as members of society*. Examples of socialisation agents include parents, brothers and sisters, teachers and the media.

Status is the general esteem given to a role by society. People sometimes choose products for their social status. A motivation for the purchase and display of such products is not to enjoy them but to let others know that one can afford them. Status-seeking is a significant source of motivation to buy appropriate products and services that the user hopes will inform others of his or her raised status.

In summary, understanding consumers' needs and the buying process is the foundation of successful marketing. By understanding how buyers go through problem recognition, information search, evaluation of alternatives, the purchase decision and post-purchase behaviour, the marketer can pick up many clues for meeting consumers' needs. Consumers' buying behaviour is the result of personal, psychological and social factors, which are useful for the marketer in identifying and understanding the consumers they are trying to influence.

---

1. Consumer analysis should be the foundation of marketing management. It assists managers in:
   a. Designing the marketing mix.
   b. Segmenting the marketplace.
   c. Positioning and differentiating products.
   d. Performing environmental analysis.
   e. Developing market research studies.
2. Consumer behaviour should play an important role in the development of public policy.
3. The study of consumer behaviour will enhance one's own ability to be a more effective consumer.
4. Consumer analysis provides knowledge of human behaviour.
5. The study of consumer behaviour provides three types of information:
   a. A consumer orientation.
   b. Facts about human behaviour.
   c. Theories to guide the thinking process.

Table 2.1: *Reasons for studying consumer behaviour*

Source: Mowen (1995).

2.5 *Organisational buying behaviour*

Organisational buyers buy products and services on behalf of the organisations they work for. The needs they are trying to satisfy are the needs of the organisation. They buy components for the products that their organisations assemble; they buy accountancy services to enable their organisation to audit their finances; they buy capital equipment so that their organisations can produce goods and services for sale. A definition of organisational buying is 'the decision-making process by which formal organisations establish the need for purchased products and services, and identify, evaluate, and choose among alternative brands and suppliers' (Kotler and Armstrong, 1995).

There are six key stages in the ***organisational buying decision-making process***:

- ***Problem recognition:*** Similar to the consumer's 'perception of need', someone in an organisation recognises that a problem may be solved by the acquisition of goods or services. Internally, this may occur due to a new product development, under-capacity or problems with quality control; externally, this may occur when a buyer sees a product report in the trade press or is offered a promotional price by a potential new supplier.

- ***Product specification:*** Often in conjunction with other members of the decision-making unit who have expertise and can give technical advice, the buyer will draw up a general description and then a precise specification of the nature and quantity of the product required.

- ***Supplier search:*** The buyer will identify potential suppliers of the specified products and may ask them to submit proposals or give sales presentations to demonstrate their capabilities and indicate their prices.

- ***Supplier selection:*** This is commonly done by ranking the desired attributes of potential suppliers in order of importance. The list is likely to include a number of purely functional attributes, such as price, delivery, quality and after-sales service, but may also include less tangible features such as corporate ethics and communication skills. Suppliers chosen will be those who most closely meet the key criteria. In many cases, organisations will choose more than one supplier for products they require on a regular basis to ensure continuity of supply in case of one supplier's default and to allow the price and service comparison of different suppliers over a period of time.

- ***Ordering:*** Placing an order with a supplier may be a one-off activity or may take the form of a contract to purchase under agreed terms over a period of time. Usually these terms will include payment terms; while consumers usually pay cash upfront before they receive their products or services, organisations usually set up accounts with their suppliers, receiving goods first and subsequently paying for them within a stipulated time period.

- ***Performance evaluation:*** Buyers collect information about the performance of their suppliers and use this as an important source of information when a similar product is required again. Sometimes this information is used as part of a system for motivating suppliers to maintain excellent performance levels.

Categories of organisational buyers

There are generally four broad *categories of organisational buyers*:

- *Industrial producers:* Typified by manufacturing companies, this category consists of all the individuals and organisations acquiring goods and services that enter into production of other products and services that are sold or supplied to others. Buyers or purchasing managers will usually be professionally trained and qualified and usually work within a separate purchasing department.

- *Commercial and reseller organisations:* This consists of all organisations such as retailers and wholesalers that acquire goods for the purpose of reselling or renting them to others at a profit. While they do not physically alter the products they handle in general, they will seek to add value through service. Their purchase decisions in respect of traded goods will be dominated by commercial criteria such as bought-in costs, resale price and profitability. The larger retail organisations with an increasingly dominant position in consumer markets have large bargaining power. In recent years some retail groups such as Marks & Spencer have taken the lead in developing stronger partnership links with preferred suppliers.

- *Government and public sector organisations:* These exhibit the most formality in their buying behaviour. Traditionally, their approach to purchasing has been highly conservative and slow moving, often subject to red tape, committees and rules and procedures. There are signs, however, that public sector purchasing is now becoming more professional and commercially driven, perhaps in response to the general containment of public sector expenditure almost everywhere.

- *Institutions:* Colleges, hospitals and voluntary organisations are similar to the public sector in their buying behaviour. Traditionally, purchasing has been a semi-formal activity. Recent external influences and policy changes, such as funding constraints, have made purchasing more professional and competitive.

Organisational buyers differ from consumers by being more formalised in their buying behaviour. Organisational buying differs from consumer buying in the following respects:

- Bigger order values in terms of finance and quantity.
- Fewer buyers, because there are fewer firms than there are individual consumers.
- More people in the decision-making process.
- More complex techniques for buying and negotiating.

- Because the purchases are more complex, organisational buyers may take longer to make their decisions.
- Buyer and seller are often more dependent on each other, which means the firms may buy each other's products as part of a negotiated deal.

Organisational consumers usually:	Individual consumers usually:
Purchase goods and services that meet specific business needs	Purchase goods and services that meet individual or family needs
Need emphasis on economic benefits	Need emphasis on psychological benefits
Use formalised, lengthy purchasing policies and processes	Buy on impulse or with minimal processes
Involve large groups in purchasing decisions	Purchase as individuals or as a family unit
Buy large quantities and buy infrequently	Buy small quantities and buy frequently
Want a customised product package	Are content with a standardised product
Experience major problems if supply fails	Experience minor irritation if supply fails
Find switching to another supplier difficult	Find switching to another supplier easy
Negotiate on price	Accept the stated price
Purchase directly from suppliers	Purchase from intermediaries
Justify an emphasis on personal selling communication	Justify an emphasis on mass media

Table 2.2: *Differences between organisational and consumer buying behaviour*

Source: Brassington and Pettitt (2006).

Types of organisational buying situations

The organisational buyer faces a number of decisions when making a purchase. The number of decisions depends on the type of buying situation. According to Robinson et al. (1967), there are three categories of buying situations:

- **Straight rebuy:** In a straight rebuy, the buyer reorders something without any modifications. When the buying task is familiar and recurring, routine ordering procedures are used to place orders with acceptable suppliers. Based on previous buying satisfaction, the buyer simply chooses from various suppliers on its list, which makes it very difficult for new suppliers to break in.

- *Modified rebuy:* In a modified rebuy, the buyer wants to modify product specifications, prices, terms or suppliers. If buyers become dissatisfied with their routine purchases for any reason, they may decide to consider new suppliers; their objectives may be to get better prices, to change the product specification, to improve the delivery times or simply to review the effectiveness of their routine purchases. This provides an opportunity for new firms to get onto the shortlist and current suppliers must reassess what they offer and prepare for the likelihood of further negotiation.
- *New task:* In a new task, the company is buying a product or service for the first time. In this situation, all the stages of the decision-making process are likely to be in evidence, though the amount of detail included in the product specification and the lengths to which buyers will go to find the best supplier are still likely to vary according to the value of the product and its importance in the operations of the organisation.

2.6 *Collaborators*

Buying materials, hiring an advertising agency or getting a loan from a bank all require that a company works together with another company. These companies are called *collaborators*. Collaborators help the company run its business without actually being part of the company. They are often specialists who provide specific services or supply raw materials, component parts or production equipment. Working with collaborators helps companies enhance their flexibility, especially in global marketing activities. Before an organisation decides how much it will work with collaborators, its managers should ascertain the company's core competencies. A *core competency* is a talent in a critical functional activity, such as technical knowledge or a particular business specialisation, that helps provide a company's unique competitive advantage. In other words, core competencies are what an organisation does best.

Important terms and concepts

consumer buying behaviour: p. 24
exchange process: p. 24
buying units: p. 24
acquisition phase: p. 25
consumption phase: p. 25
disposition phase: p. 25
personal buyer: p. 25
organisational buyer: p. 25

consumer decision-making process:
  p. 25
problem recognition: p. 26
actual state: p. 26
desired state: p. 26
information search: p. 26
personal sources: p. 27
commercial sources: p. 27

Case study: The 'Choose Cadbury' marketing strategy endeavours to have a Cadbury product for every occasion

The Cadbury brand name has existed since 1824, when John Cadbury opened his first shop in Birmingham, England. Cadbury Ireland, as a subsidiary of Cadbury Schweppes, is the fourth largest confectionary business in the world, selling chocolate, sugar and gum-based products. Cadbury Ireland is the number one confectionery company in Ireland. Cadbury products range from solid blocks to chocolate-filled bars and novelties. The Cadbury brand is associated with pleasant-tasting chocolate. Marketing managers at Cadbury are working to ensure that the association of pleasant-tasting chocolate is continually developed through their 'Choose Cadbury' marketing strategy. Key concepts of quality, taste and emotion underpin the Cadbury brand. These core values aim to differentiate Cadbury from other brands and to help its competitive advantage.

The Cadbury family of brands: The umbrella brand

In the chocolate market, the Cadbury brand has more than 50 per cent market share, selling 10 of the 20 top-selling chocolate singles (singles are individual bars sold to consumers). Research data show that Cadbury brand equity is highly differentiated from other brands by consumers. Brand equity is the value consumer loyalty brings to a brand and reflects the likelihood that a consumer will repeat purchases. The Cadbury umbrella brand has endured in a highly competitive market and has established a link in the mind of the consumer that Cadbury equals chocolate. An umbrella brand is a parent brand that appears on a number of products that may each have separate brand images. The Cadbury umbrella brand consists of four icons: the Cadbury script, the 'glass and a half', the dark purple colour and the swirling chocolate image. These images create a visual identity for Cadbury that communicates chocolate as a pleasurable experience. Consumer research is conducted frequently so that managers can learn more about how the market perceives the brand. Research has confirmed that the swirling chocolate and the 'glass and a half' are powerful marketing images, associated with a desire for chocolate, while the half-full glass suggests values of goodness and quality.

Product brands

The Cadbury brand has a strong effect on individual product brands. Brands have individual personalities aimed at specific target markets for each need; for example, TimeOut is promoted as a snack to accompany a cup of tea. These brands benefit from the Cadbury parentage, including quality and taste credentials. To help subsidiary product brands to succeed, all aspects of the parent brand are included. While a Flake, Crunchie or TimeOut, for example, are clearly different and manufactured to appeal to a variety of consumer segments, the strength of the umbrella brand is always used to support these and other Cadbury chocolate products. Consumers believe they can trust a chocolate bar that carries Cadbury branding. Some brands maintain a stronger relationship with the Cadbury brand of pure chocolate, such as Dairy Milk, while other brands have a more distant relationship, as the consumer motivation to purchase is for ingredients other than chocolate, such as Crunchie. Similarly, issues such as specific advertising or product quality of a packet of Cadbury biscuits or a single Creme Egg will in turn impact on the perception of the parent brand. At the same time, the umbrella brand has a strong brand value and a reputation that is supported by its individual brands.

Identifying brand values

We are all consciously and unconsciously affected by brands in our daily lives. For example, when we decide to purchase a pair of training shoes, we rarely make a purely practical decision. There are numerous branded and non-branded options available. For many people, a pair of trainers must sport a brand logo, as that will communicate certain values to other people. The confectionery market elicits similar conscious and unconscious feelings of passion, loyalty and enthusiasm. For many people, chocolate is Cadbury and no other brand will do. This type of consumer loyalty is critical, as a small number of consumers, in all markets, account for a large proportion of sales. Loyal customers are the most valuable customers to have because they will buy a product over and over again.

Branded products command premium prices. Consumers will happily pay that premium if they believe that the brand offers levels of quality and satisfaction that competing products do not. The most enduring brands have become associated with both tangible and intangible properties over time. The most successful brands provoke a series of emotional or aspirational associations and values in consumers' minds that go far beyond the physical product. Cadbury has identified these brand values and adjusts its advertising strategies to reflect these values in different markets. Its strategy can vary from increasing brand awareness, educating potential customers about a new product, increasing seasonal purchases or – as is currently the case in the 'Choose Cadbury' campaign – to highlight the positive emotional value of the brand. After identifying brand values, the marketing manager must match these to the specific market. For this reason it is important to identify possible segments that have specific needs and to highlight appropriate brand values that will promote the brand in that market.

Consumer lifestyles and chocolate consumption

The Cadbury core markets are currently in Great Britain, Ireland, Australia and New Zealand. The Cadbury brand is very well known in these markets and consumers have established patterns of chocolate consumption. Ireland has one of the highest chocolate consumption rates in the world, along with Switzerland. In Ireland alone, the average person eats 8 kg of chocolate and 6 kg of sweets each year. In these key geographic areas, the Cadbury brand has secured significant brand status.

The Cadbury product range aims to address the needs of any consumer, young or old, whether for impulse purchases or as special treats. In Ireland, Cadbury has identified three key consumer segments: impulse, take-home and gift. These segments reflect consumer decision-making processes. Impulse purchases, for example, are typically for products bought for immediate consumption, such as single bars. Take-home confectionery is generally bought in a supermarket and is often motivated by a specific need or usage, such as 'I need something for the lunchbox.' Here consumers tend to make more rational decisions, for example on a blend of brand influence and the price–value relationship. These areas can be further subdivided. For example, the gift sector can include special occasions (birthdays, Christmas, etc.) as well as token and spontaneous gifts. Where marketers successfully identify and isolate consumer segments in this manner, it becomes easier to target products and advertising in a more meaningful way to increase consumption.

Source: Adapted from www.business2000.ie/pdf/pdf_12/cadbury_12th_ed.pdf [accessed 19 March 2011].

Case study: The National Lottery: Facilitating online consumer buyer behaviour

The National Lottery is a state-owned business that was set up by the Government in 1987. The National Lottery mission is 'to operate a world-class lottery for the people of Ireland, raising funds for good causes, on behalf of Government'. The vision of the National Lottery is to provide exciting and engaging lottery games that bring fun and entertainment to everyone.

In 2009, overall National Lottery sales reached €815.1 million. This was achieved despite a downturn in the economy. Innovation is seen as one of the National Lottery's key elements for growing business. In 2009, a programme of game developments was implemented to keep the National Lottery's portfolio relevant and attractive. This included the launch of National Lottery Play Online.

The National Lottery recognises the increasing importance of its Internet presence, including its online media presence through outlets such as Twitter, Facebook and other mobile technologies and social networking sites. The Lottery continually evolves to remain competitive in a rapidly changing business environment, including satisfying the demands of online customers. Its website is an essential element of its interface with customers, using an attractive and easy-to-navigate website, which clarifies and reinforces its brand values.

The number of online players is growing steadily as more people become aware of the convenient option of playing National Lottery games on the Internet. Up-to-date information, including draw results, is available online. Online players can play National Lottery games from their own homes and receive an e-mail from the National Lottery when they win a prize. The website's site map, accessible from the homepage, gives a clear outline of everything available on the site. Online customers are given instructions on how to enter the Lotto draw, thus reducing the amount of basic enquiry contact customers have to make with the National Lottery. This allows for better use of resources and time, which can in turn reduce staff costs.

A number of popular draw games and instant-win games are available online once players complete the registration process. The games include Lotto, Lotto Plus, EuroMillions and EuroMillions Plus, together with instant-win games such as Blackjack, Bingo, Angels & Devils, Spin to Win and Suit Pursuit. This benefits customers, as it is both convenient and time-saving.

When introducing Play Online, the National Lottery looked at ways to ensure the games were secure and appropriate for the Irish market. As with all National Lottery games, proper system facilities and security checks are put in place to safeguard players and to guarantee integrity, credibility and fairness, which are the hallmarks of its business. A new National Lottery smartphone application has been created to allow users to check draw results. There is a 'number generator' that works by moving the mobile phone around, which initiates a random selection process similar to the 'Quick Pick' random number selection available at a National Lottery retail outlet.

SWOT analysis: Developing a business online

A SWOT analysis of a business examines its internal strengths and weaknesses and its external opportunities and threats. The objective of a SWOT analysis is to enable a firm to profitably avail of possible future opportunities.

Strengths

- Improved customer service.
- Online presence 24/7.
- Professionalism.
- Efficient and relatively inexpensive way of reaching new customers.
- Powerful, fast and efficient marketing and communication tool.
- Increases productivity.
- Better understanding of player behaviour through website analysis.
- A convenient way to play National Lottery games.

Weaknesses

- Not everyone has Internet access.
- Significant investment is required to develop and support the website systems.
- Online security systems can be expensive.

Opportunities

- Greater market reach: captures a greater number of customers.
- Increased sales and profits.
- Improved understanding of customers and their preferences.
- Potential to grow the number and type of games.
- Potential to gain greater knowledge of players.

Threats

- Fear about security of personal and financial information.
- Competition, to some extent, with existing retail networks.

Market segmentation through the web

With 65 per cent of all adults, or 2.2 million people, playing National Lottery games on a regular basis, the player base draws from all adult population segments. A breakdown of National Lottery Play Online users illustrates that 72 per cent are male and 28 per cent are female. The age profile ranges from 2 per cent of 18–24-year-olds, 34 per cent of 25–34-year-olds, 43 per cent of 35–49-year-olds, 18 per cent of 50–64-year-olds, and 3 per cent of those aged 65+ (www.lottery.ie statistics).

During 2009, the National Lottery continued its strategy of developing an overall mix of games to keep players involved and excited by the prizes on offer and the fun of playing. Having concentrated on extending the portfolio of games over the last number of years, the marketing strategy for the coming years will be to promote the various benefits of these games to existing and new players.

The Play Online facility is open to all Irish residents over the age of 18. Responding to customer needs demands that the business expands and becomes more competitive and customer focused. This type of organic growth occurs when a business offers the same product to a new market. The National Lottery website gets on average 1.3 million visits per month and 42,600 visits per day. On the day following a very large jackpot, the site can expect to get over 120,000 visits.

There is a lot of potential in the Internet-based games market. It is a strong growth area consistent with the general uptake of digital communications and expectations of today's generation of players. This should ensure growth in the overall market for games.

Benefits of technology

Being competitive is the key to successful business. Selling goods and services online is now imperative to ensure growth and increased market share. The following are some of the benefits for National Lottery customers and for the business itself.

For customers

- **Access**: Customers can access information 24/7 and access games between 7 a.m. and 10 p.m. each day.
- **Convenience**: National Lottery Play Online can offer useful features, such as play in advance, by saving favourite numbers and play history to make playing much easier.
- **Up-to-date**: The website is updated on an ongoing basis, so players can access results immediately after a draw.
- **Secure**: Top-of-the-range security measures are used and are updated on a daily basis to keep personal and financial information safe.
- **Environmental**: Online business is environmentally friendly. Information is communicated via e-mail or text, including the use of virtual tickets. This cuts down on paper costs and saves more organic resources.
- **Gaeilge**: In accordance with the Official Languages Act, the National Lottery website is available in both Irish and English. Customers can click on the 'Gaeilge' tab on the top of the homepage to access the website through Irish.
- **Accessible**: Customers with visual disabilities are provided with font sizes that can be enlarged in online browsers.

For the National Lottery

- **Time saving**: Customer needs can be met immediately, ensuring greater customer satisfaction and loyalty to the site.
- **Cost benefits**: Reduced costs of printing.
- **Driving business forward**: New customers are accessing the site every day. This increases the profile of the business and drives the business forward.
- **Maintaining competitiveness**: Online access to games is imperative to suit the ever-changing needs of society.
- **More timely service**: Any issues that arise can be dealt with immediately. Customers can e-mail any questions or concerns they may have and staff will reply within 24 hours.
- **Better understanding**: Online games allow the National Lottery to monitor customer preferences. By monitoring the options that online customers select, the National Lottery can identify and analyse customer needs and priorities. The National Lottery can communicate news – such as game results, winner information and prize details – quickly and efficiently through www.lottery.ie.
- **Better response rate from customers**: Instant access to the games means a better response rate from customers. Customers quickly become familiar with the website and find it easy to find new games that they may not have played before.
- **Instant target market**: If the National Lottery wants to launch a new game, they have immediate access to their customers. Customers can be informed and encouraged to try new games.

Overall, the launch of National Lottery Play Online should ensure the continued growth and success of the National Lottery. Expanding the variety of games on offer and how players can access games should increase the existing customer base and encourage a greater uptake by Irish residents. New games like Online Bingo can be introduced and there is potential for expanding the variety of games in order to appeal to different market segments. There is also an opportunity to make all draw games available online. The National Lottery aims to bring their games to a new generation of players and, in doing so, build on the €3.4 billion raised for good causes to date.

Source: Adapted from: http://www.business2000.ie/case_studies/national_lottery/index.html [accessed 19 March 2011].

Questions for review

1. What are the main stages of the consumer buy process?
2. Why are attitudes difficult to change?
3. Why is post-purchase behaviour important for the consumer?
4. Why is post-purchase behaviour important for the marketer?
5. Review your own decision to choose the course of study you have selected and re-create what took place at each stage of the decision process.
6. Compare the decision-making process a consumer goes through for (*a*) a high-involvement product and (*b*) a low-involvement product.
7. Compare consumer and organisational buying behaviour.
8. Outline the four broad categories of organisational buyers.

COMPANY ANALYSIS AND MARKETING PLANNING

Chapter objectives

After reading this chapter you should be able to:

- Analyse a company's capability.
- Conduct a SWOT analysis.
- Discuss Porter's three generic strategies.
- Describe the marketing planning process.
- Understand strategic business units.
- Discuss social responsibility and managerial ethics.

3.1 *The company*

The term '*company*' refers to the business or organisation in itself. A number of companies make up the industry in which a company operates: for example, Ford, Toyota, Opel, Mazda, Renault, BMW and Mercedes are companies in the car industry. Marketing, though essential, is only one functional activity of a company and must be integrated with other functional areas. In determining the costs of manufacturing a product, for example, marketing relies on information supplied by the manufacturing and accounts departments. Marketers work within the framework of the corporate objectives set by top managers, who are responsible for the company's operations.

Corporate objectives are the stated strategic aims of a company of where it wants to be. These objectives help to create guidelines for a company's marketing plans and are normally presented in the form of financial, qualitative and policy targets.

- **Financial targets** are to increase market share, sales, profit and return on investment over a set period.
- **Qualitative targets** include such matters as service levels, productivity, innovation and financial and physical resources.
- **Policy targets** are likely to be contained in a *mission statement*. This represents a vision of where the company is today and where it wants to be

in the future. It expresses the core values of a company and is intended to guide the company in its strategic development. A mission statement is a generalised statement of the overriding purpose of a company.

For example, when the Ford Motor Company was founded in 1903, Henry Ford had a clear understanding that cars need not be only for the rich – that the average American family needed economical transportation in the form of a low-priced car. Ford also had the insight to know that he could use product standardisation and assembly line technology to accomplish this mission.

• 'To make the world's information universally accessible and useful.' (Google)
• 'To build a place where people can come to find and discover anything they might want to buy online.' (Amazon)
• 'To lead in corporate citizenship through proactive programs that reflect caring for the world family of Nike, our teammates, our consumers, and those who provide services to Nike.' (Nike)
• 'Twitter is a service for friends, family, and co-workers to communicate and stay connected through the exchange of quick, frequent answers to one simple question, "What are you doing?"' (Twitter)

Table 3.1: *Examples of mission statements*

Corporate strategy

Corporate strategy concerns the allocation of resources within the company to achieve the business direction and scope specified within corporate objectives. Although the marketing department is primarily responsible for responding to perceived marketing opportunities, it cannot act without the involvement of all other areas of the company. Corporate strategy, therefore, helps to control and co-ordinate the different areas of the company, such as finance, marketing, production, research and development etc., to ensure that they are all working towards the same objectives and that those objectives are consistent with the desired direction of the company as a whole.

3.2 Analysing company capability

It is vital for an organisation to use company analysis to gain an understanding of the organisation's limiting and enabling factors and strategic capabilities. Profits can then be maximised by selecting the most effective strategies and through the successful implementation of mergers, acquisitions and divestment opportunities.

Marketing managers need to ensure the successful integration and co-ordination of activities in their company. Managers in companies that are marketing oriented regularly ask questions fundamental to the success of the company, such as:

- Which markets should we be in?
- Where are we now?
- Where do we want to get to?
- How do we get there?

It is important to analyse a company's present position but also to consider issues for the future by asking questions such as:

- Who are our existing or potential customers?
- What are their present and future needs?
- How can we satisfy these needs?
- What will our competitors be doing in three or five years' time?
- Can we assume that our current mode of operating will be good enough for the future?

These concerns are strategic, not operational, in that they affect the whole company and provide a framework for subsequent operational decisions. The focus is on the future, aligning the whole company to new opportunities and challenges within a challenging marketing environment.

When analysing a company's capability, a manager needs to measure the degree to which the needs of target customers are satisfied by the company's products or services. A manager also needs to be able to measure the company's market share and to analyse whether it is moving up or down or holding its position.

Evaluating a company's performance is also necessary for analysing the company's capability. Market share is an evaluative measure for the manager. A manager also needs to be able to answer such questions as:

- How good is our performance?
- What size is our market share?
- Is quality consistently high?

There are two basic approaches for evaluating performance: sales analysis and marketing cost analysis.

Sales analysis looks at the income generated by a company's activities. A manager can compare the sales achieved against what was forecast for the same period. The manager can also make comparisons with competitors' sales.

Marketing cost analysis looks at the costs of generating income. Costs can be broken down into direct costs, such as sales force salaries, and other costs, such as advertising for specific products and the cost of public relations that cannot be allocated to any particular product range or brand.

When a discrepancy appears between the expected performance and the actual performance, the marketing manager will need to take action. The difference between the two positions can be called the *strategic gap*. The marketing manager needs to determine the reason for the discrepancy, for example if the original plan was reasonable, if competitors seized an opportunity or if someone was at fault. The answers to these questions need to be related back to the employees concerned in order to develop a plan for correcting the discrepancy. Planning occurs so that the gap may be closed to enable the company to move from a situation it does not want to a situation that it does want.

3.3 *Situational analysis*

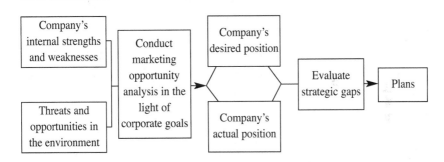

Fig. 3.1: *How situational analysis helps match opportunities to the company*

Situational analysis is the activity of interpreting environmental conditions and changes in order for a company to take advantage of potential opportunities and to ward off problems. Managers need to know the position of their company now if they are to decide where they want it to be in the future. This will involve examining the internal state of the company and examining the external environment in which the company operates. The three essentials of analysis are company, customer and competitor.

According to Murray and O'Driscoll (1999), when analysing a company's capability it is important to understand:

- The company's market position and the strengths and weaknesses of that position.
- The feasibility of proposed marketing plans.

- The opportunity to build the competence to serve new markets and to outperform new competition.

Managers can use **SWOT analysis** to examine their company's internal and external position. SWOT stands for a company's *strengths, weaknesses, opportunities* and *threats*. Strengths and weaknesses tend to concentrate on the present and past and on internal factors, such as the traditional 'four Ps'. Regarding the external environment, however, strengths and weaknesses are usually defined in relation to competitors. Low prices, for example, may be seen as a strength for a company if it is pricing below its nearest competitor but may be seen as a weakness if it has been forced by a price war into charging a low price that it cannot sustain.

Opportunities and threats tend to refer to the present and the future and take an outward-looking strategic view of likely developments and options. One company, for example, may seize an opportunity to implement new technology, but for another company new technology may be seen as a threat. The SWOT analysis, therefore, helps managers to sort information systematically. If strengths and weaknesses represent where the company is now and opportunities and threats represent where a company wants to be, then the marketing plan shows managers what they have to do to reach their desired position. The following list is an example of some questions a manager might ask when conducting a SWOT analysis.

Strengths	What are we best at?
	What financial resources have we?
	What specific skills has the workforce?
Weaknesses	What are we worst at doing?
	What is our financial position?
	What training does our workforce lack?
Opportunities	What new markets might be opening up for us?
	What new technology might be available to us?
	What weaknesses in our competitors can we exploit?
Threats	How will the economic cycle affect us?
	What social changes might threaten us?
	How do our competitors affect us?

In many competitor analyses, marketers build detailed profiles of each market competitor, focusing in particular on their relative competitive strengths and weaknesses by using a SWOT analysis. Marketing managers will examine each competitor's cost structure, sources of profits, resources and competencies, competitive positioning and product differentiation, historical responses to industry developments and other factors.

Strengths
• Specialist marketing expertise
• New innovative product or service
• Strong brand or reputation
• Quality processes and procedures
• Location of business
• Patents
Weaknesses
• Lack of marketing expertise
• Location of business
• Poor-quality goods or services
• Damaged reputation
• Undifferentiated products or services (in comparison to competitors)
Opportunities
• Developing market (e.g. China, the Internet)
• Removal of international trade barriers
• Mergers, joint ventures or strategic alliances
• Moving into new, attractive market segments
Threats
• Price war
• New regulations
• Increased trade barriers
• New competitor
• Taxation may be introduced on products or services

Table 3.2: *Sample factors in a SWOT analysis*

Having set out the SWOT elements, they are compared in order to answer questions such as: Does the company have the resources and willingness to take advantage of opportunities? Do threats pose risks against which the business is unguarded?

Understanding the SWOT analysis

The SWOT analysis, therefore, helps to sort information systematically and to classify it. The scale of opportunities and threats, and the feasibility of the potential courses of action implied by them, can really only be understood in terms of the organisation's strengths and weaknesses. If strengths and weaknesses represent 'where we are now' and opportunities and threats represent 'where we want (or don't want) to be' or 'where we could be', then the gap, representing 'what we have to do to get there', has to be filled by managerial imagination, as justified and formalised in the marketing plan.

3.4 *Establishing strategic business units*

The organisational mission and other strategic corporate goals, once established, provide a framework for determining what organisational structure is most appropriate to the organisation's marketing efforts. For a company that markets only a single product or service, the organisation will be relatively simple. In medium-sized and large organisations that engage in diverse businesses, establishing strategic business units is another aspect of corporate-level planning.

A *strategic business unit (SBU)* is a distinct unit, such as a company, division, department or product line, of the overall parent organisation with a specific market focus and a manager who has the authority and responsibility for managing all unit functions. AIB Bank, for example, has a commercial division, a trust division and a retail division, which offers traditional banking services for the general public.

SBUs operate as a 'company within a company'. The SBU is organised around a cluster of organisational offerings that share some common element, such as an industry, customer needs, target market or technology. It has control over its own marketing strategy and its sales revenues may be distinguished from those of other SBUs in the organisation. It can thus be evaluated individually and its performance measured against that of specific external competitors. This evaluation provides the basis for allocating resources.

3.5 *Marketing objectives*

The ability to exploit strengths and opportunities and to overcome threats and weaknesses allows the marketing manager to suggest directions for marketing objectives. From the SWOT analysis it should be possible to draw up *marketing objectives* that are consistent with the general corporate objectives and the vision that might be set out in a mission statement.

To be useful, there are two essential requirements for a marketing object-ive. The first is to specify what is to be achieved. The second is to state the time by which the objective is to be achieved. Marketing objectives have to be wide ranging as well as precise and they have to link closely with corporate objectives. Marketing objectives revolve around such issues as launching new products, deciding which segments to aim at or designing new promotional campaigns.

A *marketing strategy* is the means by which a company sets out to achieve its marketing objectives. It defines target markets, what direction needs to be taken and what needs to be done in broad terms to create a competitive position compatible with overall corporate strategy within those markets. It is therefore concerned with many of the aspects considered in buyer behaviour (see Chapter 2). A marketing strategy should be centred on the key concept that customer satisfaction is the main goal. It is most effective when it is an integral component of the overall organisational strategy, defining how the organisation will successfully engage customers, potential customers and competitors in the market arena. A key component of a marketing strategy is to keep marketing in line with a company's overarching mission statement.

Strategic decisions are concerned with the general direction of the company, with where the company wants to be; *tactical decisions* are concerned with how the company is going to get to its desired position.

```
┌─────────────────────────────────────────┐
│                 Mission                  │
│     A company's fundamental purpose      │
└─────────────────────────────────────────┘
                     ⇩
┌─────────────────────────────────────────────────────────┐
│                     SWOT analysis                        │
│       To formulate strategies that support the mission   │
│                                                          │
│   Internal analysis              External analysis       │
│       Weaknesses                   Opportunities         │
│       Strengths                       Threats            │
└─────────────────────────────────────────────────────────┘
                           ⇩
┌─────────────────────────────────────────────────────────┐
│                   Good strategies                        │
│          Supporting a company's mission                  │
│       Exploiting strengths and opportunities             │
│      Minimising threats and avoiding weaknesses          │
└─────────────────────────────────────────────────────────┘
```

Fig. 3.2: *Using SWOT analysis to formulate strategy*

In general, strategy deals with three areas: distinctive competence, scope and resource deployment. A ***distinctive competence*** is something a company does exceptionally well, for example Volvo's emphasis on safety. Indeed, one of the main purposes of a SWOT analysis is to discover an organisation's distinctive competencies so that the organisation can choose and implement strategies that exploit its unique organisational strengths. An organisation that possesses distinctive competencies and then exploits them in the strategies it chooses should expect to gain competitive advantage and above-normal economic performance.

The ***scope*** of a strategy specifies the range of markets in which a company will compete. ***Resource deployment*** is an outline of how a company will distribute its resources between the areas in which it competes.

It is important to distinguish between strategy formulation and strategy implementation. ***Strategy formulation*** (see Fig. 3.2) involves creating or deter-mining the strategies of a company, whereas ***strategy implementation*** involves the methods by which the established strategies are carried out.

3.6 *Alternative competitive strategies*

Competitive strategy determines how a company chooses to compete within a market, with particular regard to the relative positioning of competitors. Unless a company can create and maintain a competitive advantage, it is unlikely to achieve a strong market position. According to Porter (1980), a company should select a strategy that provides the direction for its operational decisions, which include marketing. Porter has proposed three alternative generic strategies: overall cost leadership strategy, differentiation strategy and focus strategy. Each strategy exerts different pressures on companies to ensure that their resources and capabilities are consistent with the requirements of the strategy selected. When choosing a particular strategy, however, it is important to ensure that the chosen strategy will create a ***competitive advantage***. This is a company's ability to perform in one or more ways that competitors cannot or will not match. Creating a competitive advantage involves returning to the fundamental marketing questions:

- Who are our existing and potential customers?
- What are their present and future needs?
- How do they judge value?
- When and where can these customers be reached?

A *sustained competitive advantage* is a competitive advantage that exists after all attempts at strategic imitation by competitors have ceased. *Strategic imitation* is the practice of duplicating another organisation's distinctive competence and thereby implementing a valuable strategy. A distinctive competence, however, can be difficult to imitate if based on organisational teamwork or culture. For example, competing organisations may know that a particular organisation's success is directly traceable to positive teamwork among its managers, but organisations may not be able to imitate this distinctive competence, as the same teamwork synergy can be difficult to copy.

Overall cost leadership strategy

There are a number of ways within a manufacturing environment to reduce and maintain low or lower average unit costs in comparison to competitors. *Economies of scale* suggest that as production volume increases, the unit costs decrease. The increased production gives more volume over which to spread fixed costs, thus lowering the average unit cost.

The *experience curve* is another means of building a low cost base. This concept suggests that as volume increases, so does experience in manufacturing, which might mean less wastage or higher productivity. In other words, the more you do something, the better you become at it. A company implementing overall cost leadership strategy attempts to gain a competitive advantage by reducing its own costs below the costs of its competitors. This might involve tight cost controls or low-cost production. The emphasis is on cost as a competitive weapon rather than on a range of other factors that customers might find important. Some customers, for example, might be prepared to pay more for added value or a stronger brand image. By keeping costs low, however, a company is able to sell its products at low prices and still make a profit. Ryanair is an example of a company that pursues an overall cost leadership strategy.

A leadership strategy based on cost may have the disadvantage of lower customer loyalty, as price-sensitive customers will switch once a lower-priced substitute is available. A reputation as a cost leader may also result in a reputation for low quality, which may make it difficult for a firm to rebrand itself or its products if it chooses to shift to a differentiation strategy in the future.

Differentiation strategy

A company implementing a differentiation strategy seeks to distinguish itself from competitors through offering something that its customers value and that is different from its competitors. Differentiation is usually expressed in the form of better performance, better design or better quality of products or services. Companies that successfully implement a differentiation strategy are able to charge more, because customers are willing to pay more to obtain the perceived extra value. Rolex, for example, pursues a differentiation strategy with its hand-made gold and stainless steel watches. The main advantage of a differentiation strategy is that it takes the emphasis away from price and therefore can charge a higher price. It could also generate buyer loyalty, reducing tendencies towards substitution or switching.

In order for an organisation to be successful with its differentiation strategy, the extra value offered must be valued by the customer more than the extra cost it takes to provide it. Differentiation is a viable strategy for earning above average returns in a specific business because the resulting brand loyalty lowers customer sensitivity to price. Increased costs can usually be passed on to the buyers. Buyer loyalty can also serve as an entry barrier, as new organisations must develop their own distinctive competence to differentiate their products in some way in order to compete successfully.

Focus strategy

A company implementing a focus strategy is deliberately selective and concentrates on a narrow group of customers, a specific regional market or a particular product line. It proposes to offer a selected item or service by meeting the needs of a clearly defined group far better than any of its more wide-ranging competitors. A focus strategy in itself might not be enough, however, and the company might have to combine it with cost leadership or differentiation to build competitive advantage. Fisher-Price, for example, uses focus differentiation to sell brightly coloured educational toys to parents of pre-school children. The risk with this segmentation approach is that the segment identified might not be sustainable long term or might be undermined locally by competition.

Choice of generic strategy

The actual choice of generic strategy depends on three criteria:
- The fit between the demands of the strategy and the capabilities and resources of the company.

- The main competitors' abilities on similar criteria.
- The key criteria for success in the market and their match with the capabilities of the company.

Once these criteria have been assessed, the company can select the best strategy to build a strong position. The company should take into account its potential sources of advantage and how they might best be used to exploit each alternative strategy. These sources of advantage might be:

- **Skills:** Hiring, training and developing key staff who could be in research and development, selling, quality assurance or any area that could help to implement a particular strategy.
- **Resources:** Both the level and deployment of resources, for example promotional spend, research and development investment, financial reserves, production facilities and brand strength.
- **Relationships:** The quality and long-term stability of supplier–customer relationships provides an asset that is durable in the face of many of the short-term pressures that are created by new entrants and competitors. Such relationships, for example, might tend to favour a focus strategy.

From the three generic business strategies, Porter (1980) argues that only one strategy should be adopted by a firm, and failure to do so will result in a 'stuck in the middle' scenario. He believes that trying to adopt more than one strategy will distract from the organisation's main focus, making it difficult for the organisation to establish a clear future direction. Porter adds that an organisation focusing on differentiation must avoid considering a low-cost strategy, while organisations supplying relatively standardised products with features acceptable to many customers should avoid trying to adopt differentiation strategies. Hence, cost leadership and differentiation strategies should be seen as mutually exclusive when choosing organisational direction.

3.7 The marketing audit

A *marketing audit* is to the marketing department what a financial audit is to the accounting department. The marketing audit is a method of reviewing a company's present objectives, strategies, performance and activities, and its primary purpose is to pick out the company's strengths and weaknesses so that managers can implement improvements. The marketing audit is in effect a 'snapshot' of what is happening now in the company. It should therefore be carried out fairly regularly, within the limits of time and money that can be allocated for the task. The marketing audit was defined by McDonald (1989) as 'the means by which a company can understand how it relates to the environment in which it operates. It is the means by which a company can identify its own strengths and weaknesses as they relate to external opportunities and threats. It is thus a way of helping management to select a position in that environment based on known factors.'

The marketing audit encourages management to think systematically about the environment in which their company operates and on their ability to respond, given the company's actual and planned capabilities. The marketing audit attempts to answer such questions as:

- What is happening in the environment in which we are operating?
- Does the environment pose threats or opportunities?
- What are our relative strengths and weaknesses in handling and exploiting the environment?
- How effective are we in implementing marketing activity?

An effective marketing audit should be:
- Comprehensive.
- Systematic.
- Independent.
- Periodic.

The *external audit* looks at issues such as changes in the sociocultural, technological, economic and political environments. Competition also has to be analysed very carefully on all aspects of its marketing activities, including its choice of target markets.

The *internal audit* focuses on the effectiveness in achieving the specified objectives of the company. The audit should be undertaken as part of the planning cycle, usually on an annual basis, rather than as a desperate response to a problem. The audit is a systematic attempt to assess the performance of the marketing effort.

The marketing audit should also include a product portfolio audit, which assesses the correctness of the range of products, in order to decide if modifications to an organisation's products are required. A pricing audit is also essential to monitor sales impact, market share and profits and to check if products are available at appropriate prices.

An audit of the communication strategy should also be included as part of the marketing audit. This is important, as large sums of money could be wasted if the communication strategy is not cost effective. The audit may cover the whole communication mix, including advertising, personal selling, public relations, sales promotion, perception, relationship and direct and event marketing. A detailed market audit covering all other relevant areas, such as customer service, distribution, sales, marketing research, people and processes, can provide an objective analysis of an organisation's marketing activities, and if necessary, it can correct the future direction of these activities.

3.8 *The marketing and planning process*

The term '*strategic marketing process*' refers to the entire sequence of managerial and operational activities required to create and sustain effective and efficient marketing strategies. This includes a *strategic marketing plan* and an *operational marketing plan*. The strategic marketing plan guides all planning and activities at the company level, not just in marketing but throughout the company. The operational marketing plan integrates activities, schedules resources, specifies responsibilities and provides benchmarks for measuring progress.

There are six main stages in the strategic marketing process:

- Identifying and evaluating opportunities.
- Analysing market segments and selecting target markets.
- Planning a market position and developing a marketing mix strategy.
- Preparing a formal marketing plan.
- Executing the plan.
- Controlling efforts and evaluating the results.

Stage 1: Identifying and evaluating opportunities

The ever-changing impact of environmental factors presents opportunities and threats to every organisation. Opportunities occur when environmental conditions favour an organisation attaining or improving a competitive advantage. The marketing manager must be able to accurately 'read' the environment and any changes in it and translate the analysis of trends into marketing opportunities.

Situation analysis involves interpreting environmental conditions and changes in light of the organisation's ability to capitalise on potential opportunities and ward off problems. Situation analysis requires both environmental scanning and environmental monitoring. *Environmental scanning* includes all information gathering that is designed to detect indications of changes that may be in their initial stages of development. It can be undertaken by the company itself, by professional or industry associations or by one of the various consulting agencies that specialise in forecasting. The

Internet is an extremely useful environmental scanning tool. It enables marketers to check out newspapers and their archives, relevant news stories, company press releases, journals, company reports, online magazines, government websites, etc. Diffenbach (1983) outlined some of the benefits of environmental scanning, as follows:

- An increased general awareness by management of environmental changes.
- Better planning and strategic decision-making.
- Greater effectiveness in government matters.
- Better industry and market analysis.
- Better results in foreign business.
- Improvements in diversification and resource allocations.
- Better energy planning.

Environmental monitoring involves tracking certain variables, such as sales data and population statistics, to observe whether any meaningful trends are emerging. Scanning and monitoring provide information that allows marketers to interpret environmental conditions and to determine the timing and significance of any changes. Situation analysis also requires an inward look at the organisation. The organisation should evaluate its internal strengths and weaknesses in relation to the external environment.

Stage 2: Analysing market segments and selecting target markets

A market is a group of organisations or individuals that are potential customers for the product being offered. There are many types of markets. The most fundamental distinction among them involves the buyer's use of the good or service being purchased. When the buyer is an individual who will use a product to satisfy personal or household needs, the product is being utilised by a consumer. Hence, the good or service is a consumer product sold in the consumer market. When the buyer is an organisation that will use the product to help operate its business, that organisation is buying an organisational product in the organisational market or business market.

Virtually all marketers agree that market segmentation is extremely useful and valuable. Identifying and choosing targets, rather than trying to reach everybody, allows the marketer to tailor marketing mixes to a group's specific needs. An organisation selects a target market because it believes it will have a competitive advantage in that particular segment (see Chapter 6 for further details).

Stage 3: Planning a market position and developing a marketing mix strategy

After a target market has been selected, marketing managers position the brand in that market and then develop a marketing mix to accomplish the positioning objective. A market position, or competitive position, represents how consumers perceive a brand relative to its competition. Each brand appealing to a given market segment has a position in relation to competitors in the buyer's mind. The object of positioning is to determine what distinct position is appropriate for the product. The marketing mix an organisation selects, therefore, depends on the organisation's strategy for positioning its product relative to the competition.

Planning a marketing mix requires a combination of the four Ps: product, price, place and promotion. The relative importance of each element may differ for different types of products and different positioning strategies.

Stage 4: Preparing a formal marketing plan

A formal *marketing plan* is a written statement of the marketing objectives and strategies to be followed and the specific courses of action to be taken when (or if) certain future events occur. It outlines the marketing mix, explains who is responsible for managing the specific activities in the plan and provides a timetable indicating when those activities must be performed.

The main contents of a marketing plan for medium-sized and large organisations are:

- Executive summary.
- Situational analysis.
- SWOT analysis.
- Objectives.
- Strategy.
- Action programme (the operational marketing plan itself for the period under review).
- Financial forecast.
- Controls and evaluation for monitoring performance.

A formal, written marketing plan is essential to provide an unambiguous reference point for activities throughout the planning period. One of the most important benefits of these plans, however, is the planning process itself. This typically offers a unique opportunity or forum for information-rich and productively focused discussions between the various managers involved. The plan, together with its associated discussions, then provides an agreed context for an organisation's subsequent management activities, even for those not described in the plan itself. In addition, marketing plans are included in business plans, offering data showing investors how the company will grow and, most importantly, how they will get a return on investment.

Stage 5: Executing the plan

Once marketing plans have been developed and approved, they must be executed, or carried out. *Execution*, or implementation, requires organising and co-ordinating people, resources and activities. Staffing, directing, developing and leading subordinates are major activities used to implement plans.

Stage 6: Controlling efforts and evaluating the results

The purpose of managerial control is to ensure that planned activities are completely and properly executed. The first aspect of control is to establish acceptable performance standards. Control also requires investigation and evaluation. Investigation involves 'checking up' to determine whether the activities necessary to the execution of the marketing plan are in fact being performed. Actual performance must then be assessed to determine whether organisational objectives have been met. Performance may be evaluated, for example in terms of the number of sales calls made or new accounts developed. Control activities provide feedback to alert managers because they indicate whether to continue with plans and activities or to change them and take corrective action.

The duration of marketing plans can vary. Plans that cover a year or less are called *short-range plans*; those that cover two to five years are usually called *medium-range plans*; marketing plans that extend beyond five years are generally viewed as *long-range plans*. Most marketing plans, however, are revised annually, with a detailed three-year perspective, because of the dynamic environment in which companies operate.

A marketing plan serves a number of purposes:

- It helps a company to implement its strategies and achieve its objectives.
- It specifies how resources are to be allocated.
- It heightens awareness of problems, opportunities and threats.

In conclusion, analysing a company's capability is an important task for the marketing manager, in conjunction with other departmental managers, which enables them to make more informed decisions about the present and future of the company. As suggested earlier, analysis involves three elements: customer, competitor and company. (Customer and competitor analyses are dealt with in Chapters 2 and 4.)

3.9 *Socially responsible behaviour and managerial ethics*

Society clearly expects marketers to obey the law, but a socially responsible organisation has a responsibility broader than legal responsibility. *Social responsibility* refers to the ethical consequences of a person's or an organisation's acts as they might affect the interest of others (Bennett, 1998). Corporate social responsibility is generally considered to be the 'duty' of an organisation to conduct its activities with due regard to the interest of society as a whole.

Marketing plays an important part in delivering corporate social responsibility and in building corporate brands, particularly through:

- **Products:** Issues such as product safety.
- **Advertising and promotion:** Needs to be appropriately targeted, accurate and culturally acceptable.
- **Pricing:** Needs to deliver affordability and value as well as profits.
- **Selling:** Needs to avoid perceptions of pressurising customers.
- **Distribution:** Needs to ensure fair access to products and services, particularly of life's necessities.
- **Customer service:** Needs to be effective in resolving disputes.

Baker (1990) defines a social responsibility audit as:

An evaluation or assessment of the policies and practices of an organisation to establish how and to what extent it is behaving in a socially responsible manner, e.g. in terms of employment practices, relationships with its local community, environmental protection, etc.

From this it can be seen that corporate social responsibility covers issues of interest to all business functions. However, anything that affects the way an organisation interacts with its stakeholders could be seen as a marketing issue, for example packaging of goods uses up the raw material wood, which is used for paper production. As there is a tremendous demand for paper, the forests of the world are being depleted. Significant improvements have been made in the last few years, with some firms even using their packaging policies as a selling point. Proctor & Gamble have taken this one step further. Published on their Pampers nappies is the following information: 'Pulp: Made with care for the environment. The traditional chlorine bleaching process is not used. Pampers pulp is purified with an oxidation process. With smaller bags Pampers saves raw materials and energy: less packaging, less waste and fewer lorries for transport.'

Ethics involves values about right and wrong conduct. Ethical behaviour refers to behaviour that conforms to widely accepted social norms. Unethical behaviour, therefore, is behaviour that does not conform to widely accepted social norms. A society generally adopts formal laws that reflect the prevailing ethical standards or the social norms of its citizens. *Marketing ethics* involves the principles that guide an organisation's conduct and the values it expects to express in certain situations. Ethical principles reflect the cultural values and norms of a society. *Norms* suggest what ought to be done under given circumstances. They indicate approval or disapproval, what is good or bad. Conscientious marketers face many moral dilemmas and the best thing to do is often unclear. Companies, therefore, need to develop corporate marketing ethics policies – broad guidelines that everyone in the organisation must follow. These policies should cover advertising standards, customer service, pricing, product development, distributor relations and general ethical standards. For example:

- **Products** should be honestly made and described. Commercial pressures may tempt companies to use cheaper raw materials or to use new additives to make the product perform differently. The ethical issue arises when customers are not informed of such changes.
- **Promotions** can involve deceptive or misleading advertising, manipulative sales methods and even bribery in selling situations. Salespeople often face ethical conflicts, for example either correcting a customer's mistaken belief about a product and thus losing the business or allowing the customer to continue with the false belief right up to the point of taking delivery of the goods.
- **Pricing** raises ethical issues in the areas of price fixing, for example pricing below the cost of production in order to bankrupt competitors and not revealing the full cost of purchase.
- **Distribution ethics** involve abuse of power, for example failure to pay for goods within the specified credit terms. Some stores operate no-quibble, sale-or-return contracts, which mean that manufacturers have to accept damaged goods back, even when there is no fault in the manufacture. This has been seen as unethical by some smaller manufacturers who have little negotiating power and few choices of outlet for their products.

Marketers are ethically responsible for what is marketed and for the image that a product portrays. Therefore, marketers need to understand what good ethics are and how to incorporate good ethics in various marketing campaigns to better reach a targeted audience and to gain trust from customers. Regardless of the product offered or the market targeted, marketing ethics sets guidelines from which good marketing is practised. Companies participate in ethical marketing when they create and practise high ethical standards for marketing.

Important terms and concepts

company: p. 48
corporate objectives: p. 48
mission statement: p. 48
corporate strategy: p. 49
analysing company capability: p. 49
sales analysis: p. 50
marketing cost analysis: p. 51
strategic gap: p. 51
situational analysis: p. 51
SWOT analysis: p. 52
strategic business unit: p. 54
marketing objectives: p. 54
marketing strategy: p. 55
strategic decisions: p. 55
tactical decisions: p. 55
distinctive competence: p. 56
scope: p. 56
resource deployment: p. 56
strategy formulation: p. 56
strategy implementation: p. 56
competitive strategy: p. 56
alternative competitive strategies:
  p. 56
competitive advantage: p. 56
sustained competitive advantage:
  p. 57

strategic imitation: p. 57
overall cost leadership strategy:
  p. 57
economies of scale: p. 57
experience curve: p. 57
differentiation strategy: p. 58
focus strategy: p. 58
marketing audit: p. 59
external audit: p. 60
internal audit: p. 60
marketing and planning process:
  p. 61
strategic marketing process: p. 61
strategic marketing plan: p. 61
operational marketing plan: p. 61
situation analysis: p. 61
environmental scanning: p. 61
environmental monitoring: p. 62
marketing plan: p. 63
execution: p. 64
social responsibility: p. 65
ethics: p. 66
marketing ethics: p. 66
norms: p. 66

Case study: Providing consumers with ethically sourced garments: Primark

Rapid changes in media, transport and communications technology have made the world economy more interconnected now than in any previous period of history. This is also evident in the world of textile manufacture and clothing distribution. Consumers want fashionable clothes at affordable prices. Much high street fashion is produced in many countries across the world. Businesses source clothes from countries like India, China, Bangladesh and Turkey because of lower material and labour costs in these countries. In order to meet consumer demand, Primark works with manufacturers around the world.

Primark is part of Associated British Foods (ABF), a diversified international food, ingredients and retail group. Primark has almost 200 stores across Ireland, Britain, Spain, the Netherlands, Germany, Belgium and Portugal. Primark's annual turnover accounts for a significant proportion of ABF's revenues and profit.

Primark's target customer is fashion conscious, but wants value for money. Primark can offer value for money by:

- Sourcing products efficiently.
- Making clothes with simpler designs.
- Using local fabrics and trims.
- Focusing on the most popular sizes.
- Buying in volume.
- Not spending heavily on advertising.

Primark's business growth comes from meeting these customer needs while continuing to expand stores and move into new markets. Primark works with many third-party suppliers while having a key concern to source ethically. Primark is very clear about its focus on business ethics. Important business principles for Primark include respecting human rights and setting guidelines for appropriate employment conditions in its supply factories. Primark has over 600 major suppliers across 16 countries. These companies provide employment for over 700,000 workers in three continents. Primark is committed to ensuring that its manufacturing and supply partners also act responsibly towards their employees.

Typically, textiles are manufactured in low-wage and high manual skill economies, mostly in the developing world. Factories in countries such as India or China may supply a range of goods to retailers or for brands, according to each individual retailer or brand specifications. In these circumstances, the factory sets the same wage rate to employees, regardless of which retailer the goods are made for. At least 95 per cent of the factories supplying Primark also produce for other high street retailers.

Primark works to ensure ethical sourcing in a number of ways. It has an ethical trade director whose role is to ensure Primark goods are sourced ethically and who leads a team of ethical managers and executives based in the key sourcing countries. Primark is a member of the Ethical Trading Initiative, which is an international alliance of companies, trade unions and non-government organisations working in partnership to improve the lives of workers across the globe.

Primark is able to offer value and low prices from savings based on high sales volumes and lower retail margins with minimal advertising. The company keeps costs down by buying large quantities of items, using economies of scale from buying in bulk. In addition, retail prices are kept low through lean production and efficient operational practices. Using off-season factory time for production, for example, means that the costs are lower than at peak time. This is good for Primark, but it also means factory employees get work and pay when they might not otherwise have been needed.

Primark works closely with the suppliers and factories that produce its goods. It provides training for suppliers, factory workers and its own buyers so that they understand ethical issues. It offers guidance on issues such as child labour and home working in Asia as well as on immigration and right-to-work issues. The role of Primark buyers is important for helping to support ethical business practices. When selecting new suppliers and factories, Primark requires them to go through their selection process. This enables Primark to establish if working conditions are appropriate or if improvements are necessary before the supplier can be approved. All Primark suppliers are subject to thorough independent audits and follow-up visits to make sure that the supplier is maintaining ethical practices. This involves an audit of labour standards, for example checking that the factory has the appropriate fire safety equipment and that staff have been trained how to use it, and ensuring that all employees receive the wages and benefits they are entitled to.

A key principle of Primark's business practice is to make sure that it provides its consumers with value-for-money garments while maintaining ethical manufacturing standards. This involves paying for independent audits of all its factories and working with suppliers to address issues in a sustainable manner. Primark helps to set and maintain standards by working with external agencies such as the International Labour Organization, the Ethical Trading Initiative and independent auditors. Its auditors work with suppliers over a period of time to help them meet the exacting standards set out by the Ethical Trading Initiative. This helps the supplier to become approved. Primark sees this as a programme of continuous improvement.

By making its ethical trade processes transparent, Primark aims to demonstrate its commitment to responsible manufacturing. This helps to assure its customers that the goods they are purchasing are not only fashionable and value for money, but also that they are ethically produced by workers who are fairly treated.

Source: Adapted from www.thetimes100.co.uk/case-study--providing-customers-with-ethically-sourced-garments--158-412-1.php [accessed 19 March 2011].

Case study: Developing a new business strategy: Marks & Spencer

With more than 120 years of heritage, Marks & Spencer is one of the best-known British retailers. The company has more than 450 stores in Britain and employs more than 65,000 people. It also operates outside Britain, as far afield as Hong Kong.

In recent years, Britain's retailing industry has experienced intense competition. Customers are more aware of where and how they want to shop. They also know what sort of shopping experience they require. This has made it much more difficult for retailers to survive. Responding to these challenges, Marks & Spencer developed a new business strategy. This created a period of change for the whole organisation and refocusing the business. This included the three business values of quality, value and service.

Marks & Spencer developed a promotional campaign emphasising the 'Your M&S' logo. This helped the company to connect customers with the heritage in the business. It also linked the business in the minds of customers with its two other values of innovation and trust. The process involved three key features:

- Developing products that customers wanted.
- Investing in the environment within stores.
- Providing good customer service to look after customers.

Marks & Spencer has created a business that now has a flatter organisation structure after it lost a number of layers of authority through a process of delayering.

These changes have created a business environment with more challenges for employees. Managers had to prepare employees for whatever role they would be asked to undertake in this new environment. This means that employees throughout the business have more responsibility. This enables them to make quick decisions when required. At the same time, these employees have more accountability than before. This means that they must be prepared to explain and justify the decisions that they take. In a flatter organisational structure, many employees have bigger jobs. There are higher expectations for staff to contribute more to the organisation. Marks & Spencer ensures that it keeps staff well trained to be able to respond to business needs. Marks & Spencer provides a wide range of both on-the-job and off-the-job training for all staff.

Training and development brings benefits to Marks & Spencer and to its employees. Training provides a series of planned learning experiences for individuals and builds their technical skills and business competencies.

Training also helps to improve efficiency and can motivate employees to do well. This helps to make positive changes to the way in which they work and make decisions. Development helps individuals to use the training to meet their individual needs and ambitions. By training and developing its staff well, Marks & Spencer is in a position to develop a competitive advantage over its competitors.

Business strategy

Marks & Spencer's new business strategy focuses on three main areas:

- Developing value-for-money products that customers want. Training and development bring new skills that help to add value to its products and services, for example by cutting costs. This enables the company to keep prices lower to benefit the customer.
- Investing in the environment within stores. Better technical skills in sales and stock management mean that staff can use the store to better advantage, resulting in higher sales and profitability.
- Providing good customer service to look after customers. For example, if staff have improved skills in communication, this can have a positive impact on customer service.

Training and development equips individuals with the skills they need to achieve their targeted role in the business. Although training is a cost to a business, it is also an investment. Training helps Marks & Spencer to link the people who have the right technical skills and business competencies with the roles they are best able to do. It ensures that as a person moves from a post, he or she is succeeded by the best possible replacement. This is at the heart of succession management. By acquiring technical skills and business competencies, employees can plan their career path. This gives them responsibility for achieving their career ambitions. It also helps to create the future leaders of the organisation.

By using a framework of technical skills and business competencies, Marks & Spencer is able to develop a precise link between the requirements for each post and the necessary characteristics of the people to fill each post. The process enables Marks & Spencer to plan its staffing needs with a level of certainty and to invest in appropriate areas for training. In an industry where competition is intense, developing staff has probably never been so important. The success of Marks & Spencer indicates that such investment has been worthwhile.

Source: Adapted from www.thetimes100.co.uk/studies/view-summary--the-role-training-development-career-progression--100-271.php [accessed 19 March 2011].

Questions for review

1. Distinguish between overall cost leadership strategy, differentiation strategy and focus strategy.
2. List the factors involved in conducting a SWOT analysis.
3. Why is it important for a marketer to analyse a company's capability?
4. Discuss the stages involved in the strategic marketing process.
5. Give a brief description and an example of (*a*) distinctive competence and (*b*) competitive advantage.
6. List the contents of a typical marketing plan.
7. Write a brief note on the following.
   - SWOT analysis
   - Marketing objectives
   - Mission statements
   - Marketing strategies
   - Marketing audit

4
COMPETITOR ANALYSIS

Chapter objectives

After reading this chapter you should be able to:
- Identify the various types of competition.
- Understand the competitive structure of an industry.
- Outline the steps companies undertake in analysing their competitors.
- Assess competitors' strengths and weaknesses.
- Know the strategies for competitive positions.

4.1 *Competitors*

Competitors are other companies that could provide a product or service to satisfy the needs of a specific market. According to Dibb et al. (1997), 'competitors are generally viewed by a business as those firms that market products similar to, or substitutable for, its products aimed at the same target'.

Companies often fail to recognise who their competition is. Sometimes they define 'competition' too narrowly, simply because they define their business too narrowly. For example, if a cinema defines itself solely as being in the cinema business, the management might define its competitors as other cinemas. Alternatively, if a cinema is considered to be part of the broader entertainment business, the management will recognise the competition from video shops, television, nightclubs, the Internet and restaurants.

In some industries, competition is intense and subject to rapid change. A competitor's strategies or tactics may be the most important factors determining the marketing organisation's success or failure in achieving its objectives. A change in a competitor's marketing mix, such as a change in price, may require an immediate response.

Competition comes from substitutability in goods and services. The term '*substitutable*' can be interpreted in two ways. Firstly, it can mean that the consumer is choosing among various goods or services, for example deciding whether to spend money on a new car or a holiday. Secondly, it can mean that the consumer is choosing a particular product, for example a new car from among the various manufacturers and price ranges available. Marketers generally use three terms – product class, product category and brand – to help put the matter of competition into perspective.

Product class is used to identify groups of items that may differ from each other but perform more or less the same function. Any car or beer, for example, can compete against any other member of its product class. Brands of products compete primarily, however, within product categories.

Product categories are subsets of product types contained within a product class, for example beer. There are a number of product categories in that class, including light beer, regular beer, dark beer and imported beer.

To complete their view of competition, marketing managers must consider the matter of brand. *Brands* identify and distinguish one marketer's product from its competitors'. The light beer category, for example, is made up of brands such as Miller Lite, Coors Lite, Bud Light and many others.

There are various *types of competition*, and each company must consider its present and potential competition when designing its marketing strategy.

Types of competition

Perfect competition: This involves many small producers, all supplying identical products that can be directly substituted for each other. No producer has the power to influence or determine price, and the market consists of many small buyers, who similarly cannot influence the market individually. Farm produce, such as vegetables, is often cited as an example of near-perfect competition; the product itself, however, can be differentiated, for example organic and non-organic or class I and class II quality. Farm produce, therefore, can be seen to be moving towards monopolistic competition.

Monopolistic competition: Many sellers compete to develop a differential marketing strategy to establish their own market share on a substitutable basis. The idea is that although there are many competitors in the market, each has a product sufficiently differentiated from the rest to create its own monopoly, because to the customer it is unique or any substitutes are considered to be inferior, for example Maxwell House coffee and Nescafé coffee or Barry's tea and Lyons tea.

Oligopoly: A few companies control the majority of industry sales. Each company is large enough to have a big impact on the market and on the behaviour of its competitors, for example Tesco and Dunnes Stores or Aer Lingus and Ryanair.

Monopoly: Technically a monopoly exists where one supplier has sole control over a market and there is no competition. The lack of competition may be because the monopoly is state-owned, for example Iarnród Éireann, An Post.

4.2 *Competitive structure of an industry*

The performance of a company will be influenced by the structure of the industry in which it operates, because this affects the level of competition in that market. Porter (1980) suggests that there are *five forces* that affect the level of competition (see Fig. 4.1). The five forces framework helps identify the sources of competition in an industry or sector. The framework must not be used just to give a snapshot in time, but to give an understanding of how these forces can be countered and overcome in the *future*. The five forces are *not independent* of each other. Pressures from one direction can trigger changes in another dynamic process of shifting sources of competition. For example, potential new entrants finding themselves blocked may find new routes to the market by bypassing traditional distribution channels and selling directly to consumers.

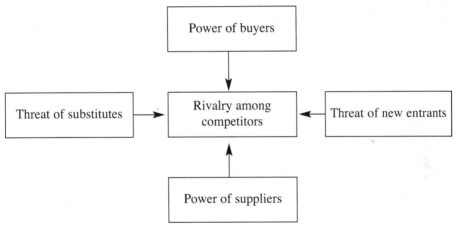

Fig. 4.1: *Porter's 'five forces' model of competition*

The bargaining power of suppliers

Suppliers are in a strong position if a marketer depends on a few powerful suppliers of raw material, and this can lead to high prices and poor product quality. If there is only a small number of suppliers controlling an important ingredient, the suppliers can use their strong position to squeeze profitability in an industry.

The bargaining power of suppliers will be high when:
- There are many buyers and few dominant suppliers.
- There are differentiated highly valued products.
- The industry is not a key customer group to the suppliers.

The bargaining power of buyers

When buyers possess strong bargaining power they will try to force prices down and set competitors against one another, all at the expense of the sellers' profitability. Buyers' bargaining power grows when they become more concentrated or organised or when the product is undifferentiated.

The bargaining power of buyers will be high when:

- There are few dominant buyers and many sellers.
- Products are standardised.
- The industry is not a key supplying group for buyers.

The threat of substitute products or services

An industry segment is unattractive when there are actual or potential substitutes for the product. The threat of substitute products or services is often not seen until it is too late. An increase in the number of substitutes can put a ceiling on growth potential and long-term profits. It can also result in problems of excess capacity.

The threat of substitute products depends on:

- Buyer willingness to substitute.
- The relative price and performance of substitutes.
- The cost of switching to substitutes.

The threat of new entrants

Additional competitors in a market will lead to increased capacity and lower prices. The attractiveness of an industry varies with the height of its entry and exit barriers. A company must consider the possible *barriers to entry* for other companies: these are business practices or conditions that make it difficult for new companies to enter the market. The higher the barriers, the more likely it is that they will deter new entrants.

High entry barriers exist in some industries, e.g. shipbuilding, whereas other industries are relatively easy to enter, e.g. restaurants. Key entry barriers include:

- Switching costs.
- Access to distribution channels.
- Economies of scale.
- Capital and other investment requirements.
- Retaliation from existing industry.
- Government policy.

The most attractive segment is one in which entry barriers are high and exit barriers are low: few firms can enter the industry and poorly performing firms can easily leave it. Additional competitors in a market will lead to increased capacity and lower prices.

Rivalry among competitors

Competitive pressures among current competitors depend on the rate of growth of the industry. Competitive rivalry is high when there are many competitors of equal size or where products or services cannot be greatly differentiated. A segment is unattractive if it already contains numerous or aggressive competitors. When market growth is slow, competition is more heated for any possible gains in market share. High fixed costs also create competitive pressures on companies to fill production capacity. Intense rivalry tends to lead to a decrease in profits.

The intensity of rivalry between competitors in an industry will depend on:

- The extent of competition.
- The degree of differentiation.
- Switching costs.
- Exit barriers.

4.3 *Analysing competitors*

The ability to understand competitors and to predict their actions is important to all customer-oriented companies. For a company to be successful in any market, it needs to know its competitors, their strengths and weaknesses, market share and positioning. Kotler et al. (1999) define *competitor analysis* as 'the process of identifying important competitors; assessing their objectives, strategies, strengths and weaknesses and reaction patterns; and selecting which competitors to attack or avoid'.

Competitor analysis is an important part of the strategic planning process. It helps management to:

- Understand its own competitive advantages and disadvantages relative to those of competitors.
- Understand competitors' past, present and future strategies.
- Inform a basis on which to develop strategies to achieve competitive advantage in the future.

To develop an effective marketing strategy, a company must carry out an analysis of its competitors. According to Murray and O'Driscoll (1999), there are seven such steps:

1. Who is the present and potential competition?
2. What is the position they have established in the market?
3. What are their missions and objectives?
4. What is their typical pattern of behaviour?
5. How strong is their resource base?
6. What important competitive advantages do they possess?
7. What are their main competitive vulnerabilities?

Step 1: Identifying competitors

Firstly, a company needs to know who its competitors are. The most obvious competitors are other firms that offer similar or identical products to the same set of customers. Some of these competitors include direct competitors, such as Vodafone, O2, Meteor and 3G, close competitors, such as Coca-Cola and Virgin Cola, and those competitors producing substitute products, such as Pepsi-Cola. Marketers should also clearly identify both existing and potential competitors.

Step 2: Competitors' positioning

Having identified its main competitors, a company must obtain information about the market segments it is pursuing and what product or service benefits it is offering (see Chapter 6). This important information will help the company to identify how good or bad the competitors are at serving their customers' needs. They may show potential gaps in the market or competitive strengths that the company would be unwise to attack.

Step 3: Competitors' mission and objectives

A marketer cannot assume that all competitors want to maximise their profits, and it must therefore act accordingly. Some competitors, for example, may want to maximise their market share. Knowing a competitor's objectives reveals to a marketer what kind of behaviour to expect from the competitor and how it might react to competitive actions, for example a price cut or the introduction of a new product.

Step 4: Pattern of competitive behaviour

The role of the marketer is to estimate competitors' likely actions and reactions. Some competitors react swiftly and strongly to certain actions, while others react slowly. There may be some who react only to certain types of pressures and not to others. At the same time, other competitors can be completely unpredictable. It is best, therefore, to build up a picture of typical behaviour patterns of competitors. This should help the marketer to decide how best to attack competitors or how best to defend one's own current position.

Step 5: Competitors' resource base

At this point the marketer should have a good idea of competitors' position in the market and their likely patterns of reaction. A company must then identify each competitor's resource base, that is, its internal resources. Competitors may call on their financial, marketing, managerial, manufacturing or technological resources when they want to implement strategies and achieve their goals. By analysing their own resources, marketers should receive a clear indication of their strengths and weaknesses.

Steps 6 and 7: Main competitive advantages and vulnerabilities

From the previous steps a marketer can identify the main advantages and disadvantages of each competitor. A company can decide how and where to compete according to these findings. For example, it might avoid the areas where its competitors are strongest and attack their weak areas.

Sources of information for competitor analysis

According to Davidson (1997), sources of competitor information can be grouped into three categories:
- **Recorded data:** This is quite easily available in published form, either internally or externally. These include competitor annual reports and accounts, product brochures, press releases, government reports, newspaper/magazine articles and presentations/speeches.
- **Observable data:** This has to be actively sought and usually needs to be assembled from several sources. Examples are competitor pricing/price lists, tenders, patent applications and promotions and advertising campaigns.
- **Opportunistic data:** Accessing this type of data requires deliberate planning and effort. Much data come from meetings; competitors' salesforces; attending competitors' trade shows, seminars and conferences; meetings with shared suppliers; discussions with customers; recruiting former employees; and social contacts with competitors.

4.4 *Direct and indirect competitors*

The most obvious competitors are other organisations which offer similar products or services. Suppliers of substitute products and services, however, highlight the indirect competitors, who must also be analysed. Five levels of competitors can be identified: direct, close, products of a similar nature, substitute products and indirect competition.

Direct competition

Pepsi-Cola is a direct competitor to Coca-Cola. Both products offer similar benefits to the same general market. The production methods employed are also very similar, although the actual formula for the basic cola essence is somewhat different in both companies since these products are in direct competition.

Close competition

Is Pepsi a competitor to Club Orange? Both products offer similar benefits to similar consumers. The difference between orange and cola flavour is easier to recognise than the difference between Coca-Cola and Pepsi, but basically the products are substitutes for each other. In any analysis of drinks, all fizzy drinks need to be considered. It could be argued that other fizzy drinks include Ballygowan sparkling mineral water and champagne, but we would be moving away from a strict interpretation of close competition.

Products of a similar nature

Perrier is a naturally sparkling water from southern France. The water comes up through a field of natural gas, hence the claim to be naturally sparkling as opposed to having added carbon dioxide, which is the case with Pepsi or other sparkling waters. Perrier, however, is targeted at an adult market, rather than the younger age targeted by Pepsi. This makes Perrier less of a close competitor. Champagne also has an alternative way of producing the fizz. 'Methode Champenoise' is a secondary fermentation of the wine after it has been bottled. It is not the different way of producing the bubbles, however, but the positioning of the product that makes it less relevant when considering competitors.

Substitute products

Is ice cream a substitute for a fizzy drink? In some situations this is a reasonable choice. Marketers need to consider those products which can substitute in this way. The study of buyer behaviour is critical in deciding how wide such a study should go.

Indirect competition

Any product that competes for the same buying power could be considered a competitor. There may be indirect competition between a foreign holiday and a new car, or for low-value items there could be a choice between a newspaper and a Sprite for a student living on a limited grant.

4.5 *Assessing competitors' strengths and weaknesses*

Marketers need to accurately identify each competitor's strengths and weaknesses. As a first step, a company gathers key data on each competitor's business over the last few years. Companies normally learn about their competitors' strengths and weaknesses through secondary data, personal experience and word of mouth. They can also increase their knowledge by conducting primary marketing research with customers, suppliers and dealers. A growing number of companies have turned to **benchmarking**, comparing the company's products and processes to those of competitors or leading firms in other industries to find ways of improving quality and performance. Benchmarking has become a powerful tool for increasing a company's competitiveness.

According to Kotler et al. (1999), a company can spend too much time and energy tracking competitors. A company can become so competitor centred that it loses its customer focus, which is even more important. A **competitor-centred company** is one whose moves are based mainly on competitors' actions and reactions. The company spends most of its time tracking competitors' moves and market shares and trying to find strategies to counter them. The company becomes too reactive, and rather than carrying out its own consistent customer-oriented strategy, it bases its moves on competitors' moves. As a result, it does not move in a planned direction towards achieving its goals. It does not know where it will end up, since so much depends on what the competitors do.

A **customer-centred company**, in contrast, focuses more on customer developments in designing its strategies. The customer-centred company is in a better position to identify new opportunities and set a strategy that makes long-term sense. By watching customer needs evolve, it can decide what customer groups and what emerging needs are the most important to serve, given its resources and objectives.

4.6 *Strategies for competitive position*

The strategy that is appropriate for a company depends on its competitive position in the industry. There are four *types of competitive position* that firms can occupy in a market: market leader, challenger, follower and nicher.

Market leader

This is the company with the highest market share. It maintains its position by changing prices, introducing new products, increasing distribution and promotion. The strategies of a market leader include:

- Expanding the total market by looking for new uses and new users and by increasing the use of its products or services.
- Protecting present market share through market diversification, continuing to innovate, extending product lines, protecting weak areas and strategic withdrawal.
- Expanding market share by acquiring other businesses.
  Examples: Microsoft, VHI, Quinn Healthcare.

Market challenger

This company is not a market leader and therefore has to fight aggressively for additional market share. Market challengers are organisations with a smaller market share, but who are close enough to pose a serious threat to the leader. However, an aggressive strategy can be costly if the challenger is thinking of attacking where there is uncertainty over winning. Before making a concerted effort to steal share, therefore, the challenger needs to ask itself whether market share really matters so much or whether there would be greater benefit from working on getting a good return on investment from existing share. The strategies of a market challenger include:

- Attacking the market leader or other companies – attacking their strengths, attacking from all directions (multi-prong approach), bypassing the competition and identifying easier markets, guerrilla attacks (annoying competitors with unpredictable attacks).
  Examples: Ryanair, Aldi, Lidl.

Market follower

This company is in a similar position to the market challenger, except that it prefers to follow rather than attack the leader. Given the resources needed, the threat of retaliation and the uncertainty of winning, many organisations favour a far less aggressive stance, acting as market followers. There are two types of followers. First, there are those who lack the resources to mount a serious challenge and prefer to remain innovative and forward thinking without disturbing the overall competitive structure in the market by encouraging open warfare. Often, any lead from the market leader is willingly followed. This might mean adopting a 'me too' strategy, thus avoiding direct confrontation and competition.

The second type of follower is the organisation that is simply not capable of challenging and is content just to survive, offering little competitive advantage. Often, smaller car rental firms operate in this category by being prepared to offer a lower price, but not offering the same standard of rental vehicle or even peace of mind should things go wrong. A recession can easily eliminate the weaker members of this category. The strategies of a market follower include:

- Holding on to present market share and trying to increase it.
- Using market segmentation.
- Using R&D efficiently.
- Maintaining high product quality.
  Examples: Independent radio stations, Dunnes Stores (its own range of breakfast cereals).

Market nicher

Some organisations, often small, specialise in areas of the market that are too small, too costly or too vulnerable for the larger organisation to contemplate. Niching is not exclusively a small organisation strategy, as some larger organisations may have divisions that specialise. The key to niching is the close matching between the needs of the market and the capabilities and strengths of the company. The specialisation offered can relate to product type, customer group, geographic area or any aspect of product/service differentiation. The strategies of a market nicher include:

- Avoiding competition in order to succeed.
- Specialising in customer, product or marketing mix lines.
- Using multiple niching.
- Finding safe market segments.

Examples: Caterpillar, Ferrari, Glenilen Farm (hand-made products with no preservatives).

4.7 The competitive triangle

The competitive triangle (Fig. 4.2) shows that customers have choices. From the top of the triangle, customers can evaluate the different product offerings of all companies and their competitors. They will choose to buy products or services from companies that best match their requirements.

As we saw in Chapter 2, the consumer buying decision process is complex. Marketers must therefore try to influence consumers in such a way that the products or services of their companies are chosen. In other words, they must endeavour to gain a *competitive advantage,* that is, something a product or a company has that is desired by consumers and not matched by competitors. In summary, to gain the strongest possible competitive advantage, a company must continuously analyse not just its present and potential customers and the company itself, but also all its competitors. To be successful it needs to sustain that competitive advantage over time and to fight off those who would like to have a share of any profitable business that is established. Sustaining a competitive advantage requires the continual collection and use of marketing information to ensure that the needs of the target markets are being met more effectively and efficiently than by the competition and that adjustments to the marketing mix are made if changes in the environment threaten the business.

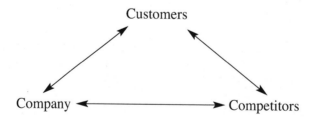

Fig. 4.2: *The competitive triangle*

4.8 Value chain analysis

To be more effective, organisational management must adopt superior skills and resources that improve competitive advantage. Competitive advantage can be sustained by value chain analysis. A *value chain* includes the discrete activities that a firm carries out in order to perform its business. These activities can include designing, producing, marketing, distributing and servicing products.

Porter (1985) suggested that the activities of a business could be classified under two headings: primary activities and support activities.

Primary activities

- Inbound physical distribution, e.g. warehousing, stock control.
- Operations, e.g. manufacturing, packaging.
- Outbound physical distribution, e.g. order processing, delivery.
- Marketing, e.g. channel management, advertising.
- Service, e.g. installation, repair, customer training.

Support activities

- Purchased inputs.
- Technology.
- Human resource management.
- The company's infrastructure, e.g. general management, finance, accounting, planning and quality management.

The activity a business undertakes is directly linked to achieving competitive advantage. For example, a business endeavouring to outperform its competitors through *differentiating* itself through higher quality will have to perform its value chain activities better than its opposition performs this (see Chapter 3). By contrast, a strategy based on seeking *cost leadership* will require a reduction in the costs associated with value chain activities or a reduction in the total amount of resources used.

Important terms and concepts

competitors: p. 73
substitutable: p. 73
product class: p. 74
product categories: p. 74
brands: p 74
types of competition: p. 74
perfect competition: p. 74

monopolistic competition: p. 74
oligopoly: p. 74
monopoly: p. 74
competitive structure of an industry:
  p. 75
'five forces' model of competition:
  p. 75

Case study: Creating competitive advantage through quality products: Portakabin

The key to superior performance is gaining and holding a competitive advantage. A competitive advantage is a clear and positive performance differential over rival producers on factors that are important to target customers. There are numerous ways to gain competitive advantage, such as through superior products, lower prices and better service. The Portakabin Group is a private company owned by the Shepherd Building Group. It specialises in modular buildings. Portakabin has undertaken efforts to achieve a competitive advantage in the hire and sale of interim (temporary) or permanent accommodation by concentrating on quality.

Portakabin operates in a very competitive market. Despite this, Portakabin has 17 per cent of the overall UK market (its nearest competitor has 14 per cent). In competing for business, the company decided early on to establish a reputation for quality. It has therefore positioned its products at the top end of the market, providing high levels of quality at premium prices. Quality is associated with consistency. A customer who is happy with the first buying experience will need and want to be equally happy on each further occasion.

Portakabin has attracted key customers who recognise that customers' reputations depend, at least in part, on the quality of accommodation and facilities they offer their own customers.

Its client base includes schools, hospitals, local authorities and public and private companies. Clients want modular buildings for a variety of reasons, such as:

- New classrooms.
- Staffrooms.
- Offices.
- Laboratories.
- Site offices.
- Reception areas.
- Outpatient clinics.
- Additional hospital ward accommodation.
- Child nurseries.

Portakabin's motto is 'Quality – this time – next time – every time'. The company believes that clients who really care about quality are willing to pay more to obtain it, as they view extra facilities and quality as worth the additional expense. Currently, the company operates in a range of European countries as well as in Britain. Portakabin's brand vision is to provide peace of mind for their customers across Europe through quality buildings and services. Quality relates to appropriate use – how well a product does what it is intended to do.

The appropriate use of quality comes from two sources, one internal and the other external to the company. Internally, Portakabin has developed its range of buildings around its own market research on the precise needs of customers. The company places an emphasis on how important it is to offer optional extras, such as high-quality carpeting, fitted furnishings and climate control systems to provide a quality working environment. Offering a combination of buildings and additional quality accessories gives the customer a one-stop-shop service. Externally, national building regulations require further additions to Portakabin specifications. Portakabin ensures that its products, whether interim or permanent, fully comply with all relevant building regulations. It also meets the demands of ISO 9001 Quality Management Systems. This is an internationally recognised standard that acts as a form of guarantee that everything the company does is managed to the highest quality standards.

Portakabin provides key services and can be employed to manage construction projects from start to finish. Their modular buildings are constructed off-site and no building may leave the production site until it complies with the demands of customer requirements and standards. Modules to be assembled come in standard shapes and sizes. The manner in which they are subsequently put together, along with the choice of interiors, is customised for each individual client. To ensure that all customers get what they want, Portakabin uses a Quality Systems approach outlined in its quality manual. A Corporate Quality Team (comprising senior managers) is responsible for ensuring that individual teams understand quality processes, and clear communication is facilitated by means of process charts using illustrations that set out the sequential processes involved, for example in creating a new set of school classrooms or laboratories.

The essentials of the Quality System are as follows.

1. Say what you do: Teams working on a process know what the job requires. Everyone involved understands the process and their role within it.
2. Do what you say: Once individuals understand the process, team members are able to implement it.
3. Record what you have done: Constructions teams record all actions taken so that they all know the current position, what has happened before and what still needs to be done.
4. Review what you have done: Records are regularly reviewed, both to ensure that delivery targets can be met and to identify any problem areas.
5. Take remedial action where necessary.
6. Start the process all over again.

Portakabin contacts its clients after delivery to check that they are satisfied. It aims to resolve any difficulties within 24 hours. Portakabin also guarantees to complete all projects on time and on budget. It also operates a Customer Charter, laying down standards customers should expect.

In a difficult economic climate and a highly competitive market, Portakabin strives to stay ahead by ensuring quality of process and by offering quality products and services to its customers.

Source: www.thetimes100.co.uk/case-study—the-importance-of-quality-in-creating-competitive-advantage—35-200-1.php [accessed 19 March 2011].

Case study: Using diversification strategy to extend its portfolio: Sisk Group

Sisk Group – Sicon Ltd is a diversified holding company based in Ireland, Britain and on the Continent, with the Sisk Group focused primarily on construction and healthcare, while Sicon owns a portfolio of investment and trading companies. The Sisk Group is a family-owned business which originated in Cork and dates back to 1859. The Sisk Group is one of the largest privately owned companies in Ireland. In 2007, turnover exceeded €1.6 billion with 2,800 people employed across all of its operations. In Ireland, the Sisk name is best known for its successful construction businesses – John Sisk & Son Ltd – the leading construction company in Ireland. In recent years, the Sisk Group has diversified its interests to include a growing number of other businesses.

In 2004 and 2005, the acquisition by Sisk of a series of healthcare distribution companies started when the Irish construction sector was at its peak, giving Sisk unprecedented turnover. While some businesses continued to pour investment back into the sector, Sisk realised that the boom times could not continue, so its shareholders agreed to invest in different portfolios. Sisk began its strategic review into what it could do if it were to sectorally diversify its business.

The group began by looking at 20 possible areas of expansion, gradually filtering it down to four or five, with healthcare at the top of the list. The rationale was that Ireland had a wealthy but ageing population and a historical under-investment in healthcare by the Irish state. The Sisk Group realised that society will always have health problems and will need healthcare regardless of the strength of the economy, so it seemed a suitable way to counterbalance Sisk's exposure to deflation in the construction sector. Over 18 months, the group invested in five medical device distribution companies, and today their healthcare business is nearing an annual turnover of €100 million.

Some of the health companies were first-generation firms that had been built from the ground up by founders who were nearing retirement and wondering about succession. Sisk promised to keep their individual brands and companies alive after the retirement of their founders by giving people the resources, the strategic capabilities and the balance sheet of being part of a 150-year-old and billion-euro-a-year-turnover business.

Early in 2010, Sisk moved into the manufacturing side of healthcare for the first time with the acquisition of Eschmann, a UK-based company that has produced medical operating tables for 180 years. Sisk was attracted to Eschmann by the international sales of its products – including to the Middle East and the Far East – and Sisk now has an office as far afield as Singapore.

The move to the healthcare sector was a radical change of direction for the group and one that initially drew some concern. This change of direction, however, built on existing knowledge of the distribution business within the Sisk Group, which now comprises 11 separate companies. The group includes

Origo, another firm (which distributes Bosch equipment in Ireland) launched in the 1950s, in response to Sisk's need to import electrical equipment from Germany for its own use. Sisk already understood what it took to make a good distribution business, even if healthcare was new territory.

While the Sisk Group had no credibility as a healthcare provider, the companies it acquired did. Sisk responded by taking a softer approach to managing its acquisitions, maintaining the acquired brands and determining to learn from the expertise of the new employees. As people came into the group, their input was acknowledged as very important to Sisk and it allowed them to influence the group's overall strategy. The Sisk Group has no immediate plans for further acquisitions, preferring instead to build on those companies already acquired. The recession is both an opportunity and an inhibition for acquisitions.

Source: Adapted from www.enterprise-ireland.com/en/Publications/The-Market/Aug-Sep-2010-Issue.pdf [accessed 19 March 2011].

Questions for review

1. What would a company hope to gain by analysing its competitors?
2. Outline the steps involved in analysing competitors.
3. What questions should a marketing manager attempt to answer when undertaking a competitor analysis?
4. How would a company analyse the competitive structure of an industry?
5. Discuss the various competitive positions in marketing and the appropriate strategies for each position.
6. Discuss direct and indirect competition.

5
MARKETING INFORMATION AND RESEARCH

Chapter objectives

After reading this chapter you should be able to:
- Recognise the importance of information to a company.
- Define the marketing information system and its elements.
- Describe the steps involved in the marketing research process.
- Understand the applications of marketing research.

5.1 *The importance of information to a company*

'Information is the principal resource used by a marketer, and decisions can only be as good as the information used' (Murray and O'Driscoll, 1999).

To apply the marketing concept, marketers require a constant flow of information on every aspect of marketing. *Data* are derived from the marketing environment and transferred into *information* that marketing managers can use in their decision-making. The difference between data and information is:
- **Data:** The most basic form of knowledge, such as the brand of yoghurt sold to a particular customer in a certain town. This statistic is of little worth in itself but may become meaningful when combined with other data.
- **Information:** Combinations of data that provide decision-relevant knowledge, such as the brand preferences of customers in a certain age category in a particular geographic region.

The proper collection of data is the cornerstone of any information system. The quality of marketing decisions is usually dependent on the quality of information that informs those decisions. A marketer requires information on a wide range of areas, including defining target markets, developing marketing mixes and formulating long-term strategic plans. Better planning, data collection and analysis lead to more reliable and useful findings and therefore marketers are able to make decisions that are more likely to satisfy the needs and wants of the target market segments.

A company that is prepared to make a marketing decision without first assessing likely market reaction runs a risk of failure. In general, gathering information offers a company a foundation on which it can adjust to the changing environment in which it operates.

5.2 *The marketing information system*

In order to serve the information needs of the organisation and to support decision-making, marketers need to focus not only on collecting data and information, but also on how to handle and manage issues of storage, access and dissemination. A research report is no use to anyone if nobody knows where it is or that it exists or if the people who need it do not have the authority or means to access it. Marketing information, therefore, has become increasingly important. As a result, many firms have designed their own systems for processing the information for use by their marketing managers. A firm needs to co-ordinate the information it collects from a variety of sources (see section 5.3) into a *marketing information system*. 'A marketing information system (MIS) is an organised set of procedures and methods by which pertinent, timely and accurate information is continually gathered, sorted, analysed, evaluated, stored and distributed for use by marketing decision makers' (Zikmund and d'Amico, 2001).

Fig. 5.1: *The marketing information system*

Fig. 5.1 summarises the elements of a marketing information system. An MIS can be one of a number of management information systems used by a firm, but it is mainly used by marketing managers. It provides marketers with timely and comprehensive information to aid their decision-making. Previously, marketing information systems stressed the collection and organisation of marketing data. An MIS now emphasises the need for the system to be easier to use so as to encourage its use by marketing managers who require ready access to information for their decisions.

Most marketing information systems use databases and high-powered computers; some use advanced scanning technology for stock control and ordering. For some companies the marketing information system may be a well-organised, formal system, whereas for others it may be much more informal.

The *elements of the marketing information system* are internal records, marketing intelligence, information analysis and marketing research.

Internal records

Internal records comprise information collected from sources within the company, including:

- Sales records.
- Accounts data.
- Production schedules.
- Purchasing details.
- Sales representatives' reports.
- Customer enquiries and complaints.
- Loyalty card schemes (e.g. Boots Advantage Card).
- Product returns.
- Research studies.

Internal records enable a manager to evaluate the company's marketing performance and to discover possible marketing problems and opportunities. Information from internal records is usually faster and cheaper to access than information from other sources, but it also has a number of limitations. Because internal information is usually collected for other purposes, it may be incomplete or in the wrong form for use in making marketing decisions.

Marketing intelligence

Marketing intelligence is everyday information about events in a company's marketing environment that helps managers to prepare and adjust marketing plans. Marketing intelligence involves developing a perspective on information that provides a competitive edge, for example the opening up of a new market segment. The sources of marketing intelligence include:

- Employees.
- Customers.
- Competitors.
- Suppliers.
- Intermediaries.
- Published reports.
- Advertisements.
- Trade fairs and conferences (e.g. Showcase Ireland, The Holiday World Show).
- Buying intelligence from research agencies.
- The Internet, search engines, company websites, Facebook, Twitter, blogs.
- Newspaper/magazine articles (printed and online versions).

Companies can also buy intelligence information from outside suppliers, such as Dun and Bradstreet (D&B), the world's leading source of information on businesses, which sells data on brand shares, retail prices and percentages of shops stocking different brands.

Information analysis

Data gathered by a company's marketing information system may require further analysis for transformation into practical, usable information. Sometimes managers experience difficulties in applying the information to its marketing problems and decisions. Computer programs that include regression analysis and correlation may help with these.

Marketing research

This is the systematic gathering, analysing and reporting of significant information relating to exchanges that take place between a company, or its products and services, and its customers. Tull and Hawkins (1992) defined marketing research as 'a formalised means of obtaining information to be used in making marketing decisions.'

A successful business depends on developing an effective two-way exchange and communication process with its customers. Research findings are essential to planning and developing marketing strategies. Information on target markets makes a vital contribution to planning the marketing mix and controlling marketing activities. This means that when adequate information about customers is available, the marketing concept can be better implemented.

Marketing research, therefore, is a scientific method of finding data on markets, analysing the information and using it as a basis for decision-making. Market research can enable a company:

- To investigate what has been happening in the past in the market.
- To understand what is happening at present.
- To try to anticipate what will happen in the future.

Marketing research can help a company to gather both **quantitative** and **qualitative information** about its customers. If the research objectives require data to be collected on how many people hold similar views or display particular characteristics, the research is described as being quantitative. Quantitative information lists how many customers and potential customers are accessible, how much they spend on the company's product and where they spend their money. If the research objectives require information to be generated about how people think and feel about issues or why they take certain decisions and behave as they do, then the research is described as being qualitative. Qualitative information lists the attitudes, opinions and preferences of customers and suggests why they prefer to buy one company's products rather than those of its competitors.

The need for marketing research sometimes arises because the organisation needs specific details about a target market, which is a well-defined, straightforward descriptive research task. Sometimes, though, the research need arises from a much broader question, such as why a new product is not achieving expected market share.

5.3 *The marketing research process*

Step 1: Define the problem and research objectives

The research process begins with the recognition of a marketing problem or opportunity. Marketing research may be used to evaluate product, promotion, distribution or pricing alternatives. Before research begins, the marketing manager and the researcher should agree on the nature of the marketing problem or opportunity to be investigated. For example, as changes occur in a company's external environment, marketing managers are faced with questions such as, 'Should we change the existing marketing mix – and if so, how?'

Make That Grade: Marketing

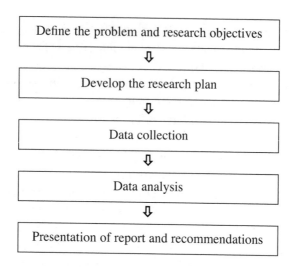

Fig. 5.2: *The marketing research process*

Definition of research objectives

The culmination of the process of problem or opportunity formulation is a statement of the **research objectives**. These consist of the precise information necessary and desired to solve the marketing problem. Objectives must be specific and limited in number: the fewer the research objectives, the easier it is to keep track of them and to make sure each is considered fully and to determine the most appropriate method. Often researchers state research objectives in the form of a hypothesis. This is a statement about a relationship between two or more variables that can be tested with empirical data. The development of research hypotheses sets the stage for creating the research plan or design.

At this early stage of the research process it is often necessary to conduct **exploratory research**. Exploratory research is usually small-scale research undertaken to define the exact nature of the problem and to gain a better understanding of the environment within which the problem has occurred. Exploratory research tends to be highly flexible, with researchers following ideas, clues and hunches. Exploratory research is conducted if the nature of a problem or issue is unclear; it is concerned with exploring possibilities rather than finding specific answers. As the researcher moves through the exploratory research process, a list of problems and sub-problems should be developed.

The research objectives may also be answered by using descriptive research or causal research. **Descriptive research** is conducted to answer 'who', 'what', 'when', 'where' and 'how' questions. It is implicit in descriptive research that the management already knows or understands the underlying relationships of the problem area. Descriptive research is used to outline the factors that will influence marketing decisions, such as the market potential for a product, customers' attitudes and competitors' strategies. An example of descriptive objectives is determining the average frequency of purchase.

In *causal research* the researcher investigates whether one variable causes or determines the value of another variable. A variable is a symbol or concept that can assume any set of values. A *dependent variable* is a variable expected to be predicted or explained; an *independent variable* is a variable in the experiment that the researcher can manipulate or change to some extent. An independent variable is expected to influence the dependent variable. An independent variable in a research project is a presumed cause of the dependent variable, which is the presumed effect. For example, does the level of advertising (independent variable) determine the level of sales (dependent variable)?

Step 2: Develop the research plan

When undertaking a marketing research project, a marketer must be careful not to duplicate research if the required information is already available from another source. A researcher should start by collecting any information that is already available and then develop a plan for collecting, analysing and presenting the information to the client. In preparing the *research plan*, the researcher must identify clearly what additional data are needed and then establish how to collect that data. This may involve collecting both primary and secondary data. Once the researcher has recognised that new information is needed that is not already available, he or she must decide the best source for that information. *Primary data* consist of original sources of information used for providing the information required for the research objectives. *Secondary data* consist of information that have already been collected for another purpose.

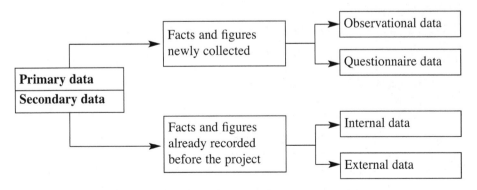

Fig. 5.3: *The differences between primary and secondary data*

There are two types of secondary data: internal and external. ***Internal data*** are obtained from within the company, for example:

- Sales statistics.
- Customer records.
- Sales representatives' reports.
- Financial statements.
- Research reports.
- Customer lists.

Once the internal sources have been consulted, a researcher should then seek external data. ***External data*** are obtained from outside the company, for example:

- Census of population (Central Statistics Office).
- Business or trade publications, both printed and online, e.g. *Checkout Ireland*, *Technology Ireland*, *Irish Kitchens*, *Top 1000 Companies in Ireland*, *The Engineers Journal*, *Franchise & Business Options*, *Retail News Directory*, *Business & Finance*, etc.
- Government departments (e.g. Enterprise, Trade and Innovation; Agriculture, Fisheries and Food).
- Universities, institutes of technology, colleges of further education.
- State agencies and other official bodies (e.g. Bord Bia, Enterprise Ireland, FÁS).
- Chambers of commerce and European business information centres.
- Local authorities (city councils and county councils).
- European Institutions (e.g. European Commission, European Parliament, European Foundation for the Improvement of Living and Working Conditions).
- Annual reports.
- Online databases (e.g. Kompass).
- Online database vendors (e.g. America Online, CompuServe, Dow Jones).
- Internet newsgroups and special interest groups.
- CD-ROM database packages (e.g. US Census Bureau offers TIGER files which map locations of all US streets, airports, etc.).
- Company websites (e.g. www.aib.ie, www.eircom.net, www.irishrail.ie, www.renault.ie, www.carlton.ie).
- Social media networks (e.g. Twitter, Facebook, YouTube, Bebo, MySpace).

Researchers generally begin by using secondary data and then continue by using primary data. Without secondary data, an expensive primary research project might be commissioned to provide information that is already available from secondary sources. Furthermore, directories such as Kompass can be very valuable when selecting a sample in an industrial marketing research project. Secondary data have a number of advantages:

- They save time, as they have already been collected and are readily available.
- They are cost effective (available free internally).
- They can be used as a source of ideas and a starting point for further primary research.

Secondary data may also have disadvantages, however:

- They may be out of date.
- The data collected for another purpose may not be specific enough for the needs of the researcher.
- There may be doubts about the accuracy of the data, such as errors in the original research design, or the sample may be inappropriate.

Gaps in secondary data can be filled through primary research, for example by *observation*, *survey* and *experiment*.

1. Observation

Observational research is used to collect information about the behaviour and actions of people or by observing the results of those actions. The data are collected by observing some action or actions of the respondent. Observation is a particularly useful technique in situations where people find it difficult to give verbal accounts of their behaviour, for example identifying the most common route taken through a supermarket. Observational research depends largely on the skills of the observer. It is less expensive than other forms of research and can be collected by personal or mechanical observation. In *personal observation* a researcher may pose as a customer in a shop and observe customers buying from a particular product category. With *mechanical observation*, companies may use mechanical tools to observe people: for example, supermarket bar code scanners continually monitor consumers' purchases; the A.C. Nielsen company monitors the viewing habits of television viewers; and tachistoscopes (measuring visual perception) and galvanometers (measuring changes in the electrical resistance of a person's skin) are used to indicate degrees of interest in advertisements.

2. Surveys

Surveying involves the collection of data directly from respondents. It is the most widely used and the most flexible method of gathering primary data.

Survey methods include face-to-face interviews, direct personal interviews, telephone questionnaires and postal questionnaires. The selection of a survey method depends on the nature of the problem, the data needed to test the hypothesis and the resources available to the researcher.

Face-to-face interviews

Focus groups involve an interviewer (known as a facilitator) chairing a discussion among a group, typically of six to 10 people. The facilitator intervenes only to keep the conversation on the right themes, preventing it from wandering from relevant topics. The researcher narrows the conversation during the session, concentrating on a specific brand, product or advertisement – hence the term 'focus group'. The discussion is ideally recorded using digital video recording devices to monitor non-verbal behaviour accompanying responses.

Advantages of this method include:
- Focus groups allow interviewers to explore issues with several people at once.
- The effects of group dynamics stimulate members to reveal beliefs and views that may not have been so freely expressed in one-to-one interviews.
- Researchers can ask probing questions to clarify responses.

Disadvantages include:
- If the group includes some dominant people, less assertive people may be discouraged from full participation.
- Focus groups usually employ small sample sizes to keep time and costs down and it may be misleading to generalise from the more limited results.

Personal interviews

This is a face-to-face meeting between an interviewer and a respondent. An interview may take place in a respondent's home or office, in the street, in a shopping centre or at an arranged venue. Trained interviewers clarify difficult questions and can hold a respondent's attention for a long time.

The advantages of personal interviews are that:
- They facilitate the researcher in probing the answers in depth.
- The product, advertisements or packaging can be shown and the reactions and behaviour of the respondent easily observed.
- In most cases, they can be conducted fairly quickly.

The disadvantages are:
- High costs (they may cost much more than the cost of telephone interviews).
- The possibility of error or interviewer bias.
- The reduced ability to reach a dispersed population.

Telephone survey

The respondent is interviewed by telephone (landline or mobile) and the interview is completed during the call. The questions must be very simple and unambiguous to enable respondents to understand them quickly and without the use of visual aids. Interviewers need to be particularly skilled, as visual communication is absent. Eircom and An Post use this method.

The advantages are that:
- They are easy to administer.
- Response rates tend to be good.
- They can be conducted quickly, which reduces costs.
- They provide a facility to probe and to gain further detail.
- They provide large-scale accessibility.
- They facilitate rapid data collection by using CATI (computer-assisted telephone interviewing).

The disadvantages include the fact that:
- It is difficult to conduct lengthy interviews.
- Cost per respondent is higher than with postal surveys.
- Increasing reluctance of general public to participate.
- Visual observation is not possible.
- Call screening can identify that the call is being made from an unknown number, with the risk of persons not wanting to take such calls.
- Inattentiveness can be a feature of the person receiving the call.

Postal survey

In postal surveys, questionnaires are sent to respondents who are encouraged to complete and return them. They are usually used when the respondents chosen for questioning are spread over a wide area and the budget for the survey is limited.

The advantages are:
- They are usually the least expensive, assuming an adequate return rate.
- Interviewer bias is eliminated, since the form is completed without the interviewer.

- Actual or promised anonymity for respondents.
- They give respondents an opportunity to reply more thoughtfully, to talk to family members and so on.

The disadvantages are:
- Inflexibility, as questionnaires must be short and simple for respondents to complete.
- No opportunity to probe respondents to clarify or elaborate on their answers.
- Low response rates.
- Difficult to obtain a complete mailing list.

Online survey

The Internet has not only changed the manner in which consumers purchase products and services, it has altered the manner in which companies interact with their markets. Many businesses are now using online surveys to obtain data they need – and for substantially lower costs. An online survey is a technique in which researchers use batch-type electronic mail to send surveys to potential respondents. The respondents key in their answers and send their replies by e-mail. It is no longer necessary to send researchers into the field to personally interview people. Equally, it is unnecessary to maintain a team that enters individual responses into statistical analysis programmes. By posting the company's questionnaire online, the data can be collected and collated automatically. This dramatically reduces the window of time between the company's survey launch and being able to take action on the responses. Additionally, by allowing respondents to complete the survey online when it is convenient for them to do so, businesses should enjoy a higher response rate. In turn, the greater number of participants replying to surveys should make data more reliable.

The advantages of online surveys are:
- E-mail is one of the applications most commonly used by Internet users.
- Rapid response rate.
- Higher response rate in comparison to postal or telephone surveys.
- Respondents may sometimes enquire about the meaning of particular questions or ask questions they might have.
- Better profile targeting, yielding more valuable data.
- More flexibility in design.
- A company can use its own website to generate contacts.
- Can be powerful, yet subtle, promotional tools for the product or service in question.

The disadvantages include:

- Every person does not have access to the Internet.
- Every Internet user does not necessarily use e-mail.
- Internet users are not a randomly chosen sample of the entire population and therefore the results cannot be used to draw conclusions about large markets.
- Competitors could get to see online research.
- Server crashes and programming errors.
- Survey fraud.

The main disadvantage of online surveys is fraud. There are several security measures that a company can use to decrease online survey cheaters and maintain integrity.

- **Invitation only:** A respondent must receive an e-mail invitation to participate in an online survey. This gives the company an opportunity to verify the address and ensure that the same name and contact information are not already assigned to another e-mail address in the system.
- **Require mailing address:** Ask for a postal address to send reward points or coupons/vouchers. If the same postal address comes up for multiple e-mail accounts, the company might have a cheater.
- **Minimum timeframe:** Set a minimum time for completing an online survey. This cuts down on cheaters who go through the survey just randomly answering questions.
- **Block 'straight line' answers:** Have the software automatically purge any surveys that come back with the same letter or number chosen for every question.
- **Block IP addresses:** If anyone is caught cheating, block his or her IP (Internet protocol) address from submitting any future surveys. It is also advisable to limit the amount of surveys that can be submitted from any one IP address to cut down on multiple submissions.
- **Demographic consistency:** Start the survey with straight demographic questions. The next couple of questions should be demographic profiling questions that verify a person's gender, age, occupation, etc. If the answers to the demographic profiling questions do not correspond with the earlier answers, the user should be blocked.
- **Open-ended questions:** Include at least one short answer, essay-type question that can be analysed for thoughtfulness. Cheaters will not take the time to answer an open-ended question multiple times with significantly different responses.

Questionnaires and questionnaire design

A *questionnaire* is a set of questions designed to generate the data required for accomplishing the objectives of the research project. Questionnaires are the most commonly used research instrument for gathering and recording information from face-to-face interviews, postal surveys, telephone surveys and online surveys.

The design of a questionnaire is critical to the findings of any survey. The style, length and layout of the questionnaire must be considered. The questionnaire must reflect the purpose of the research, collect the appropriate data accurately and efficiently and facilitate the analysis of the data. An unbiased approach to composing questions is required and questions should be clear and easy to understand. Questions should be relevant so that the length of the questionnaire can be kept to a minimum. Only questions that will elicit data to help research the objectives of the survey should be included. Technical jargon, rarely used words and ambiguous statements must all be avoided.

Two forms of questions are used: open-ended and closed-ended. With *open-ended questions* the respondent is encouraged to answer in his or her own words. The researcher does not limit the response choices. Often open-ended questions require probing from the interviewer to encourage the respondent to elaborate or continue the discussion. The interviewer may ask, 'Is there anything else?' or 'Would you elaborate on that?' The form of such a question can be: 'What do you think about Ireland's membership of the European Union?' or 'From what you know of the proposed development, do you think the company is being open and honest about its plans or not?' Such questions allow for quality in the answer and are free of bias. The main disadvantage of open-ended questions can arise in their interpretation.

A *closed-ended question* is one that requires the respondent to make a selection from a given list of responses. The primary advantage of closed-ended questions is simply the avoidance of many of the problems of open-ended questions. Bias is removed because the interviewer is simply ticking a box, circling a category, recording a number or pressing a key.

Traditionally, researchers have separated the two-item response option from the many-item type. A two-choice question is called *dichotomous*; the many-item type is called *multiple choice*. An example of a dichotomous question is: 'Do you smoke?' The answer must either be yes or no. An example of a multiple-choice question is: 'Do you smoke 10–19, 20–29 or 30–39 cigarettes a day?'

Researchers also use the *Likert scale*. This is where respondents are asked to indicate their strength of agreement or disagreement. For example, an Apple iPad represents good value:

- Strongly disagree.
- Disagree.
- Neither agree nor disagree.
- Agree.
- Strongly agree.

What to avoid in questions:
- Ambiguous words.
- Jargon or shorthand.
- Hypothetical situations.
- Complex words and phrases.
- Leading questions.
- Emotionally loaded words.
- Unnecessary questions.
- Biased questions – any questions that are phrased in such a way that they influences the respondent's answer.
- Anything that taxes the memory of respondents.

Before a questionnaire is administered it should be tested on a small-scale sample so that it can be refined before the full survey goes ahead. This is known as the pilot stage and it is very important in ensuring that the questionnaire is adequate for collecting the data required.

Criteria to evaluate a questionnaire

- **Construct validity:** Does the survey actually measure the attributes and variables that were the intended purpose of the research project?
- **Reliability:** Was the data collection methodology sound enough to provide accurate and consistent measures?
- **Internal validity:** Were extraneous variables eliminated and were rival explanations controlled?
- **External validity:** Was a sound sampling system employed given the constraints?

The advantages of questionnaires include:
- Replies tend to be more truthful because of the anonymity of respondents.
- They are useful for blanket canvassing of a wide area.
- Individual interviewer bias is eliminated.
- Easy to administer and easy for respondents to deal with.
- Can simplify the analysis of results.
- Format is familiar to most respondents.

- They provide surprisingly detailed information.
- Information is collected in a standardised way.
- They can be used for sensitive topics that users may feel uncomfortable speaking to an interviewer about.

The disadvantages include:
- They may appear impersonal.
- If a question is omitted it is not easy to go back to respondents, especially if they are anonymous.
- Response rates are low, especially from postal questionnaires.
- Those who have an interest in the subject may be more likely to respond, skewing the sample.
- Respondents may ignore certain questions.
- Questions may be incorrectly completed.
- They are not suitable for investigating long, complex issues.
- Respondents may misunderstand questions because of poor design and ambiguous language.
- They are unsuitable for some kinds of respondents, such as visually impaired.
- There is the danger of questionnaire fatigue if surveys are carried out too frequently.
- They may require follow-up research to investigate issues in greater depth and to identify ways to solve problems highlighted.

3. Experiments

Experiments are the third method researchers use in gathering data. An experiment is distinguished by the researcher changing one or more vari-ables – price, packaging, design, shelf space, advertising theme, or advertising expenditures – while observing the effects of these changes on another variable (usually sales). In experiments, data is obtained by manipulating factors under tightly controlled conditions to test cause and effect. This technique is concerned with measuring the relationship between two marketing variables that are thought to be related in some way.

The objective of experiments is to measure causality. The best experiments are those in which all factors are held constant except the ones being manipulated. This enables the researcher to observe that changes in sales, for example, can be caused by changes in the amount of money spent on advertising.

Experiments may take place under laboratory conditions or in the field. McDonald's, for example, test marketed the idea of adding a single-slice 'McPizza' to its menu. The results from the test market cities were disappointing and the company therefore decided to abandon the idea.

Sampling plan

The next part of the research plan to be decided on is the sampling plan. *Sampling* is the systematic choosing of a limited number of units to represent the characteristics of the total market or population. The sampling plan aims to achieve samples that are representative of the total population from which they are drawn. In this way researchers try to project the behaviour pattern of the target population without the effort and cost of surveying every consumer.

Sampling is one of the most important aspects of marketing research because it involves the selection of respondents on which conclusions will be based. A sampling plan consists of (*a*) a sampling frame and, in the case of probability sampling, (*b*) a sample size and (*c*) a sampling method.

The *sampling frame* is a list of the population members from which the units to be sampled are selected. The researcher must first decide *who* is to be surveyed. The age, sex and other personal characteristics of potential respondents may be relevant, depending on the objectives of the survey. All the people who are members of a sample frame for a particular survey are known as the 'population'. For example, a telephone directory might be the sample frame for a telephone survey sample. This example shows that there is seldom a perfect correspondence between the sampling frame and the population of interest. The population of interest might be all households in a city. The telephone directory, however, would not include those households that do not have telephones or have ex-directory numbers.

Once the sampling frame has been chosen, the researcher must then decide *how many* people are to be surveyed. The process of determining *sample size* for probability samples involves financial, statistical and managerial considerations. Other things being equal, the larger the sample, the smaller the sampling error. However, larger samples cost more money. Frequently the sample size for a project is determined by the budget. Financial constraints challenge the researcher to develop research designs that will generate data of adequate quality for decision-making purposes when resources are limited.

In determining the *sampling method*, the researcher must decide whether to use *probability sampling* or *non-probability sampling*. A *probability sample* is characterised by every element in the population having a known probability of being selected. Such samples allow the researcher to estimate how much sampling error is present in a given study. *Non-probability samples* include all samples that cannot be considered probability samples. Specifically, any sample in which little or no attempt is made to ensure that a representative cross-section of the population is obtained can be considered a non-probability sample. The researchers cannot statistically calculate the reliability of the sample: that is to say, they cannot determine the degree of sampling error that can be expected.

(a) Probability sampling

Random sampling is considered to be the purest form of probability sample. Random sampling provides each member of the population with an equal and known chance of being selected for the sample. As each member of the population has an equal chance of being selected and there is no bias in the selection process, this sampling procedure enables researchers to gain a very accurate reflection of the views of the population. Random sampling is appealing because it seems simple and meets all the necessary requirements of a probability sample.

(b) Stratified sampling

Stratified samples are probability samples that are distinguished by the following procedural steps. Firstly, the original population is divided into two or more mutually exclusive and exhaustive sub-sets (for example, male and female). Secondly, random samples of elements from the two or more sub-sets are chosen independently from each other.

Stratified samples are used rather than random samples because of their potential for greater statistical efficiency. This means that if there are two samples from the same population, one a properly stratified sample and the other a random sample, the stratified sample will have a smaller sampling error.

Area sampling is an alternative form of stratified sampling, where the population is divided into mutually exclusive geographical groups (such as parishes or district electoral divisions) and the researcher selects sample areas or clusters to be surveyed. However, because of the high costs and logistical difficulties of finding a random sample, non-probability sampling is far more common.

(c) Judgmental sampling

Judgmental sampling is the term given to any situation in which the researcher is attempting to draw a representative sample based on judgmental selection criteria. Judgmental samples are selected deliberately by researchers because they believe the respondents represent better sources of accurate information. Many product tests conducted in shopping centres are essentially judgmental samples. The shopping centres used for product taste tests, for example, are selected according to the researcher's judgment that they attract a reasonable cross-section of consumers who fall into the target group for the product being tested.

(d) Quota sampling

Quota samples are typically selected in such a way that demographic characteristics of interest to the researcher are represented in the sample in the same proportions as they are in the population. The researcher decides that a certain proportion of the total sample should comprise respondents conforming to selected characteristics in order to cut down bias.

Step 3: Data collection

At this stage the researcher is ready to put the research plan (step 2) into action. The collection of the data may be done by the company's marketing research staff or by outside research agencies. Interviewers must be briefed and trained for face-to-face and telephone data collection, and administrative systems must be set up for mail surveys. This stage of the process is often the most expensive and the one most subject to mistakes or problems. It is essential, therefore, that the researcher closely monitors all aspects of the fieldwork to ensure the accuracy of data collection, as important decisions may be determined by the results.

Step 4: Data analysis

This stage involves turning the raw data (that is, the responses given on the questionnaires) into useful information. A researcher must remember that it is on the basis of this analysis that important decisions are likely to be made.

The researcher will first tabulate the data and then analyse them. He or she must calculate what the average is and then measure what deviates from the average. The data must be cross-tabulated in an attempt to produce useful relationships. These types of investigation can be undertaken with relative ease, provided the data have been entered properly into appropriate computer programs. It is still, however, the researcher's own expertise, for example in identifying a trend that provides the essential component for marketing managers, that transforms the data into valuable information.

Step 5: Presentation of report and recommendations

At this final stage, conclusions have to be drawn from the findings to create information that relates to the objectives set, and this information has to be communicated to marketing decision-makers. The report is then presented orally and followed by a discussion.

The report should recount the issues and deal with the principal findings. The final outcome of the investigation is the researchers' conclusions and recommendations. The presentation of the findings should include:

• The purpose of the research: for whom and by whom it was undertaken.

- A general description of what was covered.
- The size, nature of sample and date of execution of the fieldwork.
- The research methods employed.
- A description of staff and control methods.
- A copy of the questionnaire.
- Factual data findings.

The layout of the final report should be as follows:
- Title page.
- Table of contents.
- Preface, including outline of the agreed brief, statement of objectives and scope and methods of research.
- Executive summary.
- Research methods.
- Research findings.
- Conclusions.
- Appendices.

Important terms and concepts

data: p. 91
information: p. 91
marketing information system: p. 92
elements of the MIS: p. 92
internal records: p. 93
marketing intelligence: p. 93
information analysis: p. 94
marketing research: p. 94
quantitative information: p. 95
qualitative information: p. 95
marketing research process: p. 95
research objectives: p. 96
exploratory research: p. 96
descriptive research: p. 96
causal research: p. 97
dependent variable: p. 97
independent variable: p. 97
research plan: p. 97
primary data: p. 97

secondary data: p. 97
internal data: p. 98
external data: p. 98
observation: p. 99
personal observation: p. 99
mechanical observation: p. 99
surveys: p. 99
focus groups: p. 100
face-to-face interview: p. 100
personal interview: p. 100
telephone survey: p. 101
postal survey: p. 101
online survey: p. 102
questionnaires: p. 104
open-ended questions: p. 104
closed-ended questions: p. 104
dichotomous: p. 104
multiple choice: p. 104
Likert scale: p. 104

Case study: Marketing research: Dublin Airport Authority plc (DAA)

Dublin Airport Authority plc (DAA) is a state-owned company that first began operations in 1937. It is an airport management company with more than 2,800 employees and a turnover in 2009 of €547 million. The company was originally known as Aer Rianta, but in 2004 the State Airports Act created the Dublin Airport Authority plc. The Act also established new airport authorities at Shannon and Cork airports. Headquartered at Dublin Airport, the DAA's principal activities include airport management, operation and development, domestic and international airport retail management and airport investment. The company's domestic operations include running Dublin, Cork and Shannon airports. Since 2006, the DAA has embarked on a €1.2 billion investment at Dublin Airport with the opening of a new terminal, Terminal 2, in November 2010 in addition to significant improvements to the overall airport infrastructure at Ireland's busiest airport.

DAA is an industry leader in duty free retailing, conducting international retailing through Aer Rianta International with retail operations in Europe, the Middle East, the Commonwealth of Independent States (CIS) and North America. Given the nature of air travel, the airport environment has its own set of challenges when providing a good customer experience. As a result, DAA undertook marketing research to help it to understand and improve the customer experience.

The customer is the central focus of DAA's business. This is reflected in the company's vision: 'To deliver a quality airport travel experience to the best international standards.' The company's mission statement also highlights the centrality of the customer: 'To manage our airport business profitably, meeting customers' needs and creating gateways for 21st-century Ireland.' In order for DAA to deliver a strong customer-focused strategy, it must be clear exactly who its customers are and what their needs and wants are. The following are DAA's customer groups or target markets:

- Passengers.
- Airlines.
- Ground handling agents.
- Concessionaries.
- Cargo companies.
- Local community.

The customer experience includes the customer's interaction with all aspects of infrastructure and services at its airports – all points of contact in their journey, including roads, forecourts, parking, signage, catering, toilet facilities, ATMs, trolleys, check-in, departures, arrivals, customs and security controls, retail, accessibility, baggage reclaim and customer service. One challenge for DAA is that an airline passenger is a shared customer of airlines, ground handlers, transport companies, caterers, etc. The DAA, however, believes that providing a quality travel experience to passengers yields benefits to all customers. At all times, DAA must efficiently move millions of people through its airports while also caring for the individual traveller. It realises that each customer experience is unique, while at the same time DAA must try to provide an airport to suit everyone. This means that the facilities and services must also be designed to meet the needs of people with reduced mobility, sight or hearing loss and other incapacities.

DAA conducts primary marketing research to understand the specific needs and desires of its customers and to track:

- Customer satisfaction with a range of services.
- Market trends in performance over time.
- Performance measured against other international airports.

It uses both qualitative and quantitative research. DAA carries out quantitative research by conducting surveys. These usually take place onsite, i.e. in the airport, but can also be performed via telephone or online. It carries out qualitative research by conducting focus groups and interviews on and offsite. DAA applies strict standards to ensure that the research is of high quality, timely, relevant, accurate and objective. The research is conducted in partnership with independent research and data management agencies.

Secondary research is carried out by other people. It can include reports by government agencies, industry or trade associations, aviation authorities, European Union institutions or other companies within the same industry. DAA refers to other industry analyses and to reports from its peers and uses the information gathered from customer comments and complaints.

Through marketing research and data collection, DAA is able to get a clear understanding of the demographic profile of its passengers and their needs and wants. It has gained a greater understanding of how passengers use the airports it manages (Dublin, Cork and Shannon) and of their customers' experiences. From this, DAA can develop its marketing strategies and tailor its services with these target customers in mind.

DAA's marketing research shows there are unique challenges for airport retailers in delivering a positive customer experience.

- **Limited time:** Passengers need time to check in, to go through security and to get to their boarding gate on time.
- **Anxiety:** Many people are anxious not to delay going directly to their boarding gate.
- **Confusion:** There are many regulations to consider, including carriage of liquids, duty-free and tax-free rules, and uncertainty about exchanges and refunds.
- **Baggage restrictions:** Passengers are restricted in terms of baggage weight and in the transportation of certain items, such as liquids.
- **Unsure of value available:** The loss of duty-free shopping within the European Union has led to uncertainty about the value for money of goods for sale at the airport.
- **Environment:** Crowding in some of the retail spaces due to the large numbers of people moving through Dublin Airport.
- **Wear-out:** Some airline passengers are so used to travelling that they no longer feel excited by airport shopping.

Airport retailers need a strong brand identity to help address the retailing challenges inherent in the airport environment, giving customers the information and support that they need to shop with confidence. In order to achieve this, DAA reviewed the airport shopping brand Travel Value to understand how it was perceived by customers. A number of issues were identified, in particular, low levels of brand awareness and a lack of understanding of what the brand stood for. For example, customers were unclear if Travel Value offered real value compared to downtown retailers and on the level of service it offered, such as refunds.

In 2009, a new brand, The Loop, was developed based on feedback from customers. The Loop is now the brand name for airport shopping at Dublin, Cork and Shannon airports, a replacement for Travel Value. It is an umbrella brand that includes both direct and indirect (concession) outlets. All the retail partners have to stand over the brand promises. These include a price promise for customers: 'Never beaten by downtown prices or double the difference refunded.'

Besides the price promise, The Loop aims to be recognised for the following four elements.

1. **Innovative customer service**: Provide new services to help improve the customer experience, such as its Shop & Collect service and the new Click & Pick Up (new online shopping at Dublin Airport).
2. **Knowledgeable and articulate staff**: Ensuring all staff have excellent product knowledge and excellent customer service.
3. **New and dynamic events**: To create excitement and make the customer journey more interesting, even for the more seasoned travellers, for example new product launches and product tasting.
4. **Demystifying airport shopping**: By providing easy-to-understand, accessible and up-to-date information to customers on all aspects of airport shopping, including its redesigned website (www.theloop.ie) and more informative point-of-sale material.

The creation of The Loop brand is a direct result of marketing research. It helped DAA to identify the need for rebranding its original airport shopping brand, Travel Value. The Loop focuses on value, quality and excellent customer service and includes a price promise never to be beaten by downtown prices. DAA hopes that when customers see The Loop, they should recognise it as a sign of high-quality retail, offering some of the top brands from home and around the world, with a service experience to match. The Loop aims to make the shopping experience more relevant, compelling and enjoyable for all DAA customers. The Loop has been well received by passengers and further retail innovations were launched in 2010.

Source: Adapted from www.business2000.ie/case_studies/daa/index.html [accessed 19 March 2011].

Case study: Innovative research solutions: RED C Research & Marketing Ltd

RED C was set up in Ireland in June 2003 to provide a new independent and innovative research resource in the marketplace. The mission of this fast-growing company is 'to provide a level of service and thought unrivalled by others, and to ensure that insight is generated from all of [its] surveys, through innovative research design'. It aims to help companies maximise their product positioning and marketing for sustained growth by providing clarity. RED C is a member of both AIMRO (Association of Irish Market Research Organisations) and ESOMAR (European Society for Opinion and Marketing

Research) and subscribes to the guidelines set up by both of these organisations.

The core values of RED C are as follows:

Innovation:
- Constantly striving to bring new and original ideas and products to the marketplace to empower research to deliver on its goals.
- Developing individual solutions to specific problems.

Quality:
- All fieldwork is thoroughly vetted and quality controlled by RED C executives.
- Consistent high level of relationship is maintained between RED C and clients to ensure quality account handling throughout the research process.

Clarity:
- Ensuring a thorough understanding of the topic and the issues involved to provide insight from a position of clear understanding of the market and the issues.
- Thoroughly exploring collected data to provide clear and concise findings.

Market research services and products provided by RED C include:
- **Face-to-face:** Its field force includes a team of three staff running a face-to-face panel and a nationally representative interviewer panel with 170 interviewers nationwide. RED C projects range from in-home, on-street and exit political surveys to in-store surveys.
- **Qualitative:** RED C has three experienced senior qualitative moderators, two of whom are dualist researchers. The range of its qualitative projects includes face-to-face and telephone depth interviews, accompanied shopping (where a researcher records every reaction of a customer while shopping with him or her) and focus groups throughout the island of Ireland. RED C also utilises a range of qualitative techniques, including projection, diaries, altered state groups, magazine tears, brand pentagons and decision trees.
- **CATI:** This involves carrying out computer-assisted telephone interviews. The RED C CATI centre has a 20-station capacity which runs from 9.00 a.m. until 9.00 p.m. Project types include business-to-business, consumer shopping and mystery shopping.
- **Online:** RED C uses online hosting and scripting of surveys. RED C undertakes significant research and development into sample structure and

quota analysis in order to provide representative samples of target customers online. It sees the importance of sampling, quota controls and design as essential to representative survey design. Its projects include research into business-to-business and business-to-consumers.

- **RED Express (three-day telephone omnibus):** This is used when a sample of 1,000 interviews is conducted with a random representative sample of the population across Ireland. One survey per month covers a sample of all adults aged 18+ and the second wave per month covers all adults aged 16+. A random digit dial (RDD) method is used to ensure ex-directory households are included and a sample is drawn to ensure that it is 100 per cent regionally representative. RED C is also one of the first research companies in the world to change their sampling approach in order to take account of the growing number of people who only have a mobile phone. Half of its sample is now conducted through calls to mobile numbers, again using an RDD approach. This ensures that its sample reaches 98 per cent of all adults in the population, including those people who only have a mobile phone, those who only have a landline and those who have both. In terms of the classification data available, RED Express uses age, gender, social class, working status, marital status, urban/rural, number of dependant children, nationality and basic voting intention at no additional cost. Data can therefore be run by any of these subgroups.

  The RED Express survey is designed using optimum statistical accuracy. Its sample size of 1,000 interviews provides a standard error at 95 per cent confidence of + or – 3 per cent, the same used for political polling. Fieldwork is conducted by ICM Research, a company that runs the leading market research outbound call centre in Britain, with the highest quality credentials. Quotas are set and weightings are used to ensure that data are nationally representative in terms of gender, age, social class and region. Its breakdown of age within gender is based on the latest census data. The RED Express is timed to run at least every two weeks and provides data in the same week and full charted presentations just one week after fieldwork is undertaken, rather than with the slower face-to-face omnibus surveys, where results are often not received until three to four weeks after the fieldwork has taken place. The most widely known and successful examples of these are the RED C opinion polls. RED C conducts public and private polling for a number of clients, ranging from nationwide political surveys concentrating on first preference figures to individual constituency surveys including transfer analysis.

- **RED MAP (Multiple Ad Pre-test):** The aim of this is to help marketing and brand teams to evaluate a number of possible executions quantitatively in order to aid decision-making about the most effective execution to use. The method used is hall test interviews. Hall tests are conducted in selected venues where a number of respondents can see and test products, services, advertisements or other marketing exercises. Respondents are often recruited from shopping streets near hall test venues. This allows key measures to be compared in one survey using the ABCD approach to advertisement testing. ABCD stands for Appreciation, Branding, Communication and Desired Effect on the particular brand. Measures include likeability, persuasion, affinity, branding level, message communication and overall preference.

- **RED IMPACT:** This uses below-the-line evaluation, which enables companies to evaluate the impact of their promotional below-the-line activities on key business drivers. Test and control samples of the target are recruited and interviewed, both immediately after the promotion or mailing and at a later date to determine longevity of impact. The questionnaire measures the impact of promotional activity on emotional brand drivers, including awareness, penetration, conversion, volume, disposition and affinity. It isolates any gains on these key measures driven by the promotion through the use of a control sample, thus showing the net gain exclusive of any other marketing activity.

- **RED CAN (Catchment Area Need survey):** The objective of this is to evaluate the needs of potential or current shoppers/customers so that a particular store might more successfully fulfil the needs of customers and thus maximise sales. This type of study is conducted over the telephone using CATI (computer-assisted telephone interviewing). RDD (random digit dial) sampling is used in the same manner as used for opinion polling to ensure a random representative sample of potential shoppers within a selected area. Key measures to be covered in the questionnaire for each store include usage behaviour, brand/store image, specific product/range needs (these are then rated as unimportant, essential, desired or order winning) and specific facility needs (rated as unimportant, essential, desired or order winning).

RED C clients include AIB, AXA, Coca-Cola, Diageo, Dublin Airport Authority, Dunnes Stores, the Green Party, Intel, *Irish Star*, Johnson & Johnson, McDonald's, Meteor, Nivea, RTÉ, SuperValu, Tesco, VHI and Walkers, among others.

Source: Adapted from www.redcresearch.ie/research [accessed 19 March 2011].

Questions for review

1. Distinguish between marketing information systems, marketing research and marketing intelligence.
2. Describe the typical steps in designing and conducting a marketing research assignment. Use a company of your choice to outline how each step might be conducted.
3. Discuss the various methods of collecting primary data that a company might use.
4. Outline the various sampling methods.
5. Compare and contrast primary and secondary data.
6. Distinguish between qualitative and quantitative information.
7. List some sources of secondary data.
8. What is the difference between open-ended and closed-ended questions?
9. What are the advantages and disadvantages of telephone surveys?

6
SEGMENTATION, TARGETING AND POSITIONING

Chapter objectives

After reading this chapter you should be able to:
- Discuss the purpose of segmentation.
- Define market segmentation, targeting and positioning.
- Describe the main methods of segmenting markets.
- Identify market coverage strategies.

6.1 *The purpose of segmentation*

'Market segmentation is the process of grouping customers in markets with some heterogeneity into smaller, more similar or homogeneous segments' (Dibb et al., 2006). The basic principle of *segmentation* is the division of the market into distinct groups of buyers who might require separate products or marketing mixes. Market segmentation therefore consists of dividing the total market into a number of smaller sub-markets or segments. Market segmentation and diversity are complementary concepts. Without a diverse marketplace composed of many different people with different backgrounds, countries of origin, interests, needs and wants and perceptions, there would be little reason to segment markets. Diversity in the global marketplace makes market segmentation an attractive, viable and potentially highly profitable strategy.

A market segment meets the following criteria.
- It is distinct from other segments, i.e. different segments have different needs.
- It is homogeneous within the segment, i.e. it exhibits common needs.
- It responds in a similar way to each market stimulus.
- It can be reached by a market intervention.

The term is also used when consumers with identical product and/or service needs are divided into different groups so they can be charged different amounts.

For market segments to be practical, they should be evaluated against the following criteria.

- **Identifiable:** The differentiating attributes of the segments must be measurable so that they can be clearly identified.
- **Accessible:** The company must be able to effectively reach the target segments through communication and distribution channels.
- **Substantial:** The segments should be sufficiently large to justify the resources required to reach them.
- **Unique needs:** To justify the production of separate offerings, the target segments must respond differently to the different marketing mixes.
- **Durable:** The market segments should be relatively stable to minimise the cost of frequent changes.

A good market segmentation will result in segment members that are internally homogenous and externally heterogeneous, that is, as similar as possible within the segment and as different as possible between segments.

In the mass-marketing era of the 1950s, multinational companies such as Coca-Cola had the power to sell large quantities of standardised goods to a 'homogeneous' mass market. Markets have changed considerably since then. Coca-Cola now offers caffeine free, diet, cherry and other variations that combine some or all of these attributes. The increase in the variety of products offered can be seen as an attempt to meet customers' needs more precisely.

Market segmentation has also been adopted by retailers. An example is Gap Inc. Gap (www.gap.com) targets different age, income and lifestyle segments in a diversity of retail outlets. Gap targets upscale consumers through its Banana Republic stores and somewhat downscale consumers with its Old Navy Clothing Company stores. It targets young parents (who are also likely to be Gap or Banana Republic shoppers) with its Baby Gap and Gap Kids stores.

According to Zikmund and d'Amico (2001), the assumptions underlying segmentation are:

- Not all buyers are alike.
- Sub-groups of people with similar backgrounds, behaviour, values and needs can be identified.
- The sub-groups will be smaller and more homogeneous than the market as a whole.
- It should be easier to satisfy smaller groups of similar customers than large groups of dissimilar customers.

Marketers are usually able to cluster similar customers into specific market segments with different, and sometimes unique, demands. The number of market segments in the total market depends on the ingenuity and creativity employed in identifying those segments. In the toothpaste market, for example, companies have identified a number of segments and have targeted various groups, such as children and smokers. In general, the purpose of segmenting the market is to enable the company to concentrate its efforts on pleasing one group of people with similar needs, rather than trying to please everybody using a standard product and therefore perhaps ending up pleasing very few.

There are three stages in market segmentation, as illustrated in Fig. 6.1.

Stage 1: Segmentation

- Choose bases or variables for market segmentation
- Profile the emerging segments
- Validate the emerging segments

⇩

Stage 2: Targeting

- Choose a targeting strategy
- Determine how many segments are to be targeted

⇩

Stage 3: Positioning

- Position products or services in the mind of consumers
- Satisfy consumers' perceptions

Fig. 6.1: *Three stages in market segmentation*

6.2 *Bases or variables for segmenting the consumer market*

There is rarely a single or best way to segment a market. There are many bases or variables for segmenting the consumer market, but the following are the main ones:

- Geographical.
- Psychographic.
- Behavioural.
- Demographic.

Geographical segmentation means dividing the market into different geographical units, such as countries, regions, counties, cities, urban or rural. Geographical segmentation may be carried out for a number of reasons: for example, the product may be suited to people living in a specific area because of the climate. In Mediterranean countries the demand for sun protection products is greater than in Scandinavian countries.

The Nokia communications corporation is organised according to global functions and geographical regions. Its products are sold in almost every region of the world (in over 150 countries) where mobile phones can be used. Currently, Nokia is aiming to bring more accessible telecommunications to rural regions, such as in Africa, India and some parts of Eastern Europe. Nokia has 15 production facilities in nine countries, which facilitates adapting products to meet local market requirements.

Some marketing scholars have argued that direct mail catalogues, free-phone numbers, satellite television transmission, global communication networks and especially the Internet have erased all regional boundaries and that geographic segmentation should be replaced by a single global marketing strategy. Clearly, any company that decides to put its catalogue on the Internet makes it easy for individuals all over the world to browse and become customers. For consumers who shop on the Internet, it often makes little difference if online retailers are around the corner or halfway around the world – the only factor that differs is the shipping charge.

Psychographic segmentation means dividing the consumer market according to social class, lifestyle or personality. Holiday companies often use lifestyle to segment the market, for example cruises versus inter-railing.

Social class reflects the ways people think and the beliefs they hold. A *lifestyle* is a dominant pattern in an individual's pursuit of life goals and is reflected in how the person spends his or her time and money. An individual's activities, interests, opinions and values contribute to that person's lifestyle. Quantitative measures of lifestyles are known as *psychographics*. Such measures represent an attempt to determine a person's private views, desires, thoughts and attitudes and to find out how they live their lives. There are many different lifestyles and there is no agreement about a standard set of lifestyle categories or psychographic measures. A psychographic profile is a summary of an investigation into the psychographic make-up of a person or group. It affects the ways in which people spend their money and the value they place on different types of products, for example clothing, food, furniture, etc. The psychographic profile of a consumer can be thought of as a combination of consumers' measured activities, interests and opinions (*AIOs*). As an approach to constructing consumer psychographic profiles, AIO research seeks consumers' responses to a large number of statements that measure activities (how the consumer or family spends time, e.g. playing games, watching television, gardening), interests (the consumer's or family's preferences and priorities, e.g. foreign travel, fashion, food) and opinions (how the consumer feels about a wide variety of events and political issues, such as social, economic and environmental issues). It is quite possible that people with similar demographic and/or psychographic profiles may interact differently with the same product. Segmenting a market in these terms, therefore, is known as behavioural segmentation.

Behavioural segmentation means dividing the market according to consumers' behaviour, knowledge and benefits required from a product. Clothes companies, such as Gucci and Gap, use behavioural segmentation to divide the market.

Behavioural segmentation also includes usage rate (e.g. light user, medium user, heavy user), user status (e.g. non-user, ex-user, potential user, first-time user, regular user), readiness to buy (e.g. unaware, aware, informed, interested, desirous, intending to buy), brand familiarity (e.g. recognition, non-recognition, rejection) or time of buying (e.g. Christmas, Easter, Valentine's Day, birthdays, etc.). As with usage rate, loyalty could be a useful mechanism not only for developing detail in the segment profile, but also for developing a better understanding of which segmentation variables are significant. Companies can profile consumers who are 'loyal to us', 'loyal to competitors' and '*switchers*' and then discover what other factors seem to differentiate between each of these groups.

Demographic segmentation means dividing the market into groups according to age, gender, occupation, religion, nationality and family size. Demographic variables are the most widely used bases for distinguishing consumer groups, as consumer wants, preferences and usage rates are often highly associated with demographic variables. Demographic variables are also easier to measure than most other types of variables. The grocery sector has designed individual and multi-pack products, such as yoghurts and toilet rolls. Demographic segmentation is the most commonly used method of segmenting markets because it is easy to get the relevant information about the segmenting variables.

Typically, demographic segmentation includes age breakdown, such as 18–24, 25–34, 35–49, 50–64, 65 and over. Family size breakdown normally includes: young single; young married, no children; full nest; empty nest. Companies such as Fisher-Price give full recognition to the differences that exist between children of various ages, with the result that toys are now being designed to fall into specific age categories. This makes the task of choosing toys much easier for parents, relatives and friends. On the negative side, demographics are purely descriptive and, used alone, assume that all people in the same demographic group have similar needs and wants. In most cases, however, the main use of demographic segmentation is as a foundation for other more customer-focused segmentation methods.

Mass-market strategy/total market approach/ undifferentiated strategy

When marketers determine that there is little diversity among market segments, they usually engage in mass marketing. This approach is appropriate in a market that lacks diversity of interest.

A company that uses this type of market coverage strategy deliberately ignores any differences that exist within its markets and decides instead to focus on a feature that appears to be common or acceptable to a wide variety of customers. One marketing mix is used for the entire market. A company that adopts this strategy assumes that individual customers have similar needs that can be met with a common marketing mix. At one time, Coca-Cola used this strategy with a single product and a single size of its familiar bottle. Marketers of commodity products, such as sugar and flour, are also likely to use the mass-market strategy.

Advantages:
- Potential savings on production costs, as only one product is produced.
- Marketing costs may be lower when there is only one product to promote and a single channel of distribution.

Disadvantages:
- It makes the company more susceptible to competition.
- Unimaginative products may be produced.

Single segment/niche/concentrated strategy

This is when a company selects one segment of a market for targeting its marketing efforts. As it is appealing to one segment, it can concentrate on understanding the needs of that particular segment and on developing and maintaining a highly specialised marketing mix. Small companies often use this strategy to compete effectively with much larger firms. The key to this strategy is 'specialisation'.

An organisation might concentrate on a single market niche where management believes it has a competitive advantage in dealing with the selected segment. Concentrated marketing, however, is not without its risks. Where an organisation specialises its efforts it will lack diversity, running the risk of failure if that market dries up. Similarly, where the market segment is too narrow and if growth in that segment slows, financial problems inevitably arise.

Advantages:
- Strong positioning.
- Allows small companies to compete with larger companies better.
- Can meet the needs of a narrowly defined segment better.
- Concentration of resources.
- Can control costs by advertising and distributing only to the segment it views as its primary target.

Disadvantages:
- The company can be vulnerable if powerful competitors turn their attention to that niche.
- Segment may become too small or change due to forces in the marketing environment.

Multi-segment/multiple niche strategy/differentiated approach

This is when the firm focuses on a variety of different segments and then develops a different marketing mix for each. It is often referred to as the 'rifle' rather than the 'shotgun' approach in that the firm can focus on buyers it has the greatest chance of satisfying rather than scattering the marketing effort.

Differentiated marketing is applicable to many situations and in many cases is easy to implement. Supplying different-sized packages of the same product, for example, is a common way of reaching a differentiated market, requiring relatively little extra production and marketing effort. While differentiated marketing is appropriate in many situations, it must be used with care. Costs increase when this approach becomes more elaborate and this must be taken into account when marketing managers consider the value of focusing on the needs of different segments. Decisions on adopting a differentiated market segmentation strategy will be influenced by competitive conditions, corporate objectives, available resources and alternative marketing opportunities for other product lines.

Advantages:
- Greater scope for expansion and growth than concentrated strategy.
- Greater financial success.
- Economies of scale in production and marketing.

Disadvantages:
- Requires a high level of marketing expertise.
- Higher marketing costs than concentrated strategy.
- Cannibalisation.

6.3 *Bases or variables for segmenting the industrial market*

Industrial or organisational markets may be segmented by using variables similar to those used for segmenting the consumer market. The aim of industrial segmentation is to satisfy the needs of companies for products. The following are the most common bases used for segmenting the industrial market.

Geographical location is useful for reaching industries that are concentrated in certain places and it enables salespeople to make the best use of their travelling time.

Operational characteristics, such as company size, industry type and technology, also play an important role in segmenting the corporate market. IBM, for example, segments its market according to the industry in which its customers operate, with some salespeople specialising in serving the requirements of bankers, insurers and other industries.

Purchase behaviour and usage rate are also used to segment the industrial market. Purchasing companies that use large quantities of products will expect a different service from that received by customers who buy only small quantities.

6.4 *Requirements for a usable segment*

There is no limit to the number of ways in which a market can be segmented, but if a segment is to be successfully exploited it must fulfil the following requirements:
- It must be *measurable* or *definable*. This means there must be some way of identifying the members of the segment and knowing how many are in the segment.

- It must be *substantial*. This means it must be large enough to be sufficiently profitable to justify developing and maintaining a specific marketing mix.
- It must be *accessible*. This means the segment must be easy to reach with the developed marketing mix and communication with the segment as a group must be achievable.
- It must be *stable*. This means the nature of the segment must be reasonably constant, so that marketers can make strategic decisions knowing that the segment, as such, will survive long enough.

6.5 *The advantages of market segmentation*

Segmenting the market allows companies to have a better understanding of customers' needs, wants and demands and allows them to keep in touch and to respond quickly to changes demanded by their chosen segment.

It also allows the marketer to spot market opportunities, for example if a segment is unhappy with the existing products or services.

Market segmentation also allows for more effective use of a company's resources, for example improved budget allocation for specific market segments. The obvious gain to consumers is that they can find products that seem to fit more closely with what they want. Consumers may feel that a particular company is more sympathetic towards them or is speaking more directly to them, and therefore they will be more responsive and eventually more loyal to that company.

Market segmentation helps the organisation to target its marketing mix more closely on the potential consumer and thus to meet the consumer's needs and wants more exactly. Segmentation helps to define shopping habits (in terms of place, frequency and volume), price sensitivity, required product benefits and features as well as laying the foundation for advertising and promotional decisions.

Segmentation can also help the company to allocate its resources more efficiently. If a segment is well defined, then the company will have sufficient understanding to develop precise marketing objectives and an accompanying strategy to achieve them, with a minimum of wastage.

Finally, the use of segmentation will help the organisation to achieve a better understanding of itself and the environment within which it exists. By looking outwards to the consumer, the company has to ask itself some very difficult questions about its capacity to serve that consumer better than the competition.

Dangers of segmentation

Catering for differing needs of a large number of segments can lead to fragmentation of the market, with additional problems arising from the loss of economies of scale (e.g. through shorter production runs or loss of bulk purchasing discounts on raw materials).

Within the market as a whole, if there are a number of companies in direct competition for a number of segments, then the potential proliferation of brands may simply serve to confuse the consumer.

6.6 *Targeting*

Having divided the market into segments, companies must decide which segment will be the best to target, given the overall objectives of the company. The target market and the marketing mix variables of product, price, place and promotion are the main elements of a marketing strategy that determine the success of a product in the marketplace. A *target market* consists of a set of buyers sharing common needs or characteristics that the company decides to serve. Normally, a company would choose the most profitable segment, but equally a company may decide to aim for a particular segment of the market which is currently neglected on the grounds that competitors are less likely to enter the market. The process of selecting a segment to aim for is called *targeting*. Choosing the right market and then targeting it accurately are two of the most important activities a marketer carries out. Choosing the wrong segment to target or not attempting to segment the market at all leads to lost opportunities and wasted effort. Targeting is the deliberate selection of segments by a company for its sales and marketing efforts. After carrying out detailed market research, it can then decide what to offer the target market.

Companies need to consider many factors when choosing a strategy for market targeting. Which strategy is best depends on company resources. When an organisation's resources are limited, concentrated marketing is the most useful strategy. The best strategy also depends on the degree of product variability. Undifferentiated marketing is more suited for uniform products. The product's life cycle stage must also be considered. When an organisation introduces a new product, it may be practical to launch only one version and concentrated marketing may make the most sense. In the mature stage of a product life cycle, however, differentiated marketing may be more appropriate. Competitors' marketing strategies also need to be taken into consideration. When competitors use differentiated or concentrated marketing, undifferentiated marketing may be unwise.

A marketer has to consider the following:

- What do the consumers in the target segment need and want?
- What is already available to them?
- What can the company offer that would be better than what is now available?
- What is the intensity of the competition?
- What company resources are available?
- What is the size of the company's existing market share?

According to Abell (1980), there are three basic market coverage strategies, as shown in Table 6.1.

	Definition	Example
Mass-market strategy	A company enters every possible segment of its potential market.	Pepsi-Cola Kellogg's
Single segment or niche strategy	A company directs its marketing effort towards a single market segment.	Mercedes-Benz Rolls-Royce
Multi-segment strategy	A company directs its marketing efforts towards two or more market segments.	British Airways

Table 6.1: *Market coverage strategies*

6.7 *Positioning*

Positioning has been defined by Wind (1984) as 'the place a product occupies in a given market, as perceived by the relevant group of customers; that group of customers is known as the target segment of the market'.

A product's position is the place the product occupies in the minds of the consumers. Positioning, therefore, is the process of creating an image for a product in the minds of target customers. Consumers build up a position for a product based on what they expect and believe to be the most likely features of the product. Marketers therefore need to find out what the most important features of the product are in the minds of the consumer. They can adjust their marketing mix to give the product its most effective position relative to competitors. Many marketers try to convey the clear advantages of their products over competing brands, as for example with Dunnes Stores's slogan, 'The difference is – we're Irish.'

According to Ries and Trout (2000), 'positioning is not what you do to a product; positioning is what you do to the mind of the prospect'. This emphasises the fact that the most important issue is the perception and evaluation by the potential customers of all those things that are done in marketing a product or service. Potential customers need to know:

- That the product or service exists.
- Where it can be bought.
- That they can afford it.
- That it is likely to meet the needs for which it is required.

This means that when positioning their products, marketers must ensure that the 'four As' are met:

- Awareness.
- Availability.
- Affordability.
- Acceptability.

Awareness is influenced by advertising, promotions, branding, display and personal selling. *Availability* depends on distribution and physical handling. *Affordability* depends on pricing. *Acceptability* is influenced by packaging and quality. One obvious way of making a product or service more acceptable is by adding extra features to the core product.

Positioning is an important element of the marketing planning process, since any decision on positioning has direct and immediate implications for the entire marketing mix. The marketing mix can be seen, therefore, as the tactical details of the firm's positioning strategy. For example, if a firm is pursuing a high-quality position, this needs to be reflected in the quality of the product and also in every element of the marketing mix, including price, distribution, the type of promotion and the after-sales service. Without this consistency, the credibility of the positioning strategy is dramatically reduced. Porsche, for example, is positioned in the prestige segment of the car market with a differential advantage based on performance.

Steps for positioning

1. Identify the attributes/characteristics used by consumers in a segment to understand brands.
2. Locate the firm's brand relative to other brands, based on how it is perceived by buyers.

3. Identify the ideal position for consumers in that segment.
4. Decide the best way to position the firm's product.
5. Develop the marketing mix that supports the positioning strategy the firm has selected.

In summary, positioning is developing a distinct image for the product or service in the mind of the consumer, an image that will differentiate the offering from competing ones and communicate to consumers that the particular product or service will fulfil their needs better than competing brands. Positioning is more important to the ultimate success of a product than its actual characteristics, although products that are poorly made will not succeed in the long run on the basis of image alone. The core of effective positioning is a unique position that the product occupies in the mind of the consumer. Most new products fail because they are perceived as 'me too' offerings that do not offer potential consumers any advantages or unique benefits over competitive products.

The result of a successful positioning strategy is a distinctive brand image on which consumers rely in making product choices. A positive brand image also leads to consumer loyalty, positive beliefs about brand value and a willingness to search for the brand. A positive brand image also promotes consumer interest in future brand promotions.

Important terms and concepts

segmentation: p. 119
bases for segmenting the consumer
  market: p. 121
geographical segmentation: p. 122
psychographic segmentation: p. 122
lifestyle: p. 122
psychographics: p. 122
AIOs: p. 122
behavioural segmentation: p. 123
switchers: p. 123
demographic segmentation: p. 123
mass-market strategy: p. 124
single segment strategy: p. 124

multi-segment strategy: p. 125
bases for segmenting the industrial
  market: p. 126
geographical location: p. 126
operational characteristics: p. 126
purchase behaviour and usage rate:
  p. 126
advantages of market segmentation:
  p. 127
target market: p. 128
targeting: p. 128
positioning: p. 129

Case study: Using e-marketing to target and segment the market: Bus Éireann

Bus Éireann was formed in 1987 to provide bus services throughout Ireland outside of Dublin city. The company's commitment to meeting customer needs is reflected in its mission statement: 'to succeed by providing excellent service to our customers through a committed team'. Part of the Bus Éireann logo is the Irish red setter, which has a reputation for being friendly, reliable and fast, as Bus Éireann strives to be when serving its customers. Bus Éireann employs over 2,700 people directly and operates a total fleet of over 1,300 coaches and buses. There were 48.2 million road trips taken by passengers on Bus Éireann in 2008 and in 2009 the projected online sales were €3 million, up from €1.8 million in 2008.

E-marketing

E-marketing is the marketing of products and services over the Internet and through other forms of electronic media. E-marketing is now an essential part of most communications strategies. It is estimated that seven out of 10 business-to-business deals start with an Internet search and 36 per cent of the Irish population now regularly buy online. Associated with this has been the large increase in recent years in social networking, which means that companies can directly target and speak to their existing and prospective customers. In essence, customers now expect companies not just to talk at them but also to talk with them, solidifying customer relationships. When used effectively, e-marketing allows companies to give increased customer service, which in turn increases brand loyalty and increases sales.

The Internet and e-marketing: Importance and trends

Today, companies need to strategically develop e-marketing so that they can deliver their message and their brand values to customers and to targeted potential customers. When considering this, it is worth bearing in mind that:
- A company's website is its most important calling card for communicating with existing customers and attracting new customers. Today, people expect websites and social networks to be up to date and interactive. A static website with out-of-date information creates a negative image.
- The way in which products or services are positioned online will determine if the company gets noticed by buyers.
- E-marketing enables a company to reach customers and decision-makers more cost effectively than by traditional means.

- E-marketing is not just about the website, but also about the company's 'online footprint', and this means using other online tools such as social networks.
- Over 800,000 people in Ireland have accessed the Internet on mobile phones and figures show that 44 per cent of this group are students.

E-marketing and online shopping

Put simply, e-marketing involves driving people to the website to buy online. It is interesting to look at the current trends in online shopping in Ireland, which include:

- In 2008, 36 per cent of Irish people shopped on the Internet compared with just 14 per cent in 2004 (the EU average is 32 per cent).
- The greatest concentration of online shoppers in Ireland is among 25- to 34-year-olds, at 52 per cent, followed by 35- to 44-year-olds (44 per cent) and 16- to 24-year-olds (34 per cent).

People are buying a wide range of products or services online. In the context of Bus Éireann, it is interesting to note that 21 per cent of Irish people have bought travel and accommodation online.

Bus Éireann's e-marketing strategy

Bus Éireann has identified the need to develop an innovative e-marketing strategy to target new and existing customers. This strategy can be examined under four simple headings.

1. Establish the target audience or marketing segmentation.
It is vital that the company understands its target audience and the segments within it. The idea behind segmentation is that it allows companies to describe benefits in ways that have a high impact on a particular target market. This is an effective marketing strategy because the same features in a product provide different benefits to different groups of people.

Segmenting customers into groups is more effective, as the marketing message can then be tailored to appeal to the people who are most likely to respond. Market segmentation helps companies to classify customers and to find more like them.

Bus Éireann knows that 80 per cent of its long-distance business is in the 18- to 35-year-old category, comprising a mixture of commuters (82 per cent) and students (18 per cent). The other 20 per cent of its total business comes from airport travellers, employers, school transport scheme users and day tours. It is important that the company creates a strategy that addresses each of these groups.

2. Identify the key objectives for the strategy.

- Make the company the first choice for transport.
- Promote and increase online buying of tickets and develop online loyalty.
- Stimulate demand and extend the customer base, i.e. reach new customers.
- Create a dialogue with customers and build customer relations.
- Show innovation in marketing online.
- Generate positive coverage for the company.

3. Identify the proposition.

This means identifying the key elements and unique selling points of the brand. In the case of Bus Éireann, these include:

- Efficient and friendly service with a large number of routes, including airport travel.
- An interactive website that allows users to view real-time service information, timetables, fares and journey planner and to purchase tickets online with no booking charge.
- An employer pass programme that allows employers to pass on tax savings to their employees in relation to travel costs.
- Day tours that can be purchased online at a discounted rate.
- School transport scheme that can be purchased online.
- An open-road travel pas that is a flexible pass valid for travel on Bus Éireann Expressway, local, city and town services which can be purchased online.

4. Implement the strategy and measure results.

Bus Éireann has created a strategy that will speak to all segments within its target reach, as follows.

- A redesign of its website to increase online sales and to make the site more streamlined and user friendly. This will be a communication tool for all segments.
- Create a presence on Facebook, Twitter, YouTube and Flickr. This will specifically target the 18- to 35-year-old category and will include information on discounted fares, competitions and special offers. Users will also forward and retweet this information to their friends and followers, resulting in a viral campaign (facilitating and encouraging others to pass along a marketing message). The overall intention is to drive people to the website to purchase tickets.

- Develop a national student campaign that includes database creation, online competitions and social media PR, which can be used for SMS text and e-mail communication. In addition to this, Bus Éireann has visited 38 colleges nationwide and distributed promotional material. This specifically targets the student market segment.
- Search engine optimisation will ensure that Bus Éireann comes up at the top of the list in search engines, particularly in Google, which is used the most in Ireland. This will be a communication tool for all segments.
- The company will also continue to use more traditional forms of media, such as newspaper and radio advertising. This will be a communication tool for all segments, but particularly users in the 35+ category.

Bus Éireann online

Bus Éireann will continually monitor its marketing strategy and will measure the results. Some of the current results show:

- Over 1,000 fans on Facebook and over 900 followers on Twitter (both of these accounts were set up in September 2009).
- More than 1,500 tickets sold via Twitter in the first two months since set-up.
- Positive press coverage and use of Bus Éireann in two recent business case studies on e-marketing by the Dublin Chamber of Commerce and the Institute of Public Administration.

Nearly all purchases made online get a 10 per cent discount, which is a further incentive for customers to book online. Bus Éireann's website had 200,000 individual visits a month in 2008, which was a 30 per cent increase from 2007, and this is continuing to rise. This means that Bus Éireann's site is one of the top 10 of the most visited Irish websites.

The advantages of having a strong website are many and include the following.

- Customers go directly to www.buseireann.ie and can get information on fares and routes and can buy tickets online. This is a convenient, easy-to-use and secure method of buying tickets for customers. The service is constant and instant and does not conform to traditional business hours, resulting in greater customer service and increased sales for the company.
- Better use of staff time and reduction in advertising costs.
- Possibility to get messages out quickly to a wide range of people and to create viral campaigns, resulting in users of the website posting information on their social networks. The customer is kept up to date on special offers and on new services and therefore feels better informed.

- Allows the company to get to know its customers better. This can be achieved through analysing web statistics (seeing who is using the website, the most popular pages and when they are using them) and via the linked social networking and through comment postings, etc. The overall result is that the company is developing its relationship with customers and it can respond to their needs in a meaningful way, which ultimately increases customer satisfaction and creates brand loyalty.

Overall, e-marketing is a sophisticated and cost-effective tool for directly talking to and with customers. Bus Éireann has shown through strategic e-marketing that it can reach key customers in a targeted and low-cost way through whatever medium is preferred by its customer. In addition, it can further drive sales growth on the web and deliver increased efficiencies and offer a better service to customers.

Source: Adapted from www.business2000.ie/pdf/pdf_13/bus_eireann_13th_ed.pdf [accessed 19 March 2011].

Case study: Targeting the teenage girl market: Nivea Visage Young

Nivea is an established name in high-quality skin and beauty care products. It is part of a range of brands produced and sold by Beiersdorf. Beiersdorf, founded in 1882, has grown to be a global company specialising in skin and beauty care. The continuing goal of the company is to have its products as close as possible to its consumers, regardless of where they live. Its aims are to understand its consumers in its many different markets and to delight them with innovative products for their skin and beauty care needs. This strengthens the trust and appeal of Nivea brands. The business prides itself on being consumer led and this focus has helped Nivea to grow its brand into one of the largest skin care brands in the world.

The company's continuing programme of market research showed a gap in the market. This led to the launch of Nivea Visage Young in 2005 as part of the Nivea Visage range, offering a wide selection of products aimed at young women. It carries the strength of the Nivea brand image to the target market of girls aged 13 to 19. Nivea Visage Young is designed to help girls to develop a proper skin care routine to help keep their skin looking healthy and beautiful. In 2007, having identified a gap in the market, the Nivea Visage Young range was relaunched using a balance of the right product, price, promotion and place, thus further optimising its position in the market.

How research improved the product

The first stage in building an effective mix is to understand the market. Nivea uses market research to target key market segments, identifying groups of people with the same characteristics, such as age, gender, attitude or lifestyle. The knowledge and understanding from the research helps in the development of new products. Nivea undertakes market research with consumers in a number of different ways, including:

- Using focus groups to listen to consumers directly.
- Gathering data from consumers through a variety of different research techniques.
- Product testing with consumers in different markets.

Nivea's market research identified that younger consumers wanted more specialised face care aimed at their own age group, offering a 'beautifying' benefit rather than a solution to skin problems. Nivea Visage Young is a skin care range targeted at girls who do not want medicated products but want a regime for their normal skin. Competitor products tend to be problem focused and offer medicated solutions. This gives Nivea a competitive advantage, as the product provides a unique bridge between the teenage market and the adult market.

As a result of research, Nivea improved the product to make it more effective and more consumer friendly. Nivea tested the improved products on a sample group among its target audience before finalising the range for a relaunch. This testing resulted in a number of changes to existing products. Improvements included:

- Changing the formula of some products, e.g. it removed alcohol from one product and used natural sea salts and minerals in others.
- Introducing two completely new products.
- A new modern pack design with a flower pattern and softer colours to appeal to younger women.
- Changing product descriptions and introducing larger pack sizes.

Each of these changes helped to strengthen the product range to better meet the needs of the target market.

Price

On relaunch, the price for Nivea Visage Young was slightly higher than previously. This reflected its new formulations, packaging and extended product range. However, the company also had to take into account that the target market was both teenage girls and mothers buying the product for their daughters. This meant that the price had to offer value for money or it would be out of reach of its target market. As Nivea Visage Young is one of the leading skin care ranges meeting the beautifying needs of this market segment, it is effectively the price leader. This means that it sets the price level that competitors will follow or undercut. Nivea needs to regularly review prices to ensure that its pricing remains competitive in case a competitor enters the market at the market growth stage of the product life cycle. Nivea Visage Young's pricing strategy now generates around 7 per cent of Nivea Visage sales.

Distribution channels (place)

Nivea Visage Young aims to use as many relevant distribution channels as possible to ensure the widest reach of its products to its target market. The main channels for the product are retail outlets where consumers expect to find skin care products. Market research shows that around 20 per cent of this younger target market will buy products for themselves in high street stores when shopping with friends. Research also shows that the majority of purchases are actually made by mothers buying for teenagers. Mothers are more likely to buy the product from supermarkets while doing their grocery shopping.

Nivea distributes through a range of outlets that are cost effective but that also reach the highest number of consumers. Its distribution strategies also consider the environmental impact of transport.

- It uses a central distribution point in Great Britain. Products arrive from European production plants using contract vehicles for efficiency for onward delivery to retail stores.
- Beiersdorf does not sell directly to smaller retailers, as the volume of products sold would not be cost effective to deliver, but it uses wholesalers to supply these smaller outlets.
- Nivea does not sell directly through its website, as the costs of producing small orders would be too high. However, retailers like Tesco feature and sell the Nivea products in their online stores.

Promotion

Nivea chooses promotional strategies that reflect the lifestyle of its users and the range of media available to them. Nivea realises that a one-way message using TV or the press is not as effective as talking directly to its target group of consumers. Instead, the promotion of Nivea Visage Young is consumer led as Nivea identifies ways of talking to teenagers (and their mothers) directly.

- A key part of the strategy is the use of product samples. These allow customers to touch, feel, smell and try the products. Over 1 million samples of Nivea Visage Young products were given away during 2008. These samples were available through the website, in stores or in gift bags at Visage road shows.
- Nivea Visage Young launched an interactive online magazine called *FYI* (Fun, Young & Independent) to raise awareness of the brand. The concept behind the magazine is to give teenage girls the confidence to become young women and to enjoy their newfound independence. Communication channels are original and engaging to enable teenagers to identify with Nivea Visage Young. The magazine focuses on first-time experiences of Nivea Visage Young as their first skin care routine.
- With *FYI*, Nivea Visage Young recognises the power of social network sites for this young audience, and these are added to by pages on MySpace, Facebook and Bebo. The company is therefore using the power of new media as part of the mix to grow awareness amongst the target audience.

In conclusion, Nivea Visage Young has created a clear position in the market. This shows that Nivea understands its consumers and has produced this differentiated product range in order to meet customer needs. To bring the range to market, the business has put together a marketing mix that balances the four elements of product, price, place and promotion. This mix uses traditional methods of place, such as distribution through the high street, alongside more modern methods of promotion, such as through social networking sites. This mix makes sure that the message of Nivea Visage Young reaches the right people in the right way.

Source: Adapted from www.thetimes100.co.uk/studies/view-brief-study—the-use-of-the-marketing-mix-in-product-launch—87-303.php [accessed 19 March 2011].

Questions for review

1. Identify and describe the variables or bases that can be used to segment consumer markets. Give examples of products that are segmented by such variables.
2. Describe the conditions required for effective segmentation.
3. What are the main methods used to segment industrial or corporate markets?
4. Define (*a*) segmentation, (*b*) targeting and (*c*) positioning and give examples of companies that practise each of these activities.

5. Distinguish between the three basic market coverage strategies. Illustrate your answer with appropriate examples.
6. What are the advantages of market segmentation?
7. Why do companies segment markets?
8. List the difference between single segment and multi-segment strategies.
9. Choose a product and describe how it could be best positioned in the market.

7
PRODUCT

Chapter objectives

After reading this chapter you should be able to:
- Understand product classification.
- Recognise the importance of brands.
- Outline the benefits of packaging and labelling.
- Describe the stages of the product life cycle.
- Describe the new product development process.

7.1 *The product*

The product is at the heart of the marketing exchange. If the product does not deliver the benefits the customer wanted or if it does not live up to the expectations created by the other elements of the marketing mix, then the whole exercise has been in vain. A product is defined as '**anything that is capable of satisfying customer needs**'. This definition includes physical products (e.g. electrical goods, transport vehicles, food) as well as services (e.g. medical, financial or transport services, waste disposal, marketing research, tourism, education). Consumers buy products to solve problems or to enhance their lives and thus the marketer has to ensure that the product can fully satisfy the consumer, not just in functional terms, but also in psychological terms. The product is important, therefore, because it is the ultimate test of whether the organisation has understood its customers' needs. A *product* is a good, service or idea. Murray and O'Driscoll (1999) define a product as 'a bundle of physical, service and psychological benefits designed to satisfy a customer's needs and related wants'.

The *physical benefits* of a product are the tangible elements, e.g. a personal computer, including its monitor, keyboard and mouse. The *service* aspect of a product represents all the product benefits that make the product saleable, e.g. the facilities provided, guarantees, installation, training, after-sales service and a user-friendly website with online support and a freephone number. The *psychological benefits* of a product are its symbolic aspects, including its brand name and the company's reputation and image, creating associations with certain people and lifestyles.

7.2 Product classification

It is useful for companies to define groups of products that have similar characteristics or that generate similar buyer behaviour within a market. Companies classify products to help develop similar marketing strategies for a wide range of products offered. There are two ways to classify products: by degree of tangibility or durability and by type of user.

Degree of tangibility or durability

There are three main types in this category. *Durable goods* usually last for many uses and for a long time before having to be replaced, for example cars, domestic electrical goods, stereo equipment, furniture. *Non-durable goods* are consumed in one or a few uses before they have to be replaced, for example food and drink, soap, fuel, stationery. *Services* are intangible products that consist of activities, benefits or satisfactions offered for sale, for example marketing research, education, holidays, financial services, home repairs, catering.

They involve a deed, performance or an effort that cannot be physically possessed. Services have four unique characteristics/features that distinguish them from physical goods. These four elements are referred to as the **four Is of services**.

1. Intangibility

The basic difference between physical goods and services is that services are intangible. They cannot be held, touched, seen, tasted or felt in the same manner in which goods can be sensed. Services cannot be stored and are often easy to duplicate. They cannot be protected through patents and prices are difficult to set. This characteristic makes it more difficult for marketers to communicate the benefits of an intangible service than to communicate the benefits of tangible goods.

2. Inseparability

The production and consumption of services are inseparable activities. This means that in most cases consumers cannot and do not separate the service from the provider of the service or the setting in which the service occurs. For example, to receive an education, a person may attend a third-level institution.

The quality of the education may be high, but if the student has difficulty parking or sees little or no opportunity to take part in extracurricular activity, he/she may not be satisfied with the educational experience.

3. Inconsistency

This is also referred to as heterogeneity. It means that services tend to be less standardised and uniform than physical products. As services depend on people to provide them, their quality varies because people have different capabilities and also vary in job performance from day to day.

4. Inventory

This is more commonly known as perishability. It means that services cannot be stored, warehoused or inventoried. An empty theatre seat or hotel room provides no revenue that day, therefore the revenue is lost forever. On the other hand, service providers may have to turn away customers during peak periods. It is a major challenge for marketers to find ways to synchronise supply and demand.

Product line and product mix

A *product line* is a group of brands that are closely related in terms of their functions and the benefits they provide, for example Toshiba's range of laptops and notebooks designed for home computing or Sony's Bravia cinematic range of TVs. The depth of the product line depends on the pattern of customer requirements, for example the number of segments to be found in the market, the product depth being offered by competitors and company resources. Therefore, the product line depth refers to the number of versions offered of each product in the line. For example, although customers may require wide product variations, a small and medium-sized enterprise may decide to focus on a narrow product line serving only sub-segments of the market. On the other hand, even simple products, such as Procter & Gamble's Crest toothpaste, can come in many sizes and flavours, with up to three formulations in each (standard toothpaste, gel toothpaste and liquid gel toothpaste).

A *product mix* is the total set of brands marketed by a company. It is the sum of the product lines offered. The width of the product mix can be gauged by the number of product lines that a company offers. For example, Procter & Gamble markets a wide product mix in many product lines, including the following brands:

- Air fresheners (Febreze).
- Laundry and fabric care (Bold, Bounce, Dreft Laundry, Lenor).

- Household and dishwashing cleaners (Mr Proper, Daz, Fairy).
- Paper towels (Charmin and Bounty).
- Baby hygiene (Pampers).
- Batteries (Duracell).
- Beauty and grooming (Gillette, Fusion, Wella, Max Factor, Olay, Clairol Professional, Dolce & Gabbana, Hugo Boss fragrances, etc.).
- Health and well-being (Crest, Oral-B, Always, Fixodent, Pringles, Vicks, etc.).

Type of user

Consumer goods

Consumer goods are products bought by the final consumer for personal consumption.

There are four types of consumer goods, according to consumer buying habits. *Convenience goods* are consumer goods that the consumer buys frequently, conveniently and with a minimum of buying effort, for example newspapers, toothpaste, soap, bread, chocolate. *Shopping goods* are consumer goods for which the consumer tends to shop around in order to compare quality, price or style, for example cameras, televisions, electrical appliances, clothes, computers. *Speciality goods* are consumer goods that the customer makes a special effort to search for, for example collectors' items, works of art, jewellery, designer clothes, prestige cars. *Unsought goods* are consumer goods that the consumer either does not know about or knows about but does not at first want. These require a lot of promotional activities to stimulate sales, for example insurance, smoke detectors, alarm systems.

Industrial goods

Industrial goods are items bought by individuals and companies for further production or support. The sale of industrial goods often results or is derived from the sale of consumer goods. *Capital items* consist of buildings, fixed equipment, portable factory equipment and office equipment that has to be installed for production to occur. *Supplies and services* are industrial goods that facilitate the production and efficient running of a company without any direct input. These include operating supplies (computer paper, paint), maintenance and repair (cleaning materials) and business services (legal advice, management consultancy, accountancy). *Materials and parts* are items that make up the product, either through further processing or as components. They include raw materials (crude oil, iron ore, cotton, timber, fish, fruit and vegetables) and manufactured materials and parts (cement, tyres, car batteries, yarn).

7.3 *Branding*

Branding is an important element of the tangible product, particularly in consumer markets, as it is a means of linking items with a product line or emphasising the individuality of product items. Branding can also help in the development of a new product by facilitating the extension of a product line or mix by building on the consumer's perceptions of the values and character represented by the brand name. This points to the most important function of branding: the creation and communication of a three-dimensional character for a product that is not easily copied or damaged by competitors' efforts. An important result of the way customers perceive a product is the recognition of a brand. A *brand* is a name, symbol or design that has a distinct image and that differentiates one product from another. A *brand name* is the verbal part of the brand, for example Ben & Jerry's, Sony, Harley-Davidson, Apple, Kellogg's, KFC, Hello Kitty. A brand or brand name can be almost anything a marketer wants it to be, but by itself it has no legal status. A *trademark*, on the other hand, is a legally protected brand name, logo (the name of the company written in a particular way) or symbol.

The owners of trademarks have exclusive rights to their use. A strong brand, for example Guinness, is likely to prove very difficult for competitors to copy and can offer a competitive advantage over other products.

Brand equity refers to the value of a brand. Brand equity is based on the extent to which the brand has high brand loyalty, name awareness, perceived quality and strong product associations. Brand equity also includes other intangible assets, such as patents and trademarks.

Brand image refers to the set of beliefs that customers hold about a particular brand. These are important to develop well since a negative brand image can be very difficult to shake off.

Brand extension refers to the use of a successful brand name to launch a new or modified product in a new market. Virgin is perhaps the best example of how brand extension can be applied into quite diverse and distinct markets.

Brand stretching is when an established brand name is used for brands in unrelated markets, such as the use of the Tommy Hilfiger brand on clothing, fragrances, footwear and home furnishings.

The object of branding is to attract a group of customers who are 'brand loyal', which means that they buy the brand regularly and do not change to competing brands. Branding offers advantages to both the consumer and the manufacturer. For the consumer it helps in identifying products and in evaluating their quality. Manufacturers also benefit from branding because each company's brand identifies its products, and this makes repeat buying easier for consumers. Branding helps a company to introduce a new product that carries the name of one or more of its existing products because consumers are already familiar with the company's existing brands. '*It is my conviction that what we call shareholder value is best defined by how strongly employees and customers feel about your brand. Nothing seems more obvious to me than that a product or service only becomes a brand when it is imbued with profound values that translate into fact and feelings that employees can project and customers embrace*' (Richard Branson of Virgin Airlines, 2000).

According to Ries (1995), brand names should have the following characteristics:

- They should attract the customer's attention.
- They should be memorable.
- They should be linked to a visual image.
- They should communicate something about the product or be capable of being used to communicate something about the product.
- They should be 'telephone friendly'.

To succeed in branding, a company must understand the needs and wants of its customers. It can do this by integrating its brand strategies through its business at every point of public contact.

A company's brand resides within the hearts and minds of customers and clients. It is the sum total of their experiences and perceptions, some of which a company can influence and some that it cannot.

A strong brand is invaluable in the intense and ongoing battle for customers. It is therefore important to invest time and resources in researching, defining and building a brand. After all, a brand is the source of a promise to one's customer.

7.4 Brand types

There are two main types of brand: manufacturer brands and own-label brands. *Manufacturer brands* are created by producers and bear their original brand name. The producer is responsible for marketing the brand, which they own. By building brand names, manufacturers can gain widespread distribution (e.g. by retailers who want to sell a particular brand) and build customer loyalty. Examples include iPhone, DKNY, BMW and Facebook.

Own-label brands or *distributor brands* are created and owned by retailers, wholesalers or other distributors. Sometimes the entire product mix of a distributor may be own label, e.g. Marks & Spencer's brand name, St Michael, or it may be part of the mix, as in the case of many supermarket chains. If associated with tight quality control over suppliers, own-label branding can provide consistently high value for customers and can be a source of power for the distributor over the manufacturer or supplier, as suppliers compete to win contracts to produce goods with distributor branding. The power of low-price supermarket own-label brands has focused many producers of manufacturer brands to introduce so-called fighter brands, i.e. their own low-price alternative.

7.5 *Brand name strategies*

Family branding involves using a single brand name, such as Campbell's, Del Monte or Heinz, over a whole line of fairly closely related items. The idea of family branding is to take advantage of a brand's reputation and the goodwill associated with the name. The use of family branding, however, does not guarantee success in the market. A company's other products may suffer because of problems with a product sold under the same brand name. This is one reason why some companies use individual brand names rather than family brand names.

An *individual brand* is assigned to a product within a product line that is not shared by other products in that line. Some companies use the individual branding approach because they wish to market several products that appeal to different market segments. Companies such as Procter & Gamble, for example, use individual brands for their Bold, Daz, Tide and Dreft detergents. Other companies use individual branding to capture shelf space: for example, the Mars company produces Snickers, Milky Way, M&Ms and many others; therefore, if a retailer has only got space to display 20 brands and 10 of them are Mars brands, the chances that a customer will select a Mars product are much improved.

Own-label brands are developed by wholesalers or retailers. The main characteristic of own-label brands is that the manufacturers are not identified on the product. Own-label brands give wholesalers or retailers the freedom to buy products at the lowest cost without disclosing the identity of the manufacturer. Familiar retailer brand names include St Bernard (Dunnes Stores), St Michael (Marks & Spencer), and Primark (Penneys).

A *generic brand* indicates only the product category, for example aluminium foil, and does not include the name of the company, manufacturer or distributor. The goods are plainly packaged with stark lettering that simply lists the contents. Usually generic brands are sold at prices below those of comparable branded items.

According to Dibb et al. (2006), successful brands must:

- Give priority to quality.
- Offer superior service.
- Get there first.
- Differentiate brands.
- Develop a unique positioning concept.
- Have a strong communication programme.
- Be consistent and reliable.

It is important for marketers to know if a particular brand is successful in order to capture the leading share in its market segment. If a brand is not successful, marketers need to consider removing it from their company's product range.

7.6 *The benefits of branding*

Branding is of particular value to the buyer in a complex and crowded market-place. In a supermarket, for example, brand names and visual images make it easier to locate and identify required products. Strong branding can help consumers judge whether it is their sort of product, delivering the functional and psychological benefits sought. This is particularly true for a new, untried product. Strong brands also strengthen the relationship between the consumer and the manufacturing company.

The manufacturer's key interest in branding is in the building of brand loyalty to the point where the trust, liking and preference for the brand overcome any doubts regarding price sensitivity, thus allowing a reasonable measure of premium pricing and the prevention of brand switching.

Other benefits of branding for the manufacturer are linked with segmentation and competitive positioning strategies. Different brands can be used by one organisation to target different segments. Because the different brands have clearly defined individual characteristics, the consumer does not necessarily link them and thus does not become confused about what the organisation stands for.

Strong branding is also important for providing competitive advantage, not just in terms of generating consumer loyalty, but also as a means of competing head on, competing generally across the whole market in an almost undifferentiated way or finding a niche in which to dominate.

7.7 *Packaging and labelling*

Packaging

The *packaging* element of a product refers to any container or wrapping in which it is offered for sale and on which information is communicated. It is an expensive and important part of a company's marketing strategy. Packaging not only serves a functional purpose, it also acts as a means of communicating product information and brand character. The packaging is often the consumer's first point of contact with the actual product so it is essential to make it attractive and appropriate for both the product's and the consumer's needs.

The benefits of packaging

- *Functional benefits:* Packaging plays an important functional role. It protects the product in storage, in shipment and on display (by extending its shelf life) and prevents tampering. It also helps to increase convenience for the con-sumer, as for example with toothpaste sold in pump dispensers, ring pulls on soft drink cans and resealable packets of sliced meat (Denny's cooked ham).
- *Communication benefits:* Packaging conveys information to the consumer on the composition and optimum use of the product, for example cooking instructions may accompany ingredients.
- *Perceptual benefits:* Packaging creates a perception in the consumer's mind. It can imply status, economy or product quality. Companies have to be careful when selecting colours for their packaging, as colour can affect consumers' perceptions. For example, in trying to modernise its image, Coca-Cola has redesigned its logo and package design but has held on to its established red and white colours.

Labelling

Labelling is closely related to packaging and can be used to display legally required information, for example regulations on food additives or on safety requirements, as well as additional information expected by consumers. Labels have many functions: they can identify, grade, describe and promote a product. They can describe the source of the product, its contents and principal features, how to use the product, how to care for the product, nutritional information, type and style of the product and size and number of servings. The label can play a promotional function through the use of graphics that attract attention. The label for many products includes a machine-readable bar code, which can be read electronically to identify the product and to produce stock and pricing information.

7.8 *Stages of the product life cycle*

Products, like people, are viewed as having a life cycle. Products are born, they grow, they mature, and finally they die. After a product is launched there will be times when its sales will grow and times when they will be relatively steady, and eventually it is likely that its sales will start to fall, particularly if a new product comes along that better satisfies consumers' needs, for example the decline of vinyl record sales as a result of the development of compact discs. The *product* life cycle refers to the various stages in the life of a product, which have different marketing needs over time. A product goes through four stages in the market: introduction, growth, maturity and decline (see Fig. 7.1).

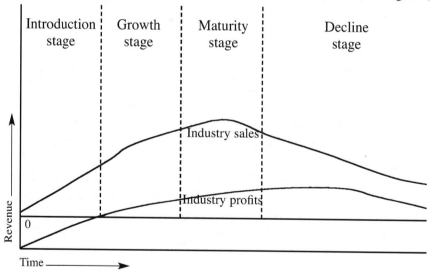

Fig. 7.1: *Stages of the product life cycle*

Introduction stage

This is when the product is first introduced to the market. The product is new, for example Blu-ray discs, so potential customers are likely to be wary of it and resistant to buying something new. High failure rates can result from over-optimism and lack of proper development before launching a product. It is sometimes difficult to encourage distributors to sell new products when they are concerned that the product might not reach the growth stage and that they might invest time and money in a product that would not bring them any long-term income.

At the introduction stage the product's sales grow slowly and the profit will be small or negative because of heavy promotion costs and production in-efficiencies. The introductory stage is a period of attempting to gain market acceptance. The marketing effort is concentrated not only on finding first-time buyers and using promotion to make them aware of the product, but also on creating channels of distribution – attracting retailers and other intermediaries to handle the product. The length of the introductory stage varies dramatically; for example, laptops and portable DVD players gained market acceptance rapidly. During this stage, prices can be either high or low. Therefore, a company has a choice between two strategies: a **skimming strategy**, which means charging a high initial price, and a **penetration strategy**, which means charging a low price in order to discourage competitors from entering the industry. (See Chapter 8 for further details on these strategies.)

Growth stage

The second stage of the product life cycle is characterised by a rapid growth in sales and increasing profits as the product becomes better known. When the product enters its growth stage, profits can be expected to be small. As sales continue to increase during this stage, profits can be expected to increase, partly because sales are increasing but also because the start-up expenses encountered earlier can be expected to diminish. If a new product satisfies customers' needs it will be fuelled by repeat purchases and word-of-mouth publicity, and new customers are attracted to the product. A product that has entered the growth stage has shown that it may have a future in the market. As a result, the number of competitors and the level of marketing activity can be expected to increase. Pioneering firms are often required to alter their products because competitors, having had the advantage of learning from the pioneer's mistakes and the time to study the market, may have improved on the original. Products still in their growth stage include mobile phones, computerised information and interactive shopping services.

Maturity stage

In the maturity stage the product is well known and well established and sales begin to level off. A change in the growth rate – indicated by sales increasing at a reducing rate – heralds the end of the growth period and the beginning of the maturity stage. When the growth rate slows down, the product requires marketing strategies and tactics appropriate for the maturity stage. Later in this stage – for reasons such as diminished popularity, obsolescence or market saturation – the product begins to lose market acceptance.

During this stage, competition is likely to be intense. Products in mature markets have solved most of the technical problems encountered early in the product's life cycle. The products require little technical improvement and changes become largely a matter of style. Portable CD players, for example, are now offered in small and large sizes. They run on mains electricity, batteries or solar power. Companies with products in mature markets whose brands are profitable typically use the funds these brands generate to support other items in the product mix. The detergent industry, for example, is in its mature stage, but the industry leader, Procter & Gamble, uses the sizeable profits generated by Tide to pay for the development and introduction of new product items and lines.

Introduction	Growth	Maturity	Decline
Third-generation mobile phones	Portable DVD players	Personal computers	Typewriters
E-conferencing	E-mail	Faxes	Handwritten letters
All-in-one racing skin suits	Breathable synthetic fabrics	Cotton T-shirts	Shell suits
Irish-based personal identity cards	Smart cards	Credit cards	Chequebooks

Table 7.1: *Products that are currently at different stages of the PLC*

Decline stage

The product is rapidly losing market share and profitability. At this stage the marketer must decide whether it is worthwhile supporting the product for a little longer or whether it should be discontinued. Supporting a product for which there is little natural demand is very unprofitable, but sometimes products can be revived and relaunched, perhaps in a different market. Survivor firms compete in an ever-smaller market, driving profit margins lower still. Eventually the decline stage ends with the withdrawal of the product from the market.

The assumption is that all products exhibit this life cycle, but the timescale will vary from one product to the next. Some products – for example computer games – may go through the entire life cycle in a matter of months.

7.9 *The new product development process*

Companies need a flow of new products in order to keep their product range up to date, their customers interested and their sales growing. Thousands of new products are developed every year in Ireland, but up to 90 per cent will fail to achieve their potential and will not survive. Failure can be expensive, particularly for a small new enterprise, which may go out of business if its only project fails.

Many factors contribute to the failure of new products:
- A target market that is too small.
- Inadequate differentiation from existing products.
- Lack of access to markets because of difficulty in distribution.
- Poor product quality.
- Bad timing – launching the product too soon or too late.
- Poor implementation of the marketing mix.

Before describing how new products are developed, we can examine *what* a new product is. The term '*new product*' is difficult to define, as there are differing degrees of newness. This can affect how a company handles that product. The product may be new from the company's point of view or from the customer's point of view.

Newness from the company's point of view

A product may be:
- New to the market (a genuine innovation, e.g. Google SketchUp 8 Pro for designing 3D structures).
- A significant innovation for the market (e.g. iPods).
- A minor innovation (e.g. Bluetooth for mobile phones).
- No innovation for the market ('copycat' products).

Newness from the customer's point of view

A product may represent:
- Continuous innovation (e.g. fast-moving consumer goods, product updates, improved washing powders).

- Dynamically continuous innovation (e.g. microchips).
- Discontinuous innovation (e.g. mobile phones, e-mail).

Why develop new products?
- To add to the company's product portfolio.
- To replace declining products.
- To take advantage of new technology.
- To maintain or increase market share.
- To keep up with rivals.
- To defeat rivals.
- To maintain competitive advantage.
- To fill a gap in the market.
- To bring in new customers.

Factors in new product success:
- Differentiation from rivals.
- Development of a unique, superior product.
- Top management support.
- Market attractiveness – the product should be aimed at markets with high potential for profit.
- Resources must be in place.
- Well-conceived and properly executed launch.
- Speed of production and timely delivery.
- Quality.
- Market-driven customer focus.

7.10 *Stages in the new product development process*

Developing and introducing new products is frequently expensive and risky. There are several stages that a product has to pass before it is ready for the market (see Fig. 7.2). A company must define the role of new products in accordance with its general corporate objectives. During this stage it scans the marketing environment to identify trends that pose either opportunities or threats. Relevant company strengths and weaknesses are also identified. The outcome of this is not new product ideas, but new markets for which new products will be developed and fresh strategic roles that new products might serve. These roles help to define the direction of new product development and to divide into externally and internally driven factors, which in turn lead to aggressive or defensive strategies.

New product strategies can be either active, leading to an allocation of resources to identifying and seizing opportunities, or reactive, which involves taking a defensive approach, that is to say, developing copycat products.

Fig. 7.2: *Stages in new product development*

Stage 1: Idea generation

Businesses seek product ideas that will help them to achieve their objectives. In doing so they should seek to exploit their special skill or competence. The majority of companies have a structured approach to generating new product ideas, while the source for more radical innovation is undoubtedly the individual inventor. The real difficulty companies have is not in generating ideas, but in generating successfully competitive ideas. New product ideas come from two main sources: internal and external.

Internal sources

- Marketing managers.
- Engineers, designers.
- Research and development departments.
- Sales representatives.
- Brainstorming of employees.
- Formal and informal suggestion schemes.

External sources

- Customers' suggestions and complaints.
- Actual and potential competitors.
- Private research agencies.
- Distributors and suppliers.
- Government agencies.

Stage 2: Screening

This stage involves the preliminary assessment of ideas with a view to determining which ones should be retained. A company may use a checklist of its requirements for the development of any new product. This should include:
- An assessment of market need.
- An estimate of the product life cycle.
- An estimate of competitive strengths, if any.
- An estimate of the costs of launching the product.

The purpose of screening is to identify good ideas and to drop poor ideas as soon as possible. Companies should seek to avoid two types of errors in this stage. ***Drop errors*** occur when the company dismisses an otherwise good idea because of lack of vision regarding its potential. For example, IBM and Eastman Kodak (unlike Xerox) did not foresee the potential of the photo-copier. If the company makes too many drop errors, its standards may be too conservative. ***Go errors*** occur when the company lets a poor idea continue on to development and commercialisation. If a company makes too many go errors, its screening criteria may not be strict enough.

Stage 3: Business analysis

The third stage involves specifying the features of the product and the marketing strategy and making financial projections. The marketing strategy reviews the new product idea in relation to the marketing programme needed to support it. This requires an assessment of the product idea to determine whether it will help or hinder sales of existing products. It is also examined to assess whether it can be sold through existing marketing channels or whether new outlets are needed.

Once the product's important features are defined, the company must then concentrate on the cost of research and development and the cost of production and marketing. Regarding financial projections, the company must forecast the likely income and market share. It should carry out a break-even analysis and should estimate the return on investment to determine the profitability of the proposed product.

Stage 4: Product development

When the idea survives screening and business analysis, it moves into product development. This begins with turning the idea on paper into a sample or prototype. This involves manufacturing the product and performing laboratory and consumer tests to ensure that it meets the standards set. Many prototypes of disposable consumer goods are used and tested by consumers in their own homes; this is referred to as product testing or field testing (for example Pepsi-Cola did this with the 'Pepsi challenge'). The product development stage seeks to determine how well the product will perform in use and its suitability and fitness for a particular purpose.

Stage 5: Test marketing

While development and testing should reduce the risks, the stakes are now raised. As a consequence, even more care and planning are required if the product is to succeed. Many otherwise excellent products have failed because of inadequate test marketing at this stage. Test marketing must be undertaken to find out what consumers say and how they perceive the product so that changes can be incorporated into the product before the launch.

Test marketing involves exposing actual products to potential consumers under realistic purchasing conditions to see if they will buy. Test marketing is a limited introduction of a product in areas chosen to represent the interested or target market. It is a sample launch of the entire marketing mix and its purpose is to determine probable buyer reaction. It allows marketers to:
- Expose a product in its real marketing environment.
- Obtain a measure of sales.
- Correct any weaknesses before commercialisation.
- Vary some of the elements of the marketing mix.

There are risks with test marketing:
- It is expensive.
- It forewarns competitors.
- It can create negative bias if the wrong area is tested.

After the market tests, the company can modify the product if required before increasing production for the full launch.

Stage 6: Commercialisation

The surviving product is now brought to the point of *commercialisation*, which is the full launch of the product. During this stage the company will spend large amounts of money promoting the new product. As the introduction of new products is expensive, it often involves huge risks, which may result in long delays between the development of the idea and the introduction of the product to the market. To limit these risks, companies may decide against an immediate national launch and instead have a phased introduction (a 'rolling launch'). Detailed planning and strict control will also help to minimise losses and to maximise effectiveness.

Stage 7: Monitoring and evaluation

The company must monitor the entire process so far, including the final launch of the product. Sometimes this involves setting performance criteria (volume targets) before the product is even launched. This allows forecast performance to be compared with actual performance. Any differences need to be thoroughly analysed and taken into account in the future. As we have seen, mistakes in managing the new product development process can lead to go errors or to drop errors. At all stages in the process, therefore, the company must balance the risks involved by monitoring and evaluating the entire process.

Important terms and concepts

product: p. 141
physical benefits: p. 141
service benefits: p. 141
psychological benefits: p. 141
product classification: p. 142
durable goods: p. 142
non-durable goods: p. 142

services: p. 142
intangibility: p. 142
inseparability: p. 142
inconsistency: p. 143
inventory: p. 143
product line: p. 143
product mix: p. 143

Case study: Extending the product life cycle: Kellogg's

The Kellogg Company is the world's leading producer of breakfast cereals and convenience foods such as cereal bars. Its product lines include ready-to-eat cereals (excluding cereals that requiring cooking, such as porridge) and nutritious snacks, such as cereal bars. Kellogg brands are household names around the world and include Rice Krispies, Special K and Nutri-Grain, while some of its brand characters, like Snap, Crackle and Pop, are among the most well known in the world. It has achieved this position not only through strong brands and strong brand value, but also through a strong commitment to corporate responsibility. This means that all of the Kellogg's business aims are set within a particular context or set of ideals. Central to this is the Kellogg's commitment to its business, its brands and its food, and all associated with the promotion of healthy living.

Each brand, e.g. Kellogg's Corn Flakes, has to endeavour to hold its market share in a competitive market. Brand managers monitor the success of brands in terms of market share, growth and performance against the competition. Key decisions have to be made about the future of any brand that is not succeeding. For example, Kellogg's recognised that they had a problem with the Nutri-Grain brand and used business tools to relaunch the brand and return it to market growth.

Each product has its own life cycle of birth, development, growth and even eventually death. Some products, like Kellogg's Corn Flakes, have retained their market position across a century. Others may have their success undermined by decreasing market share or by competitors. The product life cycle shows how sales of a product change over time. Nutri-Grain was originally designed to meet the needs of busy people who had missed breakfast. It aimed to provide a healthy cereal breakfast in a portable and convenient format.

1. **Launch:** Many products do well when they are first brought out and Nutri-Grain was no exception. From its launch in 1997 it was immediately successful, gaining an almost 50 per cent share of the growing cereal bar market in just two years.

2. **Growth:** Nutri-Grain's sales steadily increased as the product was promoted and became well known. It maintained growth in sales until 2002 by expanding the original product with new developments in flavour and format. This was relatively inexpensive, as these changes did not require investment in new equipment for production. The market position of Nutri-Grain also subtly changed from a 'missed breakfast' product to an 'all-day' healthy snack.

3. **Maturity:** Successful products attract other competitor businesses for similar markets. This indicates the third, or maturity, stage of the life cycle. This is usually the time of maximum profitability, when profits can be used to continue to build the brand. However, competitor brands from within Kellogg's itself (e.g. All Bran bars) and from other manufacturers (e.g. Alpen bars) offered the same benefits and this reduced Nutri-Grain's market position. Kellogg's continued to support the development of the brand, but some products (such as Minis and Twists) struggled in a crowded market. Although Elevenses continued to succeed, this was not enough to offset the overall sales decline. Not all products follow these stages precisely and time periods for each stage will vary widely. For example, growth may take place over a few months or, as in the case of Nutri-Grain, over several years.

4. **Saturation:** This is the fourth stage of the life cycle and the point when the market is deemed to be full, that is, when the market's maximum numbers of customers have the product and when there are other, possibly better or cheaper, competitor products. This is called market saturation and this can lead to a decline in sales. By mid-2004, Nutri-Grain found its sales declining while the overall market continued to grow at a rate of 15 per cent.

5. **Decline:** Clearly, at this point Kellogg's had to make a key business decision. Sales were falling, the product was in decline and losing its position. Should Kellogg's let the product die, i.e. withdraw it from the market, or should it try to extend its life?

When a company recognises that a product has gone into decline or is not performing as well as it should, a strategic decision needs to be made and within the context of the overall aims of the business. Kellogg's had a strong position in the market for both healthy foods and convenience foods. Nutri-Grain fits in well with its main aims and objectives and therefore was deemed to be a product and a brand worth rescuing. Kellogg's aims included the development of great brands, great brand value and the promotion of healthy living. Kellogg's decided to try to extend the life of the product rather than to withdraw it from the market. This meant developing an extension strategy for the product. Ansoff's matrix is a tool that helps analyse which strategy is appropriate. It shows both market-orientated and product-orientated possibilities.

Extending the Nutri-Grain cycle – identifying the problem

Kellogg's had to decide if the problem with Nutri-Grain was the market, the product or both. The market had grown by over 15 per cent and the competitors' market share had increased while Nutri-Grain sales in 2003 had declined. The market in terms of customer tastes had also changed, as more people missed breakfast and therefore needed such a snack product. The choice of extension strategy indicated by the matrix was either product development or diversification. Diversification carries much higher costs and risks. Kellogg's decided that it needed to focus on changing the product to meet the changing market needs.

Research showed there were several issues to address:

- The brand message was not strong enough in the face of competition. Consumers were not sufficiently impressed by the product to choose it over competitors.

- Some of the other Kellogg's products, e.g. Minis, had taken the focus away from the core business.
- Core products like Nutri-Grain Soft Bake and Elevenses between them represented over 80 per cent of sales but received a small proportion of advertising and promotion budgets.
- Those successful sales were being driven by promotional pricing, i.e. discounted pricing, rather than the underlying strength of the brand.

Implementing the extension strategy for Nutri-Grain

Having identified the problems, Kellogg's developed strategies to rebrand and relaunch the product in 2005.

1. Fundamental to the relaunch was the renewal of the brand image. Kellogg's looked at the core features that made the brand different and modelled the new brand image on these. Nutri-Grain is unique, as it is the only product of this kind that is baked. This provided two benefits: (*a*) the healthy grains were soft rather than gritty and (*b*) the eating experience is closer to the more indulgent foods that people could be eating, such as cakes and biscuits. The unique selling point (USP), therefore, needed to be on the 'soft bake' element.
2. Researchers also found that a key part of the market was a group termed 'realistic snackers'. These are people who want to snack on healthy foods but still crave a great-tasting snack. The relaunched Nutri-Grain product needed to help this key group to fulfil both of these desires.
3. Kellogg's decided to refocus investment on the core products of soft bake bars and Elevenses, as these had maintained their position. Three existing soft bake bar products were improved, three new ranges introduced and poorly performing ranges (such as Minis) were withdrawn.
4. New packaging was introduced to unify the brand image.
5. An improved pricing structure for stores and supermarkets was developed.

The marketing mix

Using this information, the relaunch focused on the four parts of the marketing mix.

- **Product:** Improvements to the recipe and a wider range of flavours, repositioning the brand as 'healthy and tasty', not a substitute for a missed breakfast.
- **Promotion:** A new and clearer brand image to cover all the products in the range along with advertising and point-of-sale promotional materials.

- **Place (distribution):** Better offers and materials to stores that sold the product.
- **Price:** New price levels were agreed that did not rely on promotional pricing. This improved revenue for both Kellogg's and the retail stores.

As a result, soft bake bar year-on-year sales went from a decline to substantial growth, with Elevenses sales increasing by almost 50 per cent.

The Nutri-Grain brand achieved a retail sales growth rate of almost three times that of the market and, most importantly, growth was maintained after the initial relaunch. Kellogg's was able to see that while Nutri-Grain fits its strategic profile – as a healthy, convenient cereal product – it was underperforming in the market. This information was used, along with the aims and objectives of the business, to develop a strategy for restoring its success. Nutri-Grain now remains a growing brand and product within the Kellogg's product family.

Source: Adapted from www.thetimes100.co.uk/case-study--new-products-from-market-research--6-388-1.php [accessed 19 March 2011].

Case study: Hi-Tec Sports: Using viral marketing to position a brand

A business needs to be distinctive in order to gain market share and to attract new customers. It needs customers to think about its products in a particular way. This helps customers to distinguish its products from those of its competitors. A single brand image and message should combine the positive characteristics and attributes of its products, thus giving the brand a unique place in the minds of consumers. This is called 'positioning a brand'.

In the past, Hi-Tec shoes were associated only with sport. Today, its shoes are promoted as an outdoor brand associated with a leisure lifestyle. More than 500 styles are now available throughout the world. Hi-Tec develops attractive and comfortable shoes that are lightweight and of high quality, yet are sold in the mid-price market segment. Founded in 1974, Hi-Tec Sports is a privately owned British company. Its products are sold in over 100 countries worldwide. It is the global number two outdoor brand in terms of sales value.

While Hi-Tec shoes always had a high-technology focus, the brand's unique selling proposition (USP) now includes emphasis on the company's four core values:

- Pride: Hi-Tec delivering more than the competition.
- Honesty: Products delivering on their promises.

- Fun: Working creatively to provide positive solutions.
- Hunger: A desire to improve products.

To deliver these values to the consumer, Hi-Tec offers high-quality shoes at a price that represents good value for money. The same technologies that are used to produce sports shoes are used to create lightweight and comfortable outdoor footwear. Over the recent years, Hi-Tec has undertaken a market research programme to know how best to encourage consumers to engage emotionally with Hi-Tec products. As it wanted its brand to be recognised both for sports and for an outdoor lifestyle, the brand theme selected for the new market position was that Hi-Tec products are 'inspired by life'. In targeting holidaymakers with high-technology cushioned sandals, for example, the emphasis is on having 'happy holiday feet'. Trail shoes for runners promote the ethos that 'feet feel free', with runners being encouraged to think 'where next?'

The marketing mix

Hi-Tec's key marketing objective is to reposition its brand to open up new markets, and this in turn should increase market share and revenues. At the heart of the marketing process is the marketing mix. Key factors in the marketing mix for Hi-Tec shoes include:

- Product: Innovative footwear that provides high performance.
- Price: Sold at value-for-money prices.
- Place: Sold online or through premium retailers.
- Promotion: A mix of targeted promotional channels and methods to achieve market penetration and increased sales.

Above-the-line promotion

Above-the-line promotion is based on advertising in mass media, such as newspapers, television, radio, cinema and the World Wide Web. This type of promotion reaches a wide audience, but it can be difficult to measure and assess its impact. Above-the-line promotion can be used to inform the audience and raise awareness of a product or service as well as to persuade people to buy.

Hi-Tec's advertising emphasises the USP for its brand and its core values. The imagery chosen to represent the brand values focuses on people in action – running, hiking, walking – in order to capture the fun element. Hi-Tec's above-the-line activities include:

- Television advertisements for raising awareness with the wider public, for example in key TV advertising slots during peak programmes, such as sports, in order to attract relevant viewers.

- Press advertisements in trade or consumer publications. Hi-Tec deals both with retailers and directly with consumers through its online shop.
- Banner advertising on selected websites. This form of paid-for advertising allows the business to measure responses through 'click-through' rates.
- Billboards at locations relevant to the chosen audience, for example a sports track.

Below-the-line promotion

Below-the line promotion aims to reach consumers more directly through forms of communication other than traditional advertising channels. It uses character branding to promote its products. This means that it appoints ambassadors, such as Alexandre Poussin, the world explorer, and Martin Dreyer, from the world of extreme sports, to endorse its products. Hi-Tec also uses sponsorship to promote its brand. For example, it sponsors Amr Shabana, one of the world's leading squash players.

The company also uses other below-the-line activities:

- Direct mail: Hi-Tec e-mails customers, linking the message to the e-commerce part of Hi-Tec's website. This means people can go directly to the Hi-Tec online shop to buy goods.
- Exhibitions: Hi-Tec promotes at trade and consumer shows. These allow Hi-Tec to give retailers and consumers the opportunity to see the products first hand.
- Sales promotions: Hi-Tec offers both retailers and consumers a range of sales incentives, including discounts, to encourage them to stock or to buy its products.
- Branding: Hi-Tec supplies retailers with point-of-sale materials, such as packaging and store displays, and provides training for retail staff within stores.
- Promotional materials: Hi-Tec's extranet website shares material such as brand photography and press releases so retailers can use this material in their own promotions. This raises the profile of the Hi-Tec brand and ensures that it is represented consistently.
- Hi-Tec also uses public relations (PR) to create a positive public perception of its products. This includes issuing press releases, blogs and the use of social networking sites like Facebook.

Liquid Mountaineering: A viral marketing campaign

A more recent innovation to take advertising to a different level is through viral marketing. A key part of Hi-Tec's brand positioning has been the development of a viral marketing campaign called Liquid Mountaineering. This is a self-generating activity in which people pass on information to other consumers through the Internet. This practice can spread a marketing campaign more widely and more quickly than through traditional advertising. This allows consumers to become advocates. This campaign was inspired by the water-repellent qualities of Hi-Tec shoes. It was devised to reflect Hi-Tec's 'inspired by life' brand proposition and the brand repositioning strategy. It aims to create a sense of adventure and to push back physical boundaries. At the centre of the campaign is a video commissioned by Hi-Tec, which went live on YouTube in May 2010. This video 'documentary' shows three men apparently running on water, as though they achieved this miraculous feat because of their water-repellent shoes.

The Liquid Mountaineering campaign does not follow the usual forms of advertising and promotion. Hi-Tec wanted to emphasise the spirit of 'fun' in its brand. The video is therefore also meant to entertain:

- Although the video is based around Hi-Tec's 'hydrophobic' footwear, it does not mention the brand directly.
- The documentary style and semi-scientific approach to 'running on water' aims to get consumers talking and thinking about the brand differently.
- To add realism, one of the video participants set up a blog the previous year. This 'back story' created excitement in the build-up to the event.

In launching the campaign, Hi-Tec recognised the massive power of the Internet. It chose to host the video on YouTube, the popular video-sharing website, which had a good fit with both the attitude of the video (youthful and fun) and the target audience (prospective consumers). The fact that there was no mention of the Hi-Tec brand meant it was not perceived as a sales message. It caught the imagination of millions of people in an incredibly short space of time as viewers e-mailed or tweeted their friends about the video. There have been press articles and interviews on TV shows. Some people wrote blogs about the video. Others even set up groups to try the 'running on water' sport for themselves. The exchange of messages on sites like Facebook and Twitter gave extra impetus to the swell of viewing numbers. Having gathered impressive viewing figures in just two weeks, Hi-Tec was able to extend interest in the promotion with a new set of promotional activities:

- It put out a press release in which it explained the hoax and claimed ownership of the video.
- Hi-Tec also hosted a video on its website showing how the Liquid Mountaineering video was made.
- The symbol Hi-Tec uses for its 'ion-mask' technology shows a man running on water, linking the video messages with the real technology.

- The Hi-Tec website links directly to an online shop for the shoes.

Up to November 2010, the video had attracted more than 7.5 million viewers. This opened up the Hi-Tec brand to a worldwide market. Hi-Tec also received positive feedback on the campaign from trade organisations. This marketing boosted awareness and reinforced the fun element of the Hi-Tec brand. As a marketing process, the video was very cost effective and Hi-Tec has received a large return on the video investment. The company estimates that the Liquid Mountaineering viral marketing campaign had a return worth 10 times the initial investment. The average return on marketing investment is usually only around four times the investment.

The Liquid Mountaineering video demonstrates the power of viral marketing. It built a huge following. It got people talking, while wondering if the video was a fake or not. It opened the brand to a new global audience. This campaign helped Hi-Tec to change consumer perceptions of its brand across different continents and provided Hi-Tec with the potential to build on the campaign through other, more traditional promotional activities.

Source: Adapted from www.thetimes100.co.uk/case-study—using-promotion-to-position-a-brand—161-415-6.php#ixzz1H3pCWJRM [accessed 19 March 2011].

Questions for review

1. Describe the stages of new product development.
2. Explain the concept of product life cycle.
3. What is meant by a new product?
4. Outline the functions of packaging.
5. Explain the methods companies use to classify products.
6. Discuss and give examples of (*a*) family branding, (*b*) individual brands, (*c*) own-label brands and (*d*) generic brands.
7. Describe the key characteristics of services.
8. Explain the term 'test marketing'.
9. How do companies generate ideas for new products?
10. What characteristics should brand names have?

8
PRICE

Chapter objectives

After reading this chapter you should be able to:
- Understand the meaning of price.
- Examine various pricing objectives.
- Understand pricing strategies.
- Identify factors influencing pricing decisions.
- Discuss various pricing approaches.
- Understand pricing in industrial markets.

8.1 *What is price?*

To a buyer, *price* is the value placed on what is exchanged. Page (1995) defined price as 'that which people have to forgo in order to acquire a product or service'. Simply defined, price is the amount of money charged for a product or service. The price a company charges will be somewhere below a level that would be too high to attract worthwhile customer demand but above a level that would be too low to produce profit. Customer perceptions of the product's value will set the ceiling for prices. If customers perceive that the price is greater than the product's value, they will not buy the product. Production costs set the minimum level for prices. If a company prices the product below its costs, company profits will suffer. In setting its price between these two extremes, the company must consider a number of other internal and external factors, including its overall marketing strategy and mix, the nature of the market and demand and competitors' strategies and prices.

Price is stated in different terms for different exchanges; for example, a solicitor charges a *fee*, an insurance company charges a *premium*, a landlord charges *rent*, banks charge *interest*. The list of elements that can make up the true price of a purchase include:
- The stated monetary price.
- Taxes (for example, value-added tax).
- The time required for searching, shopping and delivery.

- The delivery cost.
- The installation cost.
- Depreciation.

Price is an important element of the marketing mix because it relates directly to the generation of total income. A product's price is a major determinant of the market demand for a product. It affects a company's competitive position and its market share. As a result, price has a considerable bearing on a company's income and net profit. It is the only element of the marketing mix that produces income; the other three elements (product, place and promotion) represent costs. It is only through price that money comes into a company.

Thus, getting the price right is a decision of fundamental importance. Much recent marketing thought has emphasised the connection between price and quality in order to defend the idea of profitable business. 'Adding value' allows a manufacturer to widen the margin of available profit by offering the consumer more benefits. Peters (1988) claims that customers, both consumer and industrial, are prepared consistently to pay more for good quality – especially if they are convinced that what they are buying is the best available. The justification for a higher price can come from any or all of the marketing mix variables:

- **Product:** Offering extra features, individual specification or innovatory design.
- **Promotion:** Increasing the prestige and reputation of the goods or services in question through regular advertising and promotion.
- **Price:** Providing credit terms that spread payment but justify a higher eventual price.
- **Place:** Guaranteeing a specific delivery date or operating hours of business that give the customer greater convenience.

The buyer's perspective

From the buyer's perspective, price represents the value they attach to whatever is being exchanged. Up to the point of purchase, the marketer will have made promises to the potential buyer about what the product is and what it can do for that customer. The customer will weigh up those promises against the price and decide if it is worth paying.

A number of factors will influence the customer when assessing price. These include:

- **Functional benefits:** Functional benefits relate to the design of the product and its ability to fulfil its desired function.

- **Quality:** A customer may expect price to reflect the quality level of the product. A customer may be prepared to pay more for a higher-quality product.
- **Operational benefits:** Operational benefits relate to ease of use of the product and the time saved as a result of using the product.
- **Personal benefits:** Personal benefits include status, comfort, self-image and psychological benefits. Personal benefits are a difficult category for marketers to gauge as they attempt to measure price against intangible factors.

The seller's perspective

Price is important for the seller, as it provides the basis for creating a profit after recovering costs from the other elements of the marketing mix.

profit = total revenue – total cost

Where total revenue is the quantity sold multiplied by the unit price, the total cost represents the costs of producing, marketing and selling the product. The quantity sold is itself dependent on price as well as on the other marketing mix elements.

The seller must ensure they think about price from the perspective of the customer. It cannot be assumed that reducing a price will lead to higher sales because more people could then afford and want the product. A low price, however, may be interpreted as making a negative statement about the product's quality, and a sudden reduction in price of an established product may be taken to mean the product's quality has been compromised in some way.

The seller must always be aware that price can never stand apart from the other elements of the marketing mix. Price interacts with those elements and must therefore give out signals consistent with those given by the product itself, place and promotion.

Price/quality relationship

Perceived product value has been described as a trade-off between the product's perceived benefits (or quality) and the perceived sacrifice – both monetary and non-monetary – necessary to acquire it. Consumers generally rely on price as an indicator of product quality. Consumers attribute different qualities to identical products that carry different price tags. Consumer characteristics such as age and income affect the perception of value. Because price is so often considered an indicator of quality, some product advertisements deliberately emphasise a high price to underscore the marketers' claims of quality. Marketers realise that, at times, products with lower prices may be interpreted as reduced quality. At the same time, when consumers evaluate more concrete attributes of a product, such as performance and durability, they rely less on the price and brand name as indicators of quality than when they evaluate the product's prestige and symbolic value. For these reasons, marketers must understand all the attributes that consumers use to evaluate a given product and include all applicable information in order to counter any perceptions of negative quality associated with a lower price.

In most situations, in addition to price, consumers also use such cues as the brand and the store in which the product is bought to evaluate its quality. In brief, consumers use price as an indicator of quality if they have little information to go on or if they have little confidence in their own ability to make the product or service choice on other grounds. When the consumer is familiar with a brand name or has experience with a product or service or the store where it is purchased, price declines as a determining factor in product evaluation and purchase.

8.2 *Pricing objectives*

Every marketing task, including pricing, should be directed towards a goal. *Pricing objectives* are general goals that describe what a firm wants to achieve through its pricing efforts. Pricing objectives must be co-ordinated with the firm's other marketing objectives. These must in turn flow from the company's overall objectives. Organisational objectives could be 'pile it high and sell it cheap', as suggested by the founder of Tesco, Sir John Cohen. More recently, however, Tesco has changed its philosophy to compete more effectively with its main competitors for the top slot in the supermarket league.

Some typical pricing objectives that companies set for themselves are:

- Profit oriented:
    - To achieve a desired return.
    - To maximise profit.
- Sales oriented:
    - To increase sales volume.
    - To maintain or increase market share.
- Status quo oriented:
    - To stabilise prices.
    - To meet competition.

Profit-oriented goals

A company may price its products to gain a certain percentage return on its sales or on its investment. This pricing policy is aimed at achieving a *target return*. Many retailers and wholesalers use a target return on net sales as a pricing objective for short periods. Target-return pricing is usually used by industry leaders because they can set their pricing goals more independently of competition than smaller companies can.

The second profit-oriented pricing objective aims at *profit maximisation*. A profit maximisation goal is likely to be far more beneficial to a company and to the public if it is practised over a long period. To do this, however, companies sometimes have to accept short-term losses. The goal should be to maximise profits on total output rather than on each product. For example, a company might maximise total profit by setting low, relatively unprofitable prices on some products in order to stimulate sales of others, as for example with various sales promotions in supermarkets.

Sales-oriented goals

In some companies the management's pricing attention is concentrated on sales volume. The management may decide to increase *sales volume* by discounting or by some other aggressive pricing strategy, perhaps even incurring a loss in the short run.

In some companies the main pricing objective is to maintain or increase *market share*.

Status-quo-oriented goals

Price stabilisation is often the goal of companies operating in industries where the product is highly standardised, such as steel, copper and bulk chemicals. Status quo objectives can have several aspects, such as maintaining a certain market share, meeting competitors' prices or maintaining a favourable public image. One reason for seeking price stability is to avoid price wars.

8.3 Pricing strategies

Premium pricing

A premium strategy uses a high price but gives good product/service in exchange. It is fair to customers and, more importantly, customers see it as fair.

Premium-priced products could include food bought from Marks & Spencer, designer clothes or a Mercedes-Benz car.

Penetration pricing

Penetration pricing is the name given to a strategy that deliberately starts offering 'super value'. This is done to gain a foothold in the market, using price as a major weapon. It could be because other products are already well established in the market, maybe at high prices. Alternatively, penetration pricing could be used as an attempt to gain a major share of a new market. It can also deter competitors who see no profit in the market. As time goes on and the product is established, prices can be raised near market levels.

Several conditions favour setting a low price. First, the market must be highly price sensitive, so that a low price produces more market growth. Second, production and distribution costs must fall as sales volume increases. Third, the low price must help to keep out the competition and the company must maintain its low-price position – otherwise the price advantage may be only temporary.

Economy pricing

Economy pricing is a deliberate strategy of low pricing. Companies could decide to offer a 'no frills' product/service, with a price reflecting this. Before a product is launched, however, it is important to decide the position it will have in the marketplace. A product that competes purely on price is vulnerable to attack from more established products.

Price skimming

Many companies that invent new products initially set high prices to avail of maximum revenues from the market, a strategy called *market-skimming pricing*. A policy of price skimming is often used for products at the introductory stage. Initially the price is pitched high, which gives a good early cash flow to offset high development costs. If the product is new and competition has not appeared, then customers might well pay a premium to acquire a product which is offering excellent features. The launch of many home computers showed this pattern. As competitors entered the market and new features were added by the new entrants, prices dropped for all products.

A number of conditions must exist in order for market skimming to be successful. First, the product's quality and image must support its higher price.

Second, buyers must not be price sensitive and a sufficient number of them must want the product at that price. Third, the costs of producing a smaller volume cannot be so high that they cancel the advantage of charging more. Finally, competitors should not be able to enter the market easily and undercut the high price.

Psychological pricing

Psychological pricing is designed to get customers to respond on an emotional rather than rational basis. It is most frequently seen in consumer markets, having less applicability in industrial markets. The most common is the use of prices such as 99 cent or €9.95. Psychological pricing relies on the buyer's perceptions of value rather than on the seller's costs.

When using psychological pricing, the seller considers the psychology of prices and not simply the economics of pricing. For example, consumers usually perceive higher-priced products as having higher quality. When they can judge the quality of a product by examining it or by recalling past experiences with it, price is less important than quality. When they cannot judge quality, however, because they lack information or skill, then price becomes an important quality signal.

Product line pricing

Companies usually develop many product lines rather than single products. In *product line pricing*, companies must decide on the price to set between the various products in a line. Product line pricing means establishing and adjusting the prices of multiple products within a product line. When marketers use product line pricing, their goal is to maximise profits for an entire product line rather than focusing on the profitability of an individual product. For example, marketers can set prices so that one product is quite profitable while another increases market share because of having a lower price than competing products. A supplier may decide to design a product suitable for all price levels, offering opportunities for a range of purchases.

Pricing variations

Off-peak pricing and other special prices such as early booking discounts, stand-by prices and group discounts are used in particular circumstances. These are used in the travel trade. Stand-by prices represent a different product, as there is no guarantee of travel.

8.4 *Factors influencing pricing decisions*

Price-setting can be complex, as no product is entirely without competition. There is almost always another way in which customers' needs are being satisfied, and as different customers have different needs, they will have differing views on what constitutes value for money. This is why markets need to be segmented carefully to ensure that the right price is being charged in each segment.

According to Dibb et al. (2006), most factors that affect pricing decisions can be grouped into one of the following eight categories.

Corporate and marketing objectives

Before setting a price, the company must decide on its target market and positioning strategy for the product. Marketers should set prices that are consistent with the company's goals and mission. Pricing decisions must be co-ordinated with product design, distribution and promotion decisions to form a consistent and effective integrated marketing programme. Decisions made for other marketing mix variables may affect pricing decisions.

If the company has selected its target market and positioning carefully, then its marketing mix strategy, including price, will be relatively straightforward.

Pricing objectives

The pricing objectives are derived from the company's general objectives, for example whether the company seeks to maximise market share or to maximise profits.

Costs

The company will want to charge a price that covers all its costs for producing, distributing and selling the product. A company's costs can take two forms: fixed and variable. *Fixed costs* (also known as overheads) are costs that do not vary with production or sales level. For example, a company must pay each month's bills for rent, heat, salaries, etc.

Variable costs vary directly with the level of production. Each product involves the cost of raw materials, packaging and other inputs. These costs tend to be the same for each unit produced, with their total varying with the number of units produced.

Total costs are the sum of the fixed and variable costs for any given level of production. A company will want to charge a price that will at least cover the total production costs at a given level of production. A company needs to watch its costs carefully. If production and selling costs are greater for a company than for its competitors, that company will have to charge a higher price or else make less profit, thereby putting it at a competitive disadvantage.

Other marketing mix variables

The marketer must consider the total marketing mix when setting prices. Pricing decisions can influence decisions and activities associated with product, distribution and promotion. For example, consumers may associate a high price with better product quality and poorer product quality with a low price. Higher-priced products, such as perfume and designer clothes, are often sold in shops such as Brown Thomas through selective or exclusive distribution. Lower-priced products may be sold in discount shops through intensive distribution. (Distribution is discussed in more detail in Chapter 9.)

Expectations of channel members

Price is also affected by the distribution channels used by a company. Channel members' costs, such as those of wholesalers and retailers, must also be met.

Buyer perceptions

Members of one market segment may be more sensitive to price than members of a different target market. Marketers must try to ascertain a consumer's reasons for buying the product and must set the price according to consumers' perceptions of the product's value. Buyers' perceptions of a product, relative to competing products, may allow a company to set a price that differs significantly from the price of competing products. If the product is considered superior to most of the competition, a company may charge a higher price for its product.

Competition

A marketer will need to know the prices competitors charge at present and will also have to take into account the possible entry of new competitors. Prices may be set higher than those of competitors in order to give an impression of exclusivity or higher quality. This is common practice in beauty salons and restaurants.

Legal and regulatory issues

Governments, through legislation to protect consumers, may influence pricing decisions. For example, price controls may be introduced to curb inflation.

8.5 *Managing price changes*

Prices are rarely static for long periods. Competitive pressures may force prices down, either temporarily or permanently, or new market opportunities might increase the price premium on a product. Changing prices, however, can have a serious effect on profit margins and on market stability. Normally, it is likely that a price cut will increase the volume of sales, and it is sometimes a very fine calculation to predict whether the profit margin earned on the extra volume gained more than compensates for the lost margin caused by the price cut. At various times, a company may be faced with the prospect of initiating price changes or of responding to competitors' price changes.

Initiating price cuts can be a dangerous activity. Nevertheless, companies still cut prices from time to time. They may do so for short-term tactical reasons, such as clearing excess stock, or as part of a more fundamental strategic 'value for money' repositioning. Much depends on whether the company sees itself as a price leader or follower in the market. A market leader may wish to make the first move, leaving competitors with the problem of whether to respond and how.

On the other hand, when a company is faced with a competitor's price rise, it has to decide whether and how to respond. There are three possible responses:

- Respond in kind by matching the competitor's move.
- Maintain price levels, but differentiate the product by emphasising how much better value it now represents.
- Or refuse to respond at all.

Many companies prefer to follow others in implementing price rises rather than take the leadership risks. Smaller companies may use the leader's price as a reference point, follow the price and continue to compete on non-price factors such as location, service and adaptability. Promoting further differentiation may be the best option for defending a niche.

Not responding at all is perhaps the highest-risk option if it is perceived as an aggressive response designed to gain market share. Smaller companies may have more flexibility in their response, as their actions are likely to have only a marginal impact. The specific response selected will primarily depend on how much the other organisations in the market want market stability and to shelter under the price umbrella created by the price leader.

Customer reactions to price changes

Customers do not always interpret price changes in a straightforward way. They may view a price cut in several ways. For example, if a company suddenly cuts its prices, a customer may think that the product is to be replaced by a newer model or that the product has some fault and might not be selling well. A customer may also believe that quality has been reduced or may think that the price will come down even further; therefore, he or she might not purchase the product but will wait and see if further reductions follow.

Similarly, if a company increases its price, a customer may believe there is big demand for the product and that it may become unobtainable unless purchased immediately. On the other hand, a customer may perceive that the company is being greedy and is attempting to exploit customers in order to make more profit.

8.6 *General pricing approaches*

Marketers need to decide what price will be regarded by customers as good value for money, while still allowing the company to make a profit. The main methods of pricing used by companies are cost based, customer based and competition based.

Item	Cost per unit
	€
Labour costs	3.50
Raw materials	5.30
Overheads	4.20
Promotion	2.50
Distribution	1.40
Total production cost per unit	16.90
Add profit of 20%	*3.38*
Net price	**20.28**

Table 8.1: *An example of cost-plus pricing*

Cost-based pricing

Two cost-based pricing methods are cost-plus pricing and mark-up pricing. *Cost-plus pricing* involves calculating all the costs of making a product (including production, promotion, distribution and overheads) and adding an amount to provide an acceptable level of profit.

This method, however, does not take account of how customers will react to the quoted prices. If they perceive that the price does not represent value for money, they will not buy the product. Alternatively, if they perceive that the price is exceptionally good value for money, the company may not have enough stock to meet the demand and competitors will be able to enter the market easily.

Mark-up pricing

Mark-up pricing is similar to cost-plus pricing and is the method used by most retailers. A retailer will buy in stock and add on a fixed percentage to the bought-in price (a mark-up) in order to arrive at the shelf price. Usually there is a standard mark-up for each product category. In some cases the mark-up will be 100 per cent or more, while in other cases it will be close to nil if the retailer believes that stocking the product will stimulate other sales.

According to Kotler and Armstrong (2008), some common mark-ups in supermarkets are 9 per cent on baby foods, 14 per cent on tobacco products, 20 per cent on bakery products, 27 per cent on dried foods and vegetables, 37 per cent on spices and extracts and 50 per cent on greeting cards.

	€
Bought-in price	2.00
Mark-up at 25%	.50
Shelf price	2.50

Table 8.2: *An example of mark-up pricing*

Mark-up pricing is a popular approach because sellers are more certain about costs than about demand. As the price is tied to cost, sellers do not have to make frequent adjustments to price as demand changes.

When all firms in the industry use this pricing method, prices tend to be similar and price competition is reduced. A disadvantage, however, is that any pricing method that ignores environmental demand and competition is not likely to lead to the best pricing structure.

Customer-based pricing

Two customer-based pricing methods are demand-based pricing and psychological pricing. Marketers sometimes use demand-based pricing rather than establishing the price of a product on its costs. *Demand-based pricing* is determined by the level of demand for the product, resulting in a high price when demand is strong and a low price when demand is weak. Demand-based pricing usually begins with the marketer assessing what the demand will be for the product at varying prices. This is usually done by asking customers what they might expect to pay for the product and seeing how many choose each price level. Table 8.3 shows the development of demand-based pricing.

Price per unit	Number of customers who said they would buy at this price
€10–11	20,000
€11–12	15,000
€12–13	10,000
€13–14	5,000

Table 8.3: *Assessment of customer reaction for demand pricing*

As the price rises, fewer customers are prepared to buy the product, as fewer will then see the product as good value for money.

The next stage in demand pricing is calculating the costs of producing the commodity, as the cost of producing each item usually falls as more are made. To use this method, a marketer must be able to estimate the quantity of a product that customers will demand at different prices. The marketer then chooses the price that generates the highest total income. The effectiveness of this method depends on the marketer's ability to estimate demand accurately.

Psychological pricing involves both prestige pricing and odd-even pricing. Higher prices are often used as an indicator of quality, so some companies will use *prestige pricing*. This method is used especially when buyers associate a higher price with higher quality. Prestige pricing is used for luxury items, such as perfumes, jewellery and clothes. Service industries, such as restaurants and hotels, often use psychological pricing because of the value added by atmosphere and service. Companies use the non-price marketing mix variables to build up perceived value in customers' minds. Price is set to match the perceived value. For example, customers expect to pay more for a cup of coffee at a five-star hotel than at a McDonald's restaurant.

Odd-even pricing is a method of psychological pricing suggesting that buyers are influenced by prices ending in different digits. Odd pricing assumes that more of a product will be sold at €9.99 than €10. Odd pricing refers to a price ending in 1, 3, 5, 7, 9, just under a round number (e.g. €0.79, €2.97, €34.95). Even pricing refers to a price ending in a whole number or in tenths (e.g. €0.50, €6.10, €55.00).

Competition-based pricing

Competition-based pricing recognises the influence of competition in the market. The marketer must decide how close the competition is in providing for customers' needs. If the products are similar, prices will need to be similar to those of the competition. This method is important if a company is serving markets in which price is the main variable of the marketing strategy.

Companies with large market share often have enough control within their industries to become price leaders. Smaller firms tend to follow the price fluctuations of the leading brands rather than basing price on demand for their own product changes or when cost changes.

8.7 The influence of the product life cycle on pricing decisions

As we saw in Chapter 7, a product passes through various stages during its life cycle. When a new product reaches the market, a company has to choose between various strategies in determining a price for its product.

Pricing during the introduction phase

Dean (1950) first identified three objectives that all companies share when pricing a new product:
- To establish the product in the market.
- To maintain market share in the face of competition from later entrants.
- To produce profits.

During this phase a company may choose pioneer pricing, market-penetration pricing or market-skimming pricing. *Pioneer pricing* involves setting a base price for a new product. This can be set high to recover research and development costs quickly or to provide a reference point for developing discount prices for different market segments. Marketers need to consider how quickly competitors will enter the market when setting base prices. If competitors can enter the market easily and quickly, the first company may adopt a base price that will discourage competitors.

Market-penetration pricing is used when a company sets a low price for a new product in order to attract a large number of buyers and a large market share. This strategy can also be used to undercut higher-priced products that are already established in the market. As time passes and the product becomes established, prices can be raised nearer market levels. Alternatively, supplier costs could fall as volume increases. In this case the consumer benefits from a continuation of the low prices. Market-penetration pricing, however, must be used carefully, as it is very difficult to restore prices to market levels.

Market-skimming pricing is the practice of starting out with a high price for a new product, then reducing the price as sales level off. A policy of price skimming is often used for products at the introductory stage of the product life cycle. If the product is new and competition has not appeared, customers might be willing to pay a higher price to acquire a product that is offering excellent features. The launch of many home computers and video recorders showed this pattern, as competitors came into the market and new features were added by new entrants, resulting in falling prices for these products.

If companies choose to use market-skimming pricing, product quality and image must support the higher price and enough customers must want the product at that price. Additionally, competitors should not be able to enter the market easily and undercut the high price.

Pricing during the growth phase

Pricing strategy during the growth phase of the product life cycle will be influenced by the choice that was made at the introductory phase between skimming and penetration strategies. For marketers who followed the skimming strategy, prices will probably need to fall during the growth phase. The reason for this might be the arrival of more competition. For marketers who followed a market-penetration strategy, the growth phase represents the best opportunity to increase prices. This is because the market is now growing in size, and even with the arrival of additional competitors there may still be enough demand to justify price increases.

Prices during the maturity phase

As demand peaks, the pressure between companies supplying the same market increases. One way in which a company can achieve sales growth is by means of price reductions, with the aim of driving the least-efficient competitors out of the market. This, however, can lead to risky or damaging price wars.

Prices during the decline phase

Prices and profitability can be expected to fall during the decline stage, as the perceived differences between brands are likely to be insignificant and there are usually only very limited opportunities to reduce costs. The fact that a product has now fully repaid its development and investment costs may still make its production and marketing profitable.

8.8 *Pricing in industrial markets*

Industrial products can be those purchased for resale, or they can be raw materials which are incorporated into manufactured products, or consumables used in industrial operations (see Chapter 2). Consumables are the convenience goods of the industrial market, but there is no need for fancy packaging to attract shoppers as in a supermarket. They therefore tend to have basic packaging for protection and can often be supplied in multiple packs. The price will reflect this. In addition, there may be a quantity discount. Business is usually done on credit and it is common to offer discounts to customers who pay their invoice within a specified number of days. There is no role for psychological pricing, but it is common for the sales negotiators to be given some freedom in the price to be charged.

Raw materials will be regular purchases and it is probably more important that suppliers are reliable. Customers will be prepared to pay a little extra to a known and trusted supplier rather than risk supply problems. A customer, however, may operate a policy of sourcing from a number of suppliers in order to compare competition prices. If the supplier builds up a strong relationship with the customer, then a good exchange of information takes place and prices are continually discussed along with other issues. There may be an annual contract between supplier and customer which confirms price for the whole year. The above pricing methods are possible because industrial markets have much more direct contact between supplier and customer through the wide use of direct personal selling in these markets.

There is one difficult area of industrial markets, however, where direct selling is not a factor. This is when suppliers are invited to submit a tender for a contract offered by a large customer, who may be a local authority or a government department. In this situation the customer specifies what they want and asks a number of suppliers to submit a bid. In such a case it is necessary not only to carry out detailed costing on what is required, but also to have an appreciation of who else is bidding for the work. Here, a pricing strategy can be based on the knowledge of the competition as well as how badly an organisation wants the contract. The final price is therefore a marketing decision and not based solely on costs.

Important terms and concepts

Case study: Maintaining competitive advantage through low-cost pricing: IKEA

IKEA was founded in 1943 by 17-year-old Ingvar Kamprad. The name IKEA was formed from the founder's initials (I.K.) plus the first letters of Elmtaryd and Agunnaryd, the farm and village where he grew up. This is a part of southern Sweden where the soil is thin and poor. The people are famous for working hard, living on small means and using their intelligence to make the best possible use of limited resources. This way of doing things is at the heart of the IKEA approach to keeping prices low.

IKEA sells low-price home furnishing products around the world. The direction for the organisation is provided by its vision, which is 'to create a better everyday life for the many people'. This acts as a guide for everybody within and outside the organisation about what IKEA wants to achieve. To meet its vision, IKEA provides many well-designed, functional products for the home. It prices its products low so that as many people as possible can afford to buy them. IKEA's cost leadership strategy has enabled it to pass on lower prices to customers, anywhere from 25 per cent to 50 per cent below those of its competitors.

At the same time, when creating low prices, IKEA is not willing to sacrifice its principles. 'Low price but not at any price' is what IKEA believes. This means it wants its business to be sustainable. IKEA supplies goods and services to individuals in a way that has an overall beneficial effect on people and on the environment. Customers all over the world have responded positively to IKEA's approach. This is evident in its increasing sales and expansion throughout the world. IKEA aims to be a responsible organisation by using resources efficiently, reducing harm to the environment. It also considers the impact on what they do and how it affects the ability of future generations to meet their needs.

IKEA designs its own products. At the design stage, IKEA checks that products meet strict requirements for function, efficient distribution, quality and impact on the environment. Low price is one of the main factors that IKEA considers in producing well-designed, functional home furnishings available to everyone. IKEA buys products from more than 1,300 suppliers in 50 countries. It uses a number of trading service offices across the world. They negotiate prices with suppliers, check the quality of materials and analyse the environmental impacts that occur through the supply chain. They also keep an eye on social and working conditions at their suppliers. Approximately 50 per cent of IKEA's 9,500 products are made from wood or wood fibres. This is a good resource as long as it comes from sustainable sources, as it can be recycled and is a renewable resource.

During manufacturing, IKEA specifies to its producers that waste should be avoided. Where waste does occur, IKEA encourages suppliers to try to use that waste in the manufacture of other products. IKEA has a code of conduct called the 'IKEA way of purchasing home furnishing products'. This contains minimum rules and guidelines that help manufacturers to reduce the impact of their activities on the environment. IKEA designs many of its products so that the smallest amount of resources can make the best products. For example, IKEA saves on resources by using hollow legs in furniture. Another example is by using a honeycomb-paper filling material instead of solid wood for the inside of tabletops.

IKEA's retail stores add value to manufactured goods by providing a form of shopping different to the usual high street experience. IKEA has more than 260 stores in over 36 countries. These meet the needs of consumers in a number of different ways.

- Each IKEA store is large and holds more than 9,500 products, giving lots of choice.

- Within each store, there are a number of realistic room settings that enable customers to see what the products would look like in their own homes.
- The IKEA store is built on a concept of 'you do half, we do half, together we save money'. This refers to, for example, the customer assembling furniture at home.
- Customers handpick products themselves using trolleys.
- IKEA provides catalogues and home delivery to save time for customers.
- IKEA stores have restaurants that provide Swedish dishes alongside local food choices.

Overall, IKEA's long-term ambition is to become the leading home furnishing company. For IKEA, however, achieving that goal is not simply about developing profitability and market share. As a global organisation, IKEA has chosen to undertake a leadership role in creating a sustainable way of working. It has educated suppliers to understand how and why sustainable production is vital. Sustainable production together with low-cost pricing has helped IKEA to differentiate itself from its competitors.

Source: Adapted from www.thetimes100.co.uk/studies/view-brief-study--building-a-sustainable-supply-chain--110-279.php [accessed 19 March 2011].

Case study: Paying a fair price to cocoa producers: Fairtrade and Nestlé Kit Kat

The Fairtrade Foundation is an independent certification body which licenses the use of the Fairtrade mark on products that meet international Fairtrade standards. This independent consumer label appears on products as a guarantee that disadvantaged producers are getting a better deal. Fairtrade is about better prices, decent working conditions, local sustainability and fair terms of trade for farmers and workers in the developing world. By requiring companies to pay sustainable prices that are never lower than the market price, Fairtrade addresses one of the injustices of conventional trade, which traditionally discriminates against the poorest, weakest producers. Fairtrade enables them to improve their position and have more control over their lives.

Fairtrade Mark Ireland is an independent non-profit organisation that licenses the use of the Fairtrade Mark on products in Ireland in accordance with internationally agreed Fairtrade standards. Fairtrade Mark Ireland was established in 1992.

The Fairtrade minimum price defines the lowest possible price that a buyer of Fairtrade products must pay the producer. The minimum price is set based on a consultative process with Fairtrade producers and traders and it guarantees that producers receive a price that covers the cost of sustainable production. When the market price is higher than the Fairtrade minimum price, the market price is payable.

In December 2009, Nestlé Ireland announced that Kit Kat, its leading confectionery brand, was to be certified Fairtrade in Ireland and Britain. In January 2010, the four-finger version of Kit Kats carrying the Fairtrade mark was introduced to the Irish market. This move followed the launch of Nestlé's global Cocoa Plan representing a €72 million investment over the next 10 years in programmes to address the key economic, social and environmental issues facing cocoa farming communities.

Focusing predominantly on the Ivory Coast (Côte d'Ivoire), the world's largest cocoa-producing country, the aim of the Cocoa Plan is to use Nestlé's agricultural and scientific know-how to improve the quality and yield of cocoa plants. Under Fairtrade terms, farmers receive the guaranteed minimum price or world market price (whichever is higher) plus the Fairtrade premium of US$150 per ton, which is used for business or social development projects. Although the world commodity market price for cocoa is currently high, smallholder farmers are often forced because of poverty to make a quick sale to brokers at a lower price, therefore not directly benefitting from the higher commodity prices. With Fairtrade, the direct relationships mean that farmers' co-operatives secure a better deal with a fair price as well as with the Fairtrade premium. The additional Fairtrade premium payments allow farmers to invest in long-term community and business development projects of their own choice, such as education and healthcare, the environment or their businesses.

Amongst the first farmers to benefit were members of the Kavokiva cocoa co-operative, which was established in 1999 and Fairtrade certified in 2004 and now numbers 6,000 farmer members. Until now, Kavokiva farmers have sold very little on Fairtrade terms. Cocoa farmers in the Ivory Coast struggle under the relentless pressures of poverty with very high levels of illiteracy and poor access to healthcare. The Ivory Coast is one of the poorest countries in the world, with the poverty level rising from 38 per cent in 2002 to 49 per cent in 2008 as a result of conflict in recent years, according to the World Bank. The country produces 40 per cent of the world's cocoa and one in four people directly or indirectly depend on cocoa farming.

The significant volumes of cocoa that go into making Kit Kat will open whole new possibilities for these farmers in the Ivory Coast, giving them a more sustainable livelihood and the chance to plan for a better future. The move will not only enable them to increase Fairtrade cocoa sales, but will also impact other Fairtrade certified co-operatives and farmer groups looking to enter the Fairtrade market. The partnership between Fairtrade and Nestlé will give income security to these farmers.

Having its cocoa sold at a fair price directly to Nestlé is a source of motivation to all farmers and it reinforces the co-operative's cohesion. It allows the co-operative to continue to help its members to produce good-quality cocoa and to increase the yields they produce. The Fairtrade premium is used to improve the life conditions of all co-operative members. A significant part of the Fairtrade premium will be used to ensure that all children from the co-operative can attend school and also to improve the services of the health centre of the co-operative. There are currently seven Fairtrade-certified cocoa co-operatives in the Ivory Coast and many are eager to gain certification. In 2010, at least 4,300 tons of cocoa for Kit Kat came from the Ivory Coast Fairtrade-certified co-operatives, including Kavokiva. The sugar in the product is also Fairtrade certified, sourced from Belize, providing additional premiums of US$60 per ton for the farmers to invest in improving their communities and farming practices.

Today, more than 7 million people – farmers, workers and their families – across 59 developing countries benefit from the Fairtrade Foundation and over 4,500 retail and catering products have been licensed to carry the Fairtrade Mark.

Source: Adapted from www.fairtrade.org.uk/press_office/press_releases_and_ statements/december_2009/kit_kat_gives_cocoa_farmers_in_cte_divoire_a_ break.aspx [accessed 19 March 2011].

Questions for review

1. What are the main factors that influence pricing decisions for a company?
2. Outline the various approaches to pricing products.
3. What are the pricing objectives a marketer considers when setting prices?
4. Discuss the influence of the product life cycle on pricing decisions.
5. Explain (*a*) demand-based pricing and (*b*) psychological pricing. Illustrate your answer with examples.
6. Outline some of the pricing strategies a marketing manager may choose from.
7. Discuss pricing in industrial markets.

9
DISTRIBUTION

Chapter objectives

After reading this chapter you should be able to:
- Understand the role of distribution in marketing.
- Discuss the aspects of physical distribution and distribution channels.
- Compare direct distribution with intermediary distribution.
- Examine the functions of distribution channels.

9.1 *Distribution in the marketing mix*

Distribution is the process by which goods or services are made available and accessible to consumers. In terms of the 'four Ps', distribution is the means by which *place* is determined. Marketers, therefore, expend considerable effort on finding the right *channels of distribution* to ensure that their products reach customers in the most efficient way. According to Dibb et al. (2006), 'a channel of distribution (or marketing channel) is a group of individuals and organisations that direct the flow of products from producers to customers'.

The main concerns for marketers in establishing a distribution network are:
- **Timing:** Will the product be available when the market expects it?
- **Location:** Will the product be in the places where consumers expect to find it?
- **Reliability:** Will the distribution system deliver what it promised or will the retailer be apologising to consumers for delays?

The purpose of any physical distribution method is to transfer the product from its point of production to the consumer in as efficient and effective a way as possible. A company's ability to satisfy consumers' needs efficiently and effectively depends on its relationships with its own suppliers. The product must arrive in good condition and must fit the target market's needs for convenience, choice or whatever else the particular segment thinks is important. Late, damaged, incorrect or inefficiently small deliveries and unsold products show a lack of proper management of the distribution process.

9.2 *Distribution channels*

Distribution channel decisions are among the most important facing managers. A company's channel decisions directly affect every other marketing decision. The company's pricing depends on whether it uses mass merchandising or high-quality specialty stores. Distribution channels manage the series of exchanges that a product or service goes through as it is transferred from its producer to its final user. Channels can be constructed of a number of go-betweens or none at all, as in the case of direct marketing. The main aim of any marketing decision relating to distribution channels is how to reach the relevant customers. This must be in the most appropriate way, given the following four major considerations.

Customers' requirements

The choice of efficient distribution channels relies on a knowledge of a particular market, and in particular it relies on the needs and wants of customers. It may not be possible to satisfy everything a particular customer wants, but that customer's decision is likely to be based on issues such as cost, availability and convenience. The decision facing potential customers is how they rate the different elements of cost and convenience. Opening times are relevant to the availability decision of customers. For example, a neighbourhood store, managed by the owner, is likely to be open for longer hours than a supermarket in an out-of-town shopping centre. The local store will have a limited choice and is likely to be slightly more expensive, but travel time to the supermarket and queues at the checkout at a peak period must be considered.

Organisational resources

The choice of channels has to be consistent with the needs and capabilities of the organisation as well as meeting the needs of customers. An organisation will normally make decisions on the market segments to which they want to offer their product first. Many companies admit they are better off working through intermediaries because they can provide the resources to cover all the potential customers in a cost-effective way, for example food manufacturers market via retailers rather than directly. One problem arising from the use of intermediaries is that it almost invariably leads to some loss of control over the way markets are served.

Competitors' and distributors' actions

Control of the distribution channel is a very effective barrier to entry in many markets. Even if it is possible to gain access to a general distributor alongside competitive products, it will not be enough if the distributor constantly recommends a competitor's product.

Legal constraints

The legal environment is important, as there are issues such as product liability laws which affect all offerings. These restrictions vary from country to country. Key legislation such as the Sale of Goods and Supply of Services Act puts responsibilities on retailers. Policies on returned stock and replacing faulty goods are a key element of distribution policy and customer service.

9.3 *Physical distribution and logistics*

Physical distribution refers to the broad range of activities concerned with the efficient movement of finished products from the end of the production line to the consumer. Physical distribution is concerned with transport methods and distribution strategy decisions are concerned with the choice of outlets for the product. Physical distribution has many objectives. According to Zikmund and d'Amico (2001), these objectives can be condensed into one general statement of purpose: to minimise cost while maximising customer service. Companies can establish competitive advantages over their competitors by more effective physical distribution. Providing more reliable or faster delivery, avoiding errors in processing orders and delivering undamaged goods are all potential competitive advantages.

Traditional physical distribution typically started with products wherever the production plant happened to be located and then tried to find low-cost solutions to get products to customers. Today, however, marketers prefer customer-centred logistics that start with the marketplace and work backwards to the factory or even to sources of supply. Marketing logistics addresses not only outbound distribution (moving products from the factory to customers), but also inbound distribution (moving products and materials from suppliers to the factory) and reverse distribution (moving broken, unwanted or excess products returned by consumers and resellers). Thus, it involves the entire supply chain management. A supply chain is a set of organisations linked by one or more of the upstream and downstream flows of products, services, finances and information from a source to a customer.

Logistics refers to the entire process of moving raw materials and component parts into the firm, products in process through the firm and finished goods out of the firm. The term includes both materials management and physical distribution of the final product; logistics management therefore involves planning, implementing and controlling both the efficient inward flow of materials and the outward flow of finished products. Logistics involves strategic decision-making about the location of warehouses, the management of materials, stock levels and information systems. Today, the complexity of logistics can be modelled, analysed, visualised and optimised by plant simulation software.

9.4 *Aspects of physical distribution*

Physical distribution involves planning, implementing and controlling the physical flow of materials and final goods from points of origin to points of use in order to meet the needs of customers at a profit. The major physical distribution cost is transportation, followed by inventory carrying, warehousing and order processing/customer service. Physical distribution, however, is more than a cost – it can help create demand. Companies can attract more customers by giving better service or lower prices through better physical distribution. On the other hand, companies lose customers when they fail to supply goods on time.

Many companies state their objective as getting the right goods to the right places at the right time for the least cost. Unfortunately, no physical distribution system can *both* maximise customer service *and* minimise distribution costs. The process of physical distribution can be looked at as a system. The main functions carried out by a physical distribution system are the following.

Order processing

This first stage in a distribution system is a crucial one from the marketing point of view. It involves contact with the customer and offers an opportunity to introduce service advantages over the competition. The system design should include speed, ease of use and efficiency.

Materials handling

Often the physical attributes of a product, for example perishability, weight and bulk, will be the decisive influence in how it is stored and transported. Balancing service levels and cost means working out the most efficient use of warehouse space, which will affect the shape, size and nature of the packaging used.

Warehousing

The geographical location of warehouses relative to production and consumption location is a key consideration for manufacturers. A company must decide on how many and what types of warehouses it needs. The more warehouses a company uses, the more quickly goods can be delivered to customers and the higher the service level. More locations, however, mean higher warehousing costs. A company must therefore balance the level of customer service against distribution costs. A company might own private warehouses, rent space in public warehouses or both. They may use storage warehouses or distribution centres. *Storage warehouses* store goods for moderate to long periods, whereas *distribution centres* are designed to move goods rather than just store them. A distribution centre is a large computerised centre designed to receive goods from various companies and suppliers, take orders, fill them efficiently and deliver goods to customers as quickly as possible. In a distribution centre, the emphasis is on throughput.

Inventory management

Adequate stocks of working materials are vital, but too much money tied up in this way can mean cash flow disaster. Carrying too little may result in costly emergency shipments, customer dissatisfaction or lost sales as unserved customers move to a competitor. Inventory decisions involve knowing both when to order and how much to order. On average, stock will account for between a third and half of the assets of most businesses. Careful thought must be given to how much to reorder and at what intervals. Typically the cost of storage averages out at about 25 per cent of the stock's value per year.

Just-in-time

In recent years many companies have greatly reduced their inventories and related costs through *just-in-time* (JIT) logistics systems. JIT aims at maximising the efficiency of the manufacturing process by carrying the minimum level of stock necessary. New stock arrives at the factory or retail outlet exactly when needed, rather than being stored in inventory until being used. JIT systems require accurate forecasting along with fast, frequent and flexible delivery so that new supplies will be available when needed. These systems result in substantial savings in inventory carrying and handling costs. By keeping the flow in the pipeline – raw materials, work in progress, finished goods – to a minimum, suppliers can enhance logistics efficiency, while ensuring that customer service objectives are regularly met.

Transport

The final aspect of physical distribution is the transport which moves the product from where it is produced to where it is used. It is one of the most frequently contracted-out aspects of distribution, although many major manufacturers will maintain their own fleets of haulage vehicles (see section 9.5).

9.5 Transport methods

Transport is the process of moving a product from where it is made to where it is bought. Methods of transport vary according to speed, cost and ability to handle the type of product concerned. The principal transport infrastructures are railways, roads, airways, water transport and pipelines. Each mode offers advantages and disadvantages and the distribution manager or transport manager must therefore consider the cost trade-offs involved in selecting one of the modes of transport. The first consideration is always the needs of the customer. Other considerations include the nature of the product, for example bulk, perishability, weight and fragility, and the cost and availability of transport methods and storage space.

Railways carry heavy, bulky goods over long distances at low cost. Railways often carry minerals, sand, timber and chemicals as well as low-value manufactured goods. The main disadvantages of the railway system are that it is relatively slow and it can be used only near railway lines. Some companies, however, establish their factories or warehouses near rail lines for convenient loading and unloading.

Motor vehicles include lorries, vans and, to a lesser extent, buses that carry packages. Lorries are the most flexible and accessible mode of transport, as they can go almost anywhere. They are often used in conjunction with forms of transport that cannot provide door-to-door delivery. Motor vehicles and their services, however, can be expensive. Lorries are most efficient at moving comparatively small deliveries over short distances and are also effective for long distances.

Air freight is the fastest but also the most expensive mode of distribution. The primary advantages of air freight are its speed and its distance capabilities. Fast transport also permits stock reductions and savings in warehousing costs. Air transport is used primarily to move goods of high unit value, perishable goods and emergency orders. High-technology manufacturers often choose to move goods on demand by air freight rather than incur the costs of carrying stock. The ground transport needed for pick-up and final delivery, however, also adds to cost and transit time.

Water transport usually offers a very low-cost means of moving products. It is most appropriate for bulky, low-value, non-perishable goods, such as grain and coal. Many markets, however, are accessible to water only with supplementary rail or road transport. The main disadvantages of water transport are its slowness and the seasonal closing of some routes and ports by ice during winter.

Pipelines are the most specialised means of transport because they are designed to carry only one or two products. They are used mainly to transport natural gas and crude petroleum, moving them from wells to storage or treatment facilities. Most pipelines are owned by the companies that use them, such as gas and oil producers. Pipelines move products slowly but continuously and at relatively low cost. They are a reliable mode of transport and ensure low rates of product damage and theft. A large part of the expense results from the construction of the pipeline itself.

Marketers select a transport mode on the grounds of cost, speed, reliability, capability, accessibility, security and traceability. They compare alternative means of transport to determine whether the benefits from a more expensive mode are worth the higher costs. The cheapest is not always the best. For example, microchips are light and therefore relatively cheap in air freight charges, without tying up capital in lengthy surface routes.

Marketers also compare *transit time,* which is the total time for transporting products, including the time required for pick-up and delivery, handling and movement between the points of manufacture and destination. The *reliability* of a mode of transport is determined by the consistency of service provided. Marketers must be able to know that their products will be delivered on time and in an acceptable condition. *Capability* refers to the provision of appropriate equipment and conditions for moving specific products, for example refrigeration. *Accessibility* is the carrier's capacity to move products over a specific route or network, for example railway lines, waterways or roads. *Security* means delivering the products in an acceptable condition, for example not losing or damaging the goods. Highly valuable items, for example, may not be easily distributed through retailers, as direct delivery may work better. *Traceability* is the means of finding products that have been lost.

9.6 *Who does what in distribution?*

Channel intermediaries fall into two main types: merchants and functional intermediaries. Merchants actually become the legal owners of the goods they then resell. The risks are substantial because if the goods do not sell it becomes the merchant's problem. However, the potential profit to be made is correspondingly higher than being an agent or functional intermediary.

Functional intermediaries never actually own the goods that pass through their hands. They earn a commission or fee for the services they provide. These can include transport, storage and finance. The following are the main types of distribution intermediaries.

Agent

A functional intermediary with a contractual agreement to work on behalf of a particular buyer or seller. Agents find customers and negotiate, but never actually own the goods in question. They receive a fee or commission for their work.

Broker

Similar to an agent, but with fewer functions. These are mainly limited to bringing together buyers and sellers. They are employed temporarily and paid by the parties hiring them. The most familiar examples are insurance brokers, auctioneering brokers and security brokers.

Cash and carry

A type of wholesaler whose customers are not offered credit and have to collect their purchases themselves. Smaller independent retailers will often use a cash and carry (e.g. Musgraves) in conjunction with traditional full-service wholesalers and company sales representatives in order to deal with their stocking needs.

Facilitator

Firms like hauliers, warehouses, banks and insurance companies help expedite exchanges without owning the goods concerned.

Franchisee

An individual or an organisation granted the exclusive right to exploit a successful business idea by its originator (franchisor) in return for profit, for example Tie Rack, Sock Shop and Body Shop.

Franchisor

The owner of a successful business idea who franchises it out to a number of franchisees.

In-home retailers

Companies that sell direct in people's homes rather than using traditional retail environments, for example Avon or Tupperware.

9.7 Marketing intermediaries

One of the major decisions facing a manufacturer is whether to sell directly to consumers or to use intermediaries, or both. Fig. 9.1 summarises the strengths and weaknesses of direct versus intermediary distribution methods. A ***direct marketing channel*** has no intermediary levels. Direct marketing has become the fastest-growing form of marketing. Years ago, the direct marketing channel was largely dominated by mail and telephone. Today, direct marketing includes all forms of online communications, including marketing offers through e-mail, websites, interactive television, mobile communications and other interactive communications media.

Direct marketing consists of direct communications with targeted individual customers to obtain an immediate response and to cultivate lasting customer relationships. Direct marketers communicate directly with customers, often on a one-to-one interactive basis. For many companies, direct marketing – especially Internet marketing and e-commerce – constitutes a new and complete model for doing business. Companies such as eBay, Dell, Amazon and Ryanair have built their entire approach around direct marketing.

Direct channels	Intermediary channels
Manufacturer	Manufacturer
⇩	⇩
Consumer	Middleman
	⇩
	Consumer

Fig. 9.1: *Direct and intermediary distribution channels*

Most, though not all, channels of distribution have **marketing inter-mediaries**. An intermediary or 'middleman' is an independent business concern that operates as a link between producers and consumers or industrial users. **Agents** do not actually buy products, but agency sales representatives call on major retailers and on wholesalers on behalf of a number of producers and take orders and arrange delivery. This saves the producer the cost of operating a large salesforce to carry perhaps only a small product range, enlisting instead, for example, insurance brokers and recruitment agencies. Agents are usually paid a fee or commission for their work. **Wholesalers** buy the goods from the manufacturers, often through an agent, then sell the goods to retailers, for example Musgrave (SuperValu and Centra). **Retailers** are companies that offer goods directly to consumers, for example local shops and supermarkets.

Direct	Intermediaries
• Enables companies to build strong relationships with consumers	• Buy more per order than individual consumers
• Puts the distribution network under the control of the manufacturer	• Are physically closer to consumers and can provide market information
• Increases margins on sales by cutting out the mark-up of intermediaries	• Can offer after-sales service in places convenient to consumers, rather than returning products to a factory for service

Table 9.1: *Direct versus intermediary distribution*

9.8 *Internet marketing*

The potential audience for Internet usage is very large, as more and more homes and businesses either get connected or develop their own websites.

Mitchell (1999) argues that the Internet has revolutionised the way in which transactions are done and can reduce interaction costs, both of which are critical aspects of exchange, whether for profit or some other benefit. Changes in technology and the rapid growth of direct and online marketing are having a profound impact on the nature and design of marketing channels. ***Direct marketing*** is a form of advertising that reaches its audience without using traditional formal channels of advertising such as television, newspapers or radio. Companies communicate directly with the consumer with advertising techniques such as fliers, catalogue distribution, promotional letters and street advertising. If the advertisement asks the potential customer to take a specific action, e.g. to call a freephone number or to visit a website, then the effort is considered to be ***direct response advertising***.

Online marketing or ***Internet marketing*** cuts out intermediaries so that products and services are sold directly to the final buyers. The interactive nature of Internet marketing in terms of providing instant responses and eliciting responses are the unique qualities of the medium. The target user is usually browsing the Internet alone, therefore the marketing messages can reach them personally. This approach is used in search marketing, where the advertisements are based on search engine keywords entered by the users.

Internet marketing is relatively inexpensive and companies can reach a wide audience for a small fraction of traditional advertising budgets. The nature of the medium allows consumers to research and purchase products and services at their own convenience. Companies therefore have the advantage of appealing to consumers in a medium that can bring results quickly.

Internet marketers also have the advantage of measuring statistics easily and inexpensively. Nearly all aspects of an Internet marketing campaign can be traced, measured and tested. Marketers can therefore determine which messages or offerings are more appealing to the audience. The results of campaigns can be measured and tracked immediately because online marketing initiatives usually require users to click on an advertisement, visit a website and perform a targeted action.

From the buyer's perspective, however, there are some limitations to Internet purchasing. For example, the inability to touch, smell, taste or experience tangible goods before making an online purchase can be limiting. However, there is an industry standard for e-commerce sellers to reassure customers by having liberal return policies.

Security is important both to companies and consumers that participate in online business. Many consumers are hesitant to purchase items over the Internet because they do not trust that their personal information will remain private.

Another security concern that consumers have with e-commerce sellers is whether or not they will receive exactly what they purchase. Online sellers have attempted to address this concern by investing in and building strong consumer brands, e.g. Amazon and eBay. Additionally, major online payment mechanisms (credit cards, PayPal, etc.) have also provided buyer protection systems to address financial security problems if they do occur.

9.9 *Distribution strategies*

Companies have to choose the optimum number of middlemen to use. Determining the number of wholesalers and the number of retailers is an important decision that will determine the number of outlets where potential customers can expect to find the product. There are three levels of distribution: intensive, selective and exclusive.

Intensive distribution seeks to obtain maximum exposure for the product at the retail level. When consumers will not go to much effort to buy a product or will readily accept substitutes when the brand is not available, the appropriate strategy is to use all available outlets for distributing a product. The goods must be available where and when customers want them. Intensive distribution at the wholesale level allows almost all appropriate wholesalers to carry the product. Coca-Cola, for example, is distributed in vending machines, supermarkets, convenience stores, restaurants and many other outlets. Cigarettes, bread and newspapers are also intensively distributed.

Selective distribution at the retail level restricts the sale of the product to a limited number of outlets. Each selected shop must meet the company's performance standards while appealing to a select target market. Selective distribution is more commonly used for speciality goods, for example with electrical appliances and photographic specialists, who can offer professional advice. Exclusive perfumes also usually fall into the specialist category, rather than convenience goods. This type of restricted distribution, however, is becoming less common, with supermarkets, pharmacies and department stores offering increasingly wider ranges of household and electrical goods.

Exclusive distribution uses only one outlet in a particular area to sell a product. When a product requires personal selling, a complete stock of the product line, repair service or other special effort, an intermediary may be granted exclusive distribution rights. Exclusive distribution is suitable for products that are bought rather infrequently, are consumed over a long period or require information to fit them to consumers' needs. It is often used as an incentive to sellers when only a limited market is available for products. Cars such as Rolls-Royce and watches such as Rolex are sold on an exclusive basis. Generally a manufacturer or wholesaler that grants a retailer exclusive distribution expects a maximum sales effort or expects to gain something from the prestige or efficiency of the retail outlet.

9.10 *Distribution and the product life cycle*

As with other aspects of the marketing mix, product and service distribution objectives will differ from phase to phase in the product's life cycle. During the introduction phase it is vital for a manufacturer to have secured an effective distribution network by the time the product is launched. If the new product is joining a company's existing range of branded products, this should not be too difficult, as the existing channels are likely to be suitable for the new product. Wholesalers and retailers, however, will expect incentives to stock a new brand in the form of discounted prices and merchandising support.

During the growth phase, wholesalers and retailers will be more likely to stock the product, as demand will be growing and intermediaries will want to be able to satisfy this. At the maturity phase, both the retailer and the manufacturer of a brand may review their strategies, for example retailers may want to decrease the number of competing brands in a product group to concentrate on bestsellers, while manufacturers may want to concentrate distribution through the most cost-effective outlets, eliminating those that take only small orders. During the decline phase, manufacturers face pressure from retailers to offer bigger discounts just to keep the brand on the shelves.

9.11 *Getting products into distribution: The push-pull methods*

There are two methods by which products get into a distribution channel. The first is through the efforts of a sales team to convince distributors to stock the product. This involves *pushing* products into the distribution channel. A good salesperson will not overload distributors with products but will try to make sure the right level of product is available to meet customers' requirements. Push tactics can be seen to be a sales-led approach, with salespersons offering special discounts, sale or return, merchandising support and dealer competitions. The use of bar codes means that sales can be tracked efficiently, and in some cases the reordering of products is assisted by automation.

Pull tactics are advertising led. Consumers can create demand, pulling products along a distribution chain, for example by ordering the product, demand pull is created. Before this can be achieved, however, awareness of the product needs to be promoted, for example through advertising or through informal recommendations. Push and pull tactics can operate quite independently of each other but work best if combined. In practice, most markets have a mixture of push and pull techniques. Both tactics are necessary to keep the flow of products and services moving.

Important terms and concepts

distribution in the marketing mix: p. 189

channel of distribution: p. 189

physical distribution: p. 191

logistics: p. 192

order processing: p. 192

materials handling: p. 193

warehousing: p. 193

distribution centre: p. 193

inventory management: p. 193

just-in-time: p. 193

transport: p. 194

railways: p. 194

motor vehicles: p. 194

air freight: p. 195

water transport: p. 195

pipelines: p. 195

transit time: p. 195

reliability: p. 195

capability: p. 195

accessibility: p. 195

security: p. 195

traceability: p. 196

agent: p. 196

broker: p. 196

cash and carry: p. 196

facilitator: p. 196

franchisee: p. 197

franchisor: p. 197

in-home retailers: p. 197

marketing intermediaries: p. 197

direct marketing channel: p. 197

agents: p. 198

wholesalers: p. 198

retailers: p. 198

direct versus intermediary distribution: p. 198

Internet marketing: p. 198

direct marketing p. 199

direct response advertising: p. 199

online marketing: p. 199

distribution strategies: p. 200

intensive distribution: p. 200

selective distribution: p. 200

exclusive distribution: p. 200

distribution and the product lifecycle: p. 201

push-pull methods: p. 201

Case study: Using the Internet to increase brand awareness: Butlers Irish Handmade Chocolates

The Irish Chocolate Company started production in 1932. The company produces several brands along with its most recognisable brand, Butlers Irish

Handmade Chocolates, which is also known simply as Butlers. These handmade chocolates are positioned at the premium end of the confectionery market. Made from quality Irish cream, butter and eggs, the products appeal to the discerning chocolate lover. The brand is instantly recognisable with the luxurious white and gold embossed presentation boxes tied with red or gold ribbons and decorated with flowers.

The Irish Chocolate Company supplies three distinct markets:

- Duty free (domestic and international).
- Domestic retail – through department stores, gift shops, craft shops and food service catering.
- International retail – through department stores.

The Irish Chocolate Company had been operating a mail order business for its chocolates for up to 20 years. Although this operation was on a small scale, the company had identified a niche and mail order provided significant business. The company believed there was a lot more opportunity in the mail order business and identified the Internet as the best method of exploiting it. They also strove to be the first Irish handmade chocolate manufacturer selling online.

In 1997, the Irish Chocolate Company began extensive market research in relation to online selling. As there were no existing manufacturers in Ireland with an Internet presence, the company researched its international competitors, most of which were located in Belgium. The Irish Chocolate Company investigated what kind of service the online suppliers were offering, where they shipped to, how the product arrived, how long it took to arrive and what kind of condition it was in when received. They soon discovered that none of their competitors at that time sold into Ireland – for example, Godiva, a leading Belgian manufacturer, shipped only to the US.

Their research also pointed out that the majority of orders placed were for gift purposes as opposed to individuals buying for themselves. Gifts arrived from their competitors packaged in plain brown boxes labelled with a plain printed address sticker, accompanied by an invoice. The Irish Chocolate Company believed that the method of shipping and the inclusion of pricing details to be inappropriate for the gift market. They recognised a big opportunity to design an overall product acceptable as a gift by concentrating on presentation, package design and gift cards. The company recognised that the area of mail ordering was potentially a very profitable market and the Internet was the best vehicle for opening up new markets and building a new customer base. No other Irish manufacturer was engaged in online ordering, so they found a niche product and an untapped market.

In 1998, the initial website was launched with an online ordering facility.

Produced by a web design company, the site allowed customers to view products and to order online. A requirement of the site was to have three separate sections targeted at distinct customer types:

- Consumer – the end customer.
- Corporate – companies.
- Trade – resellers.

It did not envisage too many domestic retailers switching to an online facility, as they specifically targeted new overseas customers. At trade shows, Butlers frequently met potential overseas retail clients who would sample the product and see the range exhibited. Clients were also informed that they could peruse all products in an interactive manner and order instantly online.

Corporate customers are also heavily targeted on the site. Specific ranges tailored for company gifts are promoted, especially around festive seasons. To market this new section, Butlers ran a postal mail shot to a database of corporations, with return mail specifying which method they would like to use to order – online or otherwise. In addition, its existing database clients were sent information electronically or via the postal service. Each individual customer was now pre-registered with the site and was e-mailed with a password.

The website has proved important as a business-to-business (B2B) portal, a gateway for the trade customers. Trade customers can benefit from a number of service options, such as a quick quote facility that provides instant quotes for orders, including delivery costs and expected delivery times. Established trade customers were accustomed to making their orders via fax or over the phone. Ensuring that the new site encouraged trade customers to move to the new online process was a primary focus of the trade section while simultaneously attracting new customers.

The website has been a success on many levels, with all objectives being reached or surpassed. Its branding objectives have been met with huge growth in the previously untapped consumer market. Averaging 235,000 hits per month, with 84 per cent of web traffic coming from the US, their extensive online web store is attracting a whole range of customers, from individuals and corporations to retail customers. Having previously focused their business on the retail and corporate market, this new market is providing an excellent new growth area directly from the Internet platform.

Source: Adapted from www.enterprise-ireland.com/ebusiness/Case_studies/butlers/butlers_p1.asp [accessed 19 March 2011].

Case study: TNT worldwide distribution service: Building a superior customer experience

TNT is the market leader in the provision of business-to-business (B2B) express delivery services. Using road or air transport, TNT delivers documents, parcels and freight securely between businesses. Ken Thomas founded TNT in Australia in 1946 with a single truck. It became Thomas Nationwide Transport (TNT) in 1958, with national networks in Australia and all major European countries, including Ireland. Today, TNT is a global company, serving customers in over 200 countries. As a global company, TNT seeks to project a consistent image across the world. It uses the global strapline 'Sure we can' on all its vehicles, aircraft and communication materials.

TNT's values underpin the way the organisation runs. These values are the core principles or standards that guide the way TNT does business. While business plans and strategies may change, the core values of a business remain the same. TNT's values are:

- Be honest.
- Aim to satisfy customers every time.
- Challenge and improve all aspects of the business.
- Be passionate about people.
- Act as a team.
- Measure success through sustainable profit.
- Work for the world.

Every aspect of TNT's business strategy focuses on 'delivering a superior customer experience'. For example, TNT uses technology to enable customers to check exactly where their deliveries are at any time. TNT Express UK delivers over 3.5 million items every week around the world and is listed among Britain's top employers, as it endeavours to provide first-class working conditions and care for its employees. The company needs high-level skills to cover a wide range of functions, including distribution, sales and marketing, finance, customer service and human resource management.

TNT's mission is to:

- Exceed customers' expectations in the transfer of their goods and documents around the world.
- Deliver value to customers by providing the most reliable and efficient solutions through delivery networks.
- Seek to lead the industry by instilling pride in employees, creating value for stakeholders and sharing responsibility around the world.

Aims and SMART objectives

The aims supporting this mission focus on efficiently transferring goods and documents, providing customer satisfaction and behaving responsibly. To achieve these aims the organisation needs to establish objectives at a number of levels. SMART objectives are designed to ensure that everyone understands what is required and by when. They make it easy to measure performance so that the business knows if and when its aims have been achieved. Where necessary, it can change its plans to overcome any problems or obstacles.

Measurable objectives cover every aspect of TNT's operations and service. The top-level objective is 'to achieve profitable growth'. Examples of SMART objectives that contribute to this include:

- 'Answer 85 per cent of calls from customers within 10 seconds.' This objective fits with the mission 'to provide the most reliable and efficient solutions' for customers. TNT's customer focus is one of the key ways in which it aims to differentiate itself from competitors.
- 'To improve TNT's carbon efficiency by 45 per cent by 2020' (measured against the 2007 baseline). This example of a long-term objective reflects TNT's aim to reduce the environmental impact of its business.

TNT's market position is based on differentiating itself from rivals through its speed, reliability and provision of services of the highest standard. TNT's strengths are based on attracting and developing high-calibre staff who are able to exceed customer expectations so that customers remain loyal to the business. TNT's strategies need to take into account a number of important areas, including:

- What goods and services to produce, for example an integrated delivery service.
- Which territories will deliver best return on investment. TNT's international operations focus on the key trading areas of Europe, Asia, North America and South America.
- How to build a competitive advantage, for example by providing the most reliable, customer-focused services.

TNT's practical measures are set out under three main headings: Operational Excellence, Customer Relationship Management and Innovation. TNT has developed a strategy map that puts the customer at the heart of everything that the business does. It communicates to everyone involved with the business how the company will meet its goals. Specifically, the strategy map acts both as a practical guide and as a framework to achieve the business objective of growing profits. The map also describes the journey that TNT is taking towards achieving long-term aims. For example:

- The map shows that operational excellence will be achieved through a solid foundation of fast, reliable and quality services.
- From there, the customer relationship is improved by understanding what different customers want. This builds a stronger allegiance and loyalty.
- Innovation is about anticipating the future needs of TNT customers. Through stronger relationships, the business can develop a joint approach and shared vision.

TNT monitors customer satisfaction through regular customer loyalty measurements. TNT's customer promise is part of its key strategy to retain customers by delivering a superior customer experience. TNT recognises that its people are the foundation on which it builds its customer-focused strategy. It needs to have the right people and skills to deliver the promises it makes. The business is committed to staff development. It promotes around 70 per cent of its managers from within the organisation, enabling people to have long-term careers. Nearly 500 staff have at least 25 years' service each. One key factor in TNT's development of its people has involved training managers to become assessors and coaches of their teams. Through appraisals, managers find out what employees' needs and aspirations are as well as their strengths. Identifying skills gaps as well as identifying who is aiming for promotion enables TNT to put together effective training programmes. All managers possess a great knowledge of the way TNT works and, with training, can pass on that knowledge to make new workers more effective more quickly.

TNT's philosophy is that there are no limits to how far the right talent can rise. The recently retired managing director, for example, originally started out as a driver. Graduates joining TNT work on major projects across the company from the outset and often progress to management positions within five years. Such projects have included the Common Systems project. This involved implementing a new computer system for improving data entry across 50 different locations. This has reduced the time spent on data input significantly and has helped to speed up service delivery.

In conclusion, creating and delivering an effective business strategy involves:

- Having clear aims and objectives.
- Building a competitive advantage by developing core competences.
- Identifying gaps and seeking to close these through development of resources.

TNT demonstrates good practice in each of these areas. The company has clear business aims and objectives that are time related. It focuses on developing competitive advantage through its strategies for customers, innovation and its people. TNT ensures that the people working for the business have adequate opportunities to grow. It meets any gaps in the ability of the workforce to deliver its strategy by training and developing its existing people. This retains their skills and offers attractive career opportunities to recruit new talent.

Source: Adapted from www.thetimes100.co.uk/case-study—delivering-a-business-strategy—162-416-1.php [accessed 19 March 2011].

Questions for review

1. What are the main elements of the physical distribution mix?
2. Compare direct and intermediary distribution.
3. Discuss the purpose of a physical distribution system.
4. List the various transport options available to a company, giving the advantages and disadvantages of each method.
5. Write a brief description of (*a*) intensive distribution, (*b*) selective distribution and (*c*) exclusive distribution.
6. What are the main factors a marketing manager needs to consider when selecting distribution channels?

10
MARKETING COMMUNICATION

Chapter objectives

After reading this chapter you should be able to:
- Define the marketing communication process and its elements.
- Explain the communication mix and the uniqueness of each tool.
- Describe the steps involved in developing a communication programme.
- Identify the factors that affect the selection of the communication mix.

10.1 *The marketing communication process*

According to Dibb et al. (1997), marketing communication can be defined as 'the communication of information which facilitates or expedites the exchange process'. Marketing communication (promotion) is the fourth element in the marketing mix. This comprises a mix of tools available to the marketer, called the *communication mix,* which consists of personal selling, advertising, sales promotion and public relations, direct marketing and e-marketing (see Fig. 10.1).

The communication mix is the direct way in which a company attempts to communicate with a variety of target audiences. The mix can be used to:
- Inform potential customers about the benefits of the product.
- Persuade customers to use the product.
- Remind customers of the benefits of using the product.

Communication is the sharing of meaning between sender and receiver. There are eight *elements* in the *marketing communication process*.

1. Source

The source (sender) of the message will be the company with a product or service to offer to a target (receiver). It is the source that instigates the communication process. A source could be, for example, a marketing manager who wishes to communicate a message to thousands of consumers through an advertisement.

2. Message

The message is what the source wants the audience to know or understand as a result of receiving the communication. It may be any combination of words, pictures or symbols.

3. Receiver

Consumers who read, hear or see the message are the receivers (the target audience).

4. Channel

The message is communicated by means of a communication channel, such as television, radio, print or personal selling.

5. Encoding

Encoding is the process of having the source transform an idea or intended message into a set of symbols.

6. Decoding

Decoding is the reverse of encoding. It involves having the receiver take a set of symbols – the message – and transform them back into an idea. Individual receivers tend to interpret incoming messages very differently depending on their attitudes, values and beliefs.

7. Feedback

Feedback is how the receiver responds to the message, for example carrying out market research to find out how successful the message has been. With mass communication, such as television advertising, feedback tends to be slow and difficult to collect. It may be so delayed or distorted that it is of no use to the source.

8. Noise

When the result of decoding is different from what was coded, noise exists. Noise includes all activity and influences that distract from any aspect of the communication process between the source and receiver. Noise can be background traffic, people talking, distracting music or the intended receiver being distracted from watching television when the advertisement is broadcast.

10.2 *The communication mix*

To communicate to consumers, a company may use one or more of four communication tools: advertising, sales promotion, personal selling and public relations, direct marketing and e-marketing. A *communication mix* is the combination of two or more of the tools a company chooses to use.

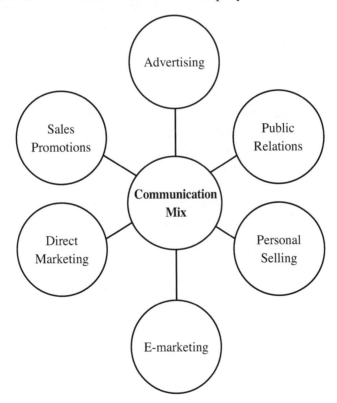

Fig. 10.1: *The tools of the communication mix*

Advertising

Kotler et.al. (2003) defines ***advertising*** as 'any paid form of nonpersonal presentation and promotion of ideas, goods or services through mass media such as newspapers, magazines, television or radio by an identified sponsor.'

Advertising has a very wide scope. When someone places a card in a local newsagent's window announcing an item for sale, this is an advertisement. This can be contrasted with a large company's commercial shown on television. Each of these examples may be successful if it achieves its objective, namely moving potential customers closer to the point of purchase for a particular product or service.

Advertising usually involves mass media, such as radio, television, cinema, magazines and the Internet. There are many factors that should be considered before advertising is undertaken. Advertisements should first be considered as part of the total communication process. The objectives, message and likely budget may well have been determined. Decisions now have to be taken on the role of advertising as part of the promotional mix. Primarily, it revolves around the balance between advertising and personal selling, as these are usually the elements where most money is committed.

Before an advertising message is made public, a company or marketer should carry out marketing research (see Chapter 5). The research will enable the company to make sure the proposed message will be understood by the target market and that the target market will actually see the medium chosen. ***Competitive advertising*** is concerned with emphasising the special features of the product or brand as a means of outselling competition. Usually the seller seeks to communicate the unique benefits, real or imaginary, that distinguishes the product and gives it its competitive edge. Given that most markets are mature and often crowded, this type of advertising is very common and very important.

Comparative advertising means making direct comparison between one product and another, showing the advertiser's product in a much more favourable light, of course. Alternatively, the comparison may be more subtle, referring to 'other leading brands' and leaving it up to the target audience to decide which rival product is intended.

Advantages of advertising

- It communicates to the mass audience a product's features, benefits and competitive advantage.
- It benefits a company by contributing to a strong long-term corporate image.

- It can help to create awareness and to build image and attitudes through reminders.
- It can reinforce positive attitudes through reminders.
- It supports the other tools of the communication mix by creating awareness, thereby helping salespeople.
- It helps to reduce sales fluctuations, which may be influenced by seasonal demand.
- It facilitates the repetition of a message many times over.

Disadvantages of advertising

- It can be very costly to produce and to advertise a message, particularly on television.
- It does not provide direct feedback, which makes it difficult for marketers to know how well a message was received.
- It is impersonal and not as persuasive as personal selling.

Advertising media

Advertising media are called on to perform the task of delivering the message to the consumer. The advertiser needs, therefore, to select the medium or media most appropriate to the task in hand, given their relative effectiveness and the budget available.

Radio

On the positive side:
- Low cost.
- Can target specific audience.
- Advertisements can be placed quickly.
- Can use sound and humour effectively.

On the negative side:
- Cannot handle complex messages.
- No visual excitement.
- Short exposure time.
- Commercial clutter.

Television

On the positive side:
- Can target specific audience.
- Excellent for demonstrating product usage.
- Digital TV will open up interactive opportunities.
- Uses picture, print, sound and motion for effect.
- Ability to reach a wide, diverse audience.

On the negative side:
- High campaign cost.
- Long lead times needed for production.
- Commercial clutter.
- Long-term advertiser commitment.
- Short life of message.

Outdoor media

On the positive side:
- Moderate cost.
- Geographic selectivity.
- High visibility.
- Opportunity for repeat exposures.
- Flexibility.

On the negative side:
- Message must be short and simple.
- Lack of demographic selectivity.
- Visual clutter.
- Subject to damage and defacement.
- Traffic hazard or eyesore.

Direct mail

On the positive side:
- Advert can be saved.
- Easy to measure performance.
- Highly selective.
- Circulation controlled by advertiser.
- Personal.
- Very flexible, 3D, pop-up advertisements, etc.

On the negative side:
- Expensive.
- Considered junk mail by many people.
- No editorial matter to attract readers.
- Invasion of privacy.

Press

On the positive side:
- Can target specific audiences.
- Handles detail well.
- Advertisements can be placed and changed.
- Advertisements can be clipped and saved.
- Can convey complex information.

On the negative side:
- Limited control of advertisement position.
- Can be low impact.
- Timing difficulties in co-ordinating appearance of the advertisement.

Internet

On the positive side:
- International communication opportunities.
- Allows the user to interact with the marketer online.
- Market research information can be obtained from people using the site.

On the negative side:
- Security, consumers giving a credit card number that can be intercepted by someone else.
- Websites need to be maintained and updated, users will become frustrated if information is out of date.
- Lack of clarity on who is browsing the web.

Sales promotion

A second promotional tool is *sales promotion*. This is a short-term inducement of value offered to stimulate interest in buying a product or service. The British Advertising Standards Authority defines sales promotion as 'those marketing techniques, which are used, usually on a temporary basis, to make goods and services more attractive to the consumer by providing some additional benefit whether in cash or in kind'.

Sales promotions are usually used in conjunction with advertising or personal selling and are rarely used in isolation. They are offered to retailers and to salespeople as well as to ultimate consumers.

Sales promotion methods

Consumer sales promotion methods

- Banded packs, e.g. toothbrush banded to a toothpaste at a reduced price for the two combined.
- Money-off coupons.
- Premium offers, e.g. items offered free or at a minimum cost.
- Stamp-collecting schemes, e.g. SuperValu promotions.
- Free sample or tasting offers.
- In-store demonstrations.
- Point-of-sale displays.
- Competitions.
- Personality promotions.

Trade sales promotion methods

- Buying allowances, e.g. temporary price reduction for buying certain quantities of a product.
- Free merchandise.
- Competitions.
- Trade shows.
- Exhibitions.
- Bonuses.
- Business meetings.
- Sales contests.
- Store demonstrations.
- Advertising allowance.

Advantages of sales promotion

- The short-term nature of these promotions often stimulates sales for their duration.
- They arouse attention and provide information.
- They offer value to the consumer, for example in the form of a money-off coupon or rebate, which provides an incentive to buy.

- They boost sales by persuading regular customers to bring forward their purchases.

Disadvantages of sales promotion

- Their gains are short term.
- To build long-term brand preference, they need advertising support.
- They lose their effectiveness if they are conducted continuously.
- They are expensive.

Personal selling

Personal selling is any paid form of interpersonal presentation of products and services. In contrast to advertising, personal selling involves face-to-face communication between the source (sender) and receiver (target audience). Murray and O'Driscoll (1999) view personal selling as 'perhaps the most powerful, certainly the most sophisticated, and often the most expensive element of the communication mix'.

The personal sales approach is the more direct and potent way of selling many products. It ranges from door-to-door insurance salespeople to assistants in a department store. Companies spend large sums of money training their salespeople in selling processes.

Personal selling processes consists of the following steps:
1. Developing a list of potential customers.
2. Pre-approach preparation.
3. Approaching the customer.
4. Presentation and demonstration.
5. Dealing with feedback.
6. Closing the sale.
7. Follow-up.

With advances in technology, personal selling also takes place by phone and through electronic mail.

Firms can choose between a *hard sell* approach and a *soft sell* approach

Hard sell strategies

- Concern for self.
- Talking.
- Pushing product.
- Presenting features.
- Advocating without acknowledging.

Soft sell strategies

- Concern for customer.
- Questions for discussion.
- Listening.
- Providing buying opportunity.
- Presenting benefits.
- Acknowledging needs.

Advantages of personal selling

- A sales representative can direct presentations at specific target sectors, thereby reducing wasted coverage.
- The salesperson can interpret the potential customer's reaction to the message.
- The feedback is immediate and allows the salesperson to modify the message accordingly.
- It is very useful for complex or technical products or services.

Disadvantages of personal selling

- It is the most expensive tool of the communication mix.
- It requires long-term commitment.
- It may lead to inconsistent communication to customers, as the people can change the message.

Public relations

Public relations (PR) deals with the quality and nature of the relationship between a company and its various 'publics'. These may include customers, shareholders, employees, suppliers, the Government, the media and pressure groups. According to Dibb et al. (1997), public relations is 'the planned and sustained effort to establish and maintain goodwill and mutual understanding between a company and its publics'. As with any marketing activity, managers must be sure that PR integrates with the rest of the organisation's promotional efforts and that it is clearly related to wider company objectives.

Marketing PR may be used for long-term strategic image building, developing credibility and raising the organisation's profile to enhance marketing activities. When used this way, it becomes a planned element of the wider promotional mix, working in synergy with the others. A new product launch or the introduction of a big new innovative advertising campaign, for instance, might benefit from planned PR aimed at specific audiences through specific media to generate interest and awareness. It can also be used to support and revive existing products, e.g. creating an event around particular successes (celebrating 50 years of *Coronation Street*) or after the first 10,000 cars of a particular model have been sold. Restaurants may invite journalists from the specialised press to encourage them to write a positive article and as a result to boost sales.

Corporate PR may be used as part of a long-term relationship-building strategy with various publics or as a short-term tactical response to an unforeseen crisis. Short-term circumstances are somewhat unpredictable, and therefore any organisation needs to have contingency plans ready so that a well-rehearsed crisis management team can go into action as soon as disaster strikes. This means, for example, that everyone should know who will be responsible for collating information and feeding it to the media and that senior management will be properly briefed and trained to face media interrogation. Such measures result in the organisation being seen to handle the crisis capably and efficiently and also reduce the chances of different spokespersons innocently contradicting each other or of the media being kept short of information because everyone thinks that someone else is dealing with that aspect.

Public relations encompasses the following techniques and activities.

- **Publicity:** This is a form of promotion that is not paid for directly. It is conducted through press statements, press conferences, press briefings and press receptions.
- **Events:** A company may hold functions or social events such as annual general meetings, factory tours and special parties on its premises for its employees, customers and at times the general public.
- **Corporate advertising:** This concentrates on establishing and reinforcing a corporate image. It is mainly targeted at the general public or broad audiences.
- **Publications:** These include written materials such as annual reports, brochures, company newsletters, magazines and audio-visual materials such as promotional DVDs, recruitment DVDs, websites and CDs. Different types of publications are used to inform publics and/or to build a favourable image with the target audiences.
- **Lobbying:** This is an exercise by which public relations practitioners try to influence decision-makers in the development and implementation of various policies.
- **Internal communication:** It is important for a company to keep its internal public – its employees – informed at all times. To achieve this, a company may use:
  - Staff/team meetings.
  - Team projects.

- Consultation.
- Open-door policies.
- Training programmes (in-service).
- Internal presentations.
- Direct mailing.
- Notice boards.
- In-house newsletters and magazines.
- Annual reports.
- Idea/suggestion boxes.
- Surveys.
- Electronic bulletin boards.
- Intranet.
- Social activities, i.e. team-building exercises such as survival weekends.
- Company diaries/pens/coffee cups/mouse mats.

• **Crisis management:** The co-ordinated effort to handle the effects of unfavourable publicity, ensuring fast and accurate communication in times of emergency.

• **Sponsorship:** The financial or material support of an event, person, organisation, group or product by private individuals or organisations. It is given with the expectation of a benefit in return. An organisation can communicate with its target audiences through sponsorship.

It is also used to create awareness or to persuade the target audience to think positively about the organisation and/or its products. Sponsorship should benefit both parties. Sponsorship and special events can be used to improve the relationship with suppliers and distributors by offering free tickets for sports or arts events. Some sponsored events are evolving towards global projects, such as the Olympic Games, the World Cup and Formula One racing.

Types of sponsorship:

- **Television and radio programme sponsorship** (e.g. the Quinn Group and *The Late Late Show*, Premier Foods and the Big Big Movie, Baileys and *Desperate Housewives*). The increasing fragmentation of television in Ireland through new digital channels is providing many more opportunities for sponsorship of this kind.

- **Sports sponsorship:** Major sporting events have the advantage of being attended and televiewed by large numbers of people. They also attract significant media coverage, e.g. Toyota Ireland's sponsorship of Munster Rugby.

- **Arts sponsorship:** Arts events or organisations are not as well attended as sports events, but are often regarded as very worthy and often fit with the image of certain businesses and brands, e.g. Guinness Cork Jazz Festival.

— **Educational sponsorship:** This can take several forms, from sponsoring individual students at college through to the provision of books and computers nationwide using the redemption of product- or store-related vouchers, e.g. Tesco's Computers for Schools.

Advantages of public relations

- It can support and complement other marketing activities.
- It is much more credible and convincing than advertisements.
- It often communicates messages to selected publics and generally influences opinion more effectively than advertising.
- In many cases, public relations objectives can be achieved at very low cost when compared to other promotional efforts.

Disadvantages of public relations

- There is no guarantee that a press statement or photograph will be published by a target newspaper.
- Effective public relations does not happen easily and so requires long-term planning.
- There is a chance that a well-devised news event or release will be removed from planned media coverage because of a more critical breaking news story, such as war news, severe weather or serious crime.
- In some areas of the world the impact of traditional news outlets is fading, forcing public relations professionals to scramble to find new ways to reach their target markets.

Direct marketing

Direct marketing attempts to acquire and retain customers by contacting them without the use of an intermediary. Unlike many other forms of communication, it usually requires an immediate response, which means that the effectiveness of most direct marketing campaigns can be assessed quantitatively. It can be defined as the distribution of products, information and promotional benefits to target customers through interactive communication in a way that allows the responses to be measured.

According to the Irish Direct Marketing Association (IDMA), companies use direct marketing to contact people with information about products and services that they may be interested in and in a way which most suits their lifestyles. Direct marketing covers online marketing, interactive television, text messages, newspaper inserts, direct mail, telemarketing and door-to-door leaflets. Direct marketing enables people to buy goods they want in the quickest and easiest way possible while providing them with value for money. This includes various activities, such as buying holidays online, donating to charities after the donor receives a fundraising pack or availing of offers in local supermarkets as a result of a door-drop leaflet. Direct marketing therefore covers a large number of the communications that people receive each day.

Many local and national organisations choose to communicate information to people using unaddressed mail and door-to-door material delivered directly to their homes. Such items can include free newspapers, free magazines, catalogues, information leaflets, advertising brochures, money-off coupons, local directories and free product samples. Organisations that communicate in this way include local authorities, utility companies (e.g. gas, water and electricity suppliers) public service organisations, charities, political parties, local shops and providers of local services. In Ireland, electronic mail (text messages, voice messages, sound messages, image messages, multimedia messages or e-mail messages) for the purpose of direct marketing cannot be sent to people without their prior consent unless it is from someone with whom they have a current customer relationship.

Direct marketing channels include:

- Direct mail.
- Door-to-door selling.
- Telemarketing (both inbound and outbound).
- Mail order catalogues.
- Direct response advertising in newspapers (coupons) and television (shopping channels).
- Electronic media (Internet, e-mail, interactive TV).
- Social media (Twitter, Facebook, YouTube, MySpace and LinkedIn).
- SMS text marketing.
- Inserts (leaflets in newspapers or magazines).
- Customer care lines.
- Publicity post (leaflet delivery by An Post).
- Free newspapers.
- Free magazines.
- Loyalty marketing.

The Internet and new media (e.g. mobile phones or PDAs – personal digital assistants), are now proving popular for direct marketing. Consumers have many sources of supply and suppliers have access to many markets. There is even room for niche marketers, e.g. Irish salmon can be ordered online, packed, chilled and sent to customers throughout the world by courier.

Direct marketing is used by many industries, including, for example, low-cost airlines, where there are no intermediaries or agents and customers book tickets directly with the airlines over the Internet. Information can be processed quickly and then categorised into complex relational databases. For example, special offers or new flight destinations can then be communicated directly to customers using e-mail campaigns. Data is not only collected on markets and segments, but also on individuals and on their individual buyer behaviour. Companies such as Amazon are booksellers, i.e. they do not write or publish them, so they use customer relationship management and marketing communications targeted directly at individual customers.

Advantages of direct marketing

- It can focus limited resources where they are most likely to produce results. E-mail is an extremely cheap form of direct marketing, as a message can be sent to thousands of recipients at very little cost.
- It allows a business to measure the success of campaigns accurately by analysing responses.
- Mobile phone users tend to take their phones with them, making it easier to reach them with time-sensitive messages.
- Messages can be sent out to groups of people quickly and relatively cheaply (via e-mail or SMS).
- Precise targeting of prospective customers – e-mail or social networking are the easiest ways to target the individual people a company needs to reach.
- May generate greater margins, as there is no profit margin added for the intermediary.
- Small markets are easily reached.
- New technologies have made it possible to produce eye-catching electronic newsletters and websites with built-in response mechanisms.
- Direct marketing can be highly effective in both business and consumer markets if it is properly planned and researched.

Disadvantages of direct marketing

- The results of direct marketing are not guaranteed. For example, a badly designed mail shot could simply be discarded or it may irritate recipients and damage the business reputation as a result.
- E-mail contacts go out of date faster than either addresses or telephone numbers, so a business needs to regularly clean up its database.
- The persistent problem of spam (unsolicited e-mail) means that marketing e-mails will need to stand out if they are not to be deleted before being read.

- Sophisticated anti-spam software also means that many marketing e-mails are deleted before they arrive at their destination.
- The amount of information one can send via SMS is limited, making it harder to get one's message across.
- The personal nature of mobile phones means that some people may find unwanted SMS messages intrusive.
- There has been a big rise in the use of fraudulent SMS messages, which has made some people wary of responding to unexpected messages.
- Direct mail is often dismissed as junk mail.
- Ethical issues.
- Growth of legislative constraints (Data Protection Act, etc.).
- Some aspects of direct marketing are seen as a public nuisance.

E-marketing

E-marketing is the product of the meeting between modern communication technologies and the age-old marketing principles that people have always applied. E-marketing, or electronic marketing, refers to the application of marketing principles and techniques via electronic media and more specifically through the Internet. The terms 'e-marketing', 'Internet marketing' and 'online marketing' are frequently interchanged and can often be considered synonymous.

E-marketing is the process of marketing a brand using the Internet. It includes both direct response marketing and indirect marketing elements and it uses a range of technologies to help businesses to connect to customers. Through these methods, e-marketing encompasses all the activities a business conducts via the worldwide web with the aim of attracting new business, retaining current business and developing its brand identity.

E-marketing includes the following.

- **Affiliate programmes:** These are a form of advertising on the web that rewards the self-selected advertisers for driving traffic to the advertiser or for subsequent transactions. It uses a multi-level marketing concept where consumers (affiliates) attract additional consumers, e.g. Amazon.com.
- **Viral marketing:** Word of mouth has an Internet version called 'word of mouse' (computer mouse). With greatly increased speeds, people refer items via e-mail and social networking to their friends and families, spreading the word through the Internet throughout the world. All viral programmes that are available are based on the same simple concept. They use the power of referrals and 'word of mouse' publicity to multiply how many people see your message. In 2010, for example, the Old Spice

marketing campaign was very successful as a result of viral marketing.

- **Newsgroups:** Discussion groups on the Internet. Newsgroups are classified by subject matter and do not necessarily deal with journalism or news. A 'buzz' can be generated about a company on a newsgroup.
- **Online branding:** Building an online branding scheme to match the company's offline branding.
- **Online advertising:** Different advertising methods on the internet, e.g. banner advertisements, affiliate programmes, pay per click, etc.
- **Online marketing:** The different methods of marketing a business online.
- **Online competitions:** Setting up online competitions to enhance a business's online marketing.
- **Reciprocal links:** Drive appropriate traffic to a business's website by using reciprocal links.
- **Search engine marketing:** Also referred to as optimisation or positioning, such as organic search listings, paid search engine submission and pay per click (PPC). For example, more and more companies are learning the value of search engine marketing. Search engine placement is one of the most effective means of driving highly pre-qualified prospective customers to a website. The most controllable form of search engine placement is the PPC model. PPC search listings allow companies to bid for placement within the search results users select. Those willing to pay more can appear higher in the search results. Companies bid for specific search terms in which their listings will appear as a result of the search. When a user searches for or is using a search term a business has bid for, the business listing will be displayed as one of the search results. Overture and Google AdWords are the major players in offering PPC.
- **Web personalisation:** Personalisation applications that deliver intuitive content about the site's users, e.g. cookies, member login areas and a website privacy policy.

Advantages of e-marketing

- Very low risk.
- Reduction in costs through automation and the use of electronic media. A properly planned and effectively targeted e-marketing campaign can reach the right customers at a much lower cost than traditional marketing methods.
- Faster response to both marketers and the end user.
- Trackable, measurable results – e-marketing methods make it easier to establish how effective a company's campaign has been. It can obtain detailed information about customers' responses to its advertising.

- One-to-one marketing – e-marketing lets a business reach people who want to know about its products and services instantly.
- More interesting campaigns – e-marketing allows a business to create interactive campaigns using music, graphics and videos. It could send its customers a game or a quiz – whatever it thinks will interest them.
- 24-hour marketing – with a website, a company's customers can find out about its products even if its office is closed.
- Global reach – a website can reach anyone in the world who has Internet access. This allows businesses to find new markets and compete globally for only a small investment.
- Boundless universal accessibility.

Disadvantages of e-marketing

- Depends on technology.
- Security and privacy issues.
- Maintenance costs due to a constantly evolving environment.
- Higher transparency of pricing and increased price competition.
- Worldwide competition through globalisation.

10.3 *Developing a communication programme*

Step 1: Identifying the target audience

The marketing manager must decide who exactly the target audience (receiver) is for the communication programme, for example the target audience may be children. The target audience may also be potential or existing customers and may be made up of individuals, groups, or the general public. The type of audience chosen will influence the message, how it will be transmitted, when it will be transmitted, where it will be transmitted and who will transmit it.

Step 2: Defining the communication objectives

Once the target audience has been selected, the company must decide on the objectives of the programme. This means it has to define what responses it is looking for. For example, it needs to know what stage of the 'product adoption process' the consumer is at and to what stage he or she needs to be moved. The stages of the **product adoption process** include (*a*) **awareness** – the person becomes aware that a product exists but has little information about it; (*b*) *interest* – the person seeks information about the product; (*c*) *evaluation* – the consumer decides whether the product will meet their individual needs; (*d*) *trial* – the consumer uses or experiences the product for the first time; and (*e*) *adoption* – the consumer decides to make full and regular use of the product.

The purpose of the programme, therefore, is to move the consumer along these stages to the adoption process. For a communication programme to be successful, the objectives must be precise, practical and measurable.

Step 3: Choosing a message

The next step in the communication programme is developing what the actual message should be. A marketer must decide on the content, structure and form of the message, that is, what the company wants to say, how it will say it and what sight, sound, colour or other stimuli it will use.

Step 4: Selecting the media

The marketing manager can decide what channel or channels of communication to use to get the message to the desired audience so that the objectives set out in step 2 can be achieved. There are two types: *personal communication channels,* for example face to face, telephone, word of mouth, salespeople, well-known personalities and opinion leaders, and *impersonal communication channels,* for example print media, television and radio, signs, posters and the World Wide Web.

Step 5: Deciding on a budget

It is important that a company develops a realistic budget so that it can achieve its objectives. It is difficult to determine this amount because there is no way to measure the precise effects of investing in a promotion.

There are four ways of deciding on how much a company should spend on promoting its product or service:

- The *affordable method*: The budget is set at what the company can afford.
- The *percentage of sales method*: The budget is set at a certain proportion of current or future sales.
- The *competitive parity method*: The budget is set to match or exceed what the competition is spending on promotion.
- The *objective and task method*: The budget is based on the analysis and costing of the communication objectives and tasks.

Step 6: Selecting the communication mix

Once the budget has been developed, the next step is to divide it among the tools of the communication mix. The company can select its communication mix by analysing each of the tools individually (see section 10.2).

Step 7: Implementing and evaluating results

This step involves putting the communication plan into action. To produce new brochures, for example, a company will invest time and effort in drafting, designing and producing this communication plan. The communication plan must then be implemented in accordance with the company's objectives and its progress must be monitored against what was originally proposed. Finally, gathering information by means of marketing research (qualitative and quantitative) may be used to assess the performance of the communication plan.

10.4 *Selecting a communication mix*

When developing a communication programme, the marketing manager has to select a communication mix that achieves the company's objectives within a defined budget. This will determine whether it is appropriate to use advertising as opposed to personal selling or whether the company should use a combination of the communication tools. To do this the company needs to be aware of the factors that affect the selection of a communication mix. These are as follows:

- The company's *communication objectives*: Awareness of the product (refer to step 1 of the communication programme above).
- Budget and resources: This determines the available budget and if the company has adequate resources to employ the communication tool (or tools).
- Type of market: If the company is dealing with a consumer market it should use mass communication, that is, advertising; if it is an industrial market it should use personal selling.
- *Communication strategy*: This can be either a push strategy or a pull strategy (described in Chapter 9).

The following quotation from Kotler (1999) sums up the role of marketing communication in relation to the marketing mix: 'Although the promotion mix is the company's primary communication activity, the entire marketing mix –

promotion, product, price and place – must be co-ordinated for the greatest communication impact.'

10.5 *Integrated marketing communications (IMC)*

Ideally, marketing communications from each communication mix element (advertising, sales promotions, advertising and public relations) should be integrated. In other words, the message reaching the consumer should be the same regardless of whether it is from a TV advertisement, a salesperson, a newspaper article or a free sample in a supermarket. Unfortunately, this is not always the case. When planning communication programmes, many marketers fail to integrate their communication efforts from one element of the mix to the next.

This unintegrated approach to marketing communication has propelled more companies to adopt the concept of ***integrated marketing communications (IMC)***. IMC is the method of carefully co-ordinating all promotional activities – advertising, sales promotions, personal selling and public relations as well as sponsorship, direct marketing and other forms of promotion – to produce a consistent, unified message that is customer focused. Marketing managers carefully work out the roles the various marketing communication tools will play in the marketing mix. The timing of various marketing communication activities is co-ordinated and the results of each campaign are carefully monitored to improve future use of the promotional mix elements. Normally, a marketing communications director is appointed. He/she has overall responsibility for integrating the company's marketing communications. Hewlett-Packard, for example, created 'marketing councils' within the company to devise strategies by which all marketing messages flow for both current campaigns and new product launches.

Important terms and concepts

marketing communication process:
  p. 209
communications mix: p. 209
elements of the marketing
  communication process: p. 209
tools of the communications mix:
  p. 211
advertising: p. 212

competitive advertising: p. 212
comparative advertising: p. 212
advertising media: p. 213
sales promotion: p. 215
personal selling: p. 217
hard sell strategies: p. 217
soft sell strategies: p. 218
public relations: p. 218

Case study: Directing marketing – Concern: Haiti Emergency Appeal

Concern Worldwide works with the poorest people and in the poorest countries of the world to help improve their lives. Sustained by the concern of its many supporters, it seeks out those who most urgently need its support and works with them to tackle poverty, hunger and disaster. Concern is supported by generous donors. It also receives money from governments and other partners. Eighty-eight per cent of its budget is spent on relief and development. The remainder goes on fundraising, education and governance.

Challenge

On 12 January 2010, a strong earthquake hit Haiti. Up to 200,000 people lost their lives and hundreds of thousands more Haitians were left injured and homeless. The Haiti emergency was a prime news story in the two weeks following the earthquake. A quick response was essential to this appeal. The challenge facing Concern was to raise €1 million from an integrated fundraising campaign in Ireland for the emergency response. The existing 130,000 Concern supporters were mailed and segmented based on their most recent donation, value and donation type. The aim was to deliver an emergency appeal to existing donors as quickly as possible following the earthquake and to benefit from heightened awareness of the crisis among the public and maximise donations as a result.

Mailing

A simple letter was developed with a reply envelope included. Written from the perspective of a field staff worker, the aim was to portray the harsh realities on the ground in the immediate aftermath of the quake, bringing the situation closer to the donor and reinforcing the urgent need for immediate support. Donors were prompted to respond via phone, web or post. Overall the response to the campaign from donors was huge, raising in excess of €5 million in total (combined income from all elements of the integrated campaign).

Source: Adapted from www.anpost.ie/AnPost/AnPostDM/KNOWLEDGE Centre/Case+Studies/Charities/Charities.htm#concern [accessed 19 March 2011].

Case study: Start spreading the news: Tourism Ireland

Tourism Ireland was established under the framework of the Belfast Agreement, which was signed on Good Friday, 1998. It is jointly funded by the Irish Government and the Northern Ireland Executive on a two to one ratio and operates under the auspices of the North–South Ministerial Council through the Department of Enterprise, Trade and Investment in Northern Ireland and the Department of Tourism, Culture and Sport in the republic.

Tourism Ireland employs 160 people in key source markets, such as Great Britain, the US, Canada, France, Germany, the Netherlands, Denmark, Belgium, Italy, Spain, Austria, Switzerland and Australia. It also has offices in Coleraine and Dublin and has now extended its reach to include emerging tourist markets such as Japan, South Africa, New Zealand, India, China, Poland, Israel, Asia and the Middle East.

Tourism Ireland works with the two tourist boards in Ireland, Fáilte Ireland and the Northern Ireland Tourist Board, who are responsible for product and enterprise development and marketing to tourism consumers within the island of Ireland. Tourism Ireland devises and delivers marketing programmes in over 20 markets across the world and works in close co-operation with industry partners on the island of Ireland as well as with the travel trade, online operators, media and air and sea carriers overseas to encourage consumers to 'go where Ireland takes you'.

To maximise exposure for Northern Ireland and the 'Experience Northern Ireland – *Titanic* and More' showcase, Tourism Ireland put in place a major marketing communications programme, which reached over 20 million potential holidaymakers in the New York and tri-state area. This was presented by Tourism Ireland in association with its partners – National Museums Northern Ireland, Northern Ireland Tourist Board, Belfast Visitor and Convention Bureau and Continental Airlines. On 24–29 September 2010, New York's iconic Vanderbilt Hall was filled with the sounds, tastes and images of Northern Ireland. This experiential extravaganza saw an array of vibrant characters from the worlds of theatre, music and dance.

Print promotions

This included full-page adverts in *Time Out*, *Irish America*, the *Irish Examiner USA*, *Irish Voice* and *Irish Echo*. A campaign with *am New York* included a cover wraparound which was highlighted by a 150-strong street team that distributed the newspaper at all subway stations in Manhattan and encouraged commuters to visit the Northern Ireland showcase.

Website

A prominent Northern Ireland display featured on the home page of Tourism Ireland's website (www.discoverireland.com) linking to a special landing page with the full schedule of events during the week-long promotion. Visits to the website increased by over 45 per cent during the campaign period, with a significant increase in traffic to the Northern Ireland pages.

Web promotions

Online adverts featured on popular websites such as TimeOut.com, Irishcentral.com and Weather.com. Approximately 110,000 online subscribers to *The New Yorker* and *TimeOut New York* received details by e-mail about the Northern Ireland showcase from Tourism Ireland.

TV and radio

Northern Ireland adverts aired on NBC during the popular *Weekend Today Show* and on popular radio stations, including 1010 WINS, WOR and WCBS.

Publicity

Over 3 million listeners to popular radio stations 1010 WINS and WOR heard Tourism Ireland's staff highlight Northern Ireland as a unique holiday destination for Americans and listeners were invited to go to Grand Central Terminal to see the showcase for themselves.

Social media

A Northern Ireland promotion on Tourism Ireland's US Facebook page as well as frequent posts and updates on the event, plus a competition inviting submissions on people's favourite Van Morrison song to grow awareness of the new iPhone app and the music of Northern Ireland, led to a major increase in engagement and comments by fans and an increase of 10,000 Facebook fans during the three-week campaign.

Source: Adapted from www.tourismireland.com/Home/about-us/corporate-publications/contact-magazine.aspx [accessed 19 March 2011].

Questions for review

1. What are the elements of the marketing communication process?
2. Discuss each tool of the communication mix. Illustrate your response with examples.
3. Describe the steps involved in developing a communication programme.
4. What factors affect the selection of the communication mix?
5. Think of a product or service with which you are familiar. Identify the tools used to promote it.

BIBLIOGRAPHY

Abell, D. (1980), *Defining the Business: The Starting Point of Strategic Planning,* Englewood Cliffs (NJ): Prentice Hall.

Baker, M. (1990), *Dictionary of Marketing and Advertising*, London: Macmillan.

Bennett, P.D. (1998), *Marketing Terms*, Chicago: American Marketing Association, p. 189.

Brassington, F. and Pettitt, S. (2006), *Principles of Marketing* (4th edn), London: Financial Times Prentice Hall.

Dibbenbach, J. (1983), 'Corporate environmental analysis in large US corporations', *Long Range Planning*, Vol. 16, No. 3, pp. 107–16.

Dibbs, S., Simkin, L., Pride, W. and Ferrell, O. (2006), *Marketing: Concepts and Strategies*, New York: South Western.

Harrell, G. D. (2002), *Marketing – Connecting with Customers*, New Jersey: Prentice Hall.

Kotler, P. and Armstrong, G. (2008), *Marketing: An Introduction* (12th edn), Englewood Cliffs (NJ): Prentice Hall.

Kotler, P., Armstrong, G., Saunders, J. and Wong, V. (2002), *Principles of Marketing* (4th European edition), London: Prentice Hall.

Langer, E. and Imba, L. (1980), 'The role of mindlessness in the perception of deviance', *Journal of Personality and Social Psychology*, Vol. 38, pp. 360–7.

Lindstrom, M. (2010), *Brand Sense: Sensory Secrets Behind the Stuff We Buy* (2nd edn), London: Kogan Page.

MacDonald, M. (1989), 'Ten barriers to marketing planning,' *Journal of Marketing Management,* Vol. 5, No. 1, pp. 1–8.

Mitchell, A. (1999), 'Marketers must grasp the Net or face oblivion', *Marketing Week*, 18 February, pp. 30–1.

Mowen, J. (1995), *Consumer Behavior* (4th edn), Englewood Cliffs (NJ): Prentice Hall.

Murray, J. and O'Driscoll, A. (1999), *Managing Marketing: Concepts and Irish Cases,* Dublin: Gill & Macmillan.

Page, S. (1995), *Introductory Marketing,* Cheltenham: Stanley Thornes.

Peters, T. (1988), *Thriving on Chaos*, New York: Pan.

Porter, M. (1980), *Competitive Strategy: Techniques for Analysing Industries and Competitors,* New York: Free Press.

Ries, A. (1995), 'What's in a name?', *Sales and Marketing Management,* October, pp. 36–7.

Ries, A. and Trout, J. (2001), *Positioning: The Battle for Your Mind*, London: McGraw-Hill.

Robinson, P.J., Farris, C.W. and Wind, Y. (1967), *Industrial Buying Behaviour and Creative Marketing*, London: Allyn and Bacon.

Tull, D. and Hawkins, D. (1992), *Industrial Marketing Research*, London: Kogan Page.

Wind, Y. (1984), 'Going to market: new twists for some old tricks', *Wharton Magazine*, 4.

Zikmund, W.G. and d'Amico, M. (2001), *Marketing: Creating and Keeping Customers in an E-commerce World* (7th edn), Cincinnati (OH): South-Western College Publishing.

Intro   3   ✓

MM -   3   ✓

Product   3   ✓

P   4   /
P   4   /
P   4   X — 5?

Cust   5   ✓

Comp   6   ✗   7?
con   7   ✓   ✗
B:S   8   ✓

2463